A Publication of
the Council on Foundations

The Council on Foundations is a nonprofit membership organization for grantmakers. Founded in 1949, the Council's mission is to promote and strengthen organized philanthropy. The Council represents grantmakers, their concerns, and their interests to public policymakers, the media and the general public. Membership includes almost 1200 independent, operating, community, public and company-sponsored foundations, corporate giving programs, trust companies, and international foundations. Members of the Council represent more than $67 billion in assets and contributed more than $3.6 billion in 1989 for programs in such fields as education, social welfare, health, science and research, environment, the arts, urban planning and economic development, religious charity, and international development. Through their subscription to a set of principles and practices for effective grantmaking, Council members provide leadership in the area of public accountability for the field of philanthropy.

Programs. Council programs help members achieve their charitable goals and foster a broad public understanding of philanthropy and its impact within society. The Council provides education and professional development opportunities for grantmakers through workshops, conferences, publications, and other information and technical assistance. The Council also has programs in government relations, communications and public affairs, research, special support services, and special initiatives to promote the growth of organized philanthropy.

Meetings. The Council sponsors an annual conference to focus on current global political, economic, and social issues confronting the United States and the world and their implications for organized philanthropy. Other educational programs and seminars held throughout the year concentrate on specific program issues, tax and regulatory policies, management and administrative practices, communications, and other areas.

Publications. The Council publishes *Foundation News,* a bimonthly magazine featuring coverage of the nonprofit sector and current philanthrophic issues and activities. The Council also publishes a biweekly newsletter, an occasional paper series, and other periodic surveys, reports, and studies on issues related to grantmaking.

COUNCIL ON FOUNDATIONS
1828 L STREET NW WASHINGTON, DC 20036 (202)466-6512

THE CORPORATE CONTRIBUTIONS HANDBOOK

James P. Shannon, Editor

THE CORPORATE
CONTRIBUTIONS
HANDBOOK

Devoting Private Means
to
Public Needs

Jossey-Bass Publishers

San Francisco   •   Oxford   •   1991

THE CORPORATE CONTRIBUTIONS HANDBOOK
Devoting Private Means to Public Needs
   by James P. Shannon, Editor

Copyright © 1991 by: Jossey-Bass Inc., Publishers
                      350 Sansome Street
                      San Francisco, California 94104

                      &

                      Jossey-Bass Limited
                      Headington Hill Hall
                      Oxford OX3 0BW

Library of Congress Cataloging-in-Publication Data

The Corporate contributions handbook : devoting private means to
   public needs / James P. Shannon, editor.—1st ed.
      p.   cm.—(The Jossey-Bass nonprofit sector series)
   "A publication of Council on Foundations"—T.p. verso.
   Includes bibliographical references and index.
   ISBN 1-55542-320-5
   1. Corporations—United States—Charitable contributions.
   I. Shannon, James P., 1921-   . II. Council on Foundations.
   III. Series.
   HV91.C677   1991
   658.15'3—dc20   90-28637
                                                             CIP

Manufactured in the United States of America

The paper in this book meets the guidelines for
permanence and durability of the Committee on
Production Guidelines for Book Longevity of the
Council on Library Resources.

JACKET DESIGN BY WILLI BAUM

FIRST EDITION

Code 9120

 A Publication of the COUNCIL ON FOUNDATIONS

The Jossey-Bass
Nonprofit Sector Series

CONTENTS

ix

PREFACE

Ever since colonial days, the nonprofit sector has performed a vital function in the economy of the United States. Funded by private means and staffed largely by volunteers, this third, or independent, sector has grown to meet public needs that government and business are either unable or unwilling to fill. Within the past decade, because of the magnitude of the federal debt and the correlative paucity of state funds, the services of the nonprofit sector have become crucial to the maintenance of adequate health care, educational opportunities, social services, and a reasonable range of cultural amenities for all segments of our society.

Corporations are by no means *the* major player in support of the nonprofit sector, but they are certainly *a* major player. Between 1980 and 1988, the total measurable monetary contributions of all businesses to the nonprofit sector grew from $2.35 billion to almost $4.75 billion, or roughly 5 percent of all monetary gifts reported to the Internal Revenue Service (*Giving USA,* 1989). The value of nonmonetary corporate contributions, such as gifts in-kind, use of corporate facilities, gifts of products, loaned executives, and the time of employee volunteers, would likely exceed $5 billion a year if it could be measured.

Unfortunately, for each of the last four years for which we have records (1986–1989), after adjusting for inflation, corporate monetary giving has not kept pace with the rise in the cost of the services provided by nonprofit organizations. Projections by professional fund raisers and by nonprofit agencies seem to agree that this discrepancy between available corporate funds and nonprofit needs will continue to grow in the 1990s. If so, it is an indication that society cannot assume that corporate support for nonprofit agencies will increase or even remain constant in the near term. This discrepancy is also a signal that in the coming decade more sophisticated managerial skills will be expected of corporate grants managers as well as of grantseekers who need corporate dollars to balance their budgets. *The Corporate Contributions Handbook* is intended to help corporate donors and nonprofit agencies rise to this challenge.

Audience

Alert corporate leaders are increasingly aware that their companies are expected, by society at large and by government, to use their resources to address high-priority public needs. To shoulder these new burdens, well-run companies are realizing that their giving programs deserve a higher priority in company planning, better management, and measurable standards of accountability. But in many corporations the office charged with overseeing contributions is still poorly staffed, poorly funded, and poorly managed.

Although there are some books and many articles that address the topics covered in *The Corporate Contributions Handbook*, no single volume is available in which the several discrete elements of corporate grantmaking are assembled for easy reference as they are in this book. It is my hope and the hope of the Council on Foundations that this volume will be a useful guide for executives charged with managing company contributions, employees who report to these managers, and senior corporate officers to whom these managers report. It is also our hope that this book will be a helpful reference for grantseekers who want a better understanding of how corporate contributions are made and how applicants for corporate support might work as equal partners, not adversaries, with their peers in corporate offices.

We also hope that this book will help undergraduate and graduate students see more clearly the catalytic role corporate contributions play in the nonprofit sector. Until now it has been axiomatic among those of us in this field to say that we "lucked into our positions," there being no clear path in place to learn the elements of this craft before starting our work. Within the past decade, however, more than a score of new graduate academic programs and a host of undergraduate curricula have been organized for study and research in the nonprofit sector. The promise of these programs is enormous, both for students and for the future of the sector. Ideally, these students will find *The Corporate Contributions Handbook* responsive to many of their current needs for information, and in due time their insights might well provide new material for future editions.

Since 1981, our federal, state, and local governments have steadily decreased their share of financial support for the nonprofit sector. Business faces increasing pressure to make up this lost revenue. Consequently, corporate grants officers, with shrinking staffs, today face growing demands to fund worthy causes in the arts, education, health care, and social service.

The downsizing of corporate staffs means that fewer corporate employees are now expected to manage an increasing number of requests from a burgeoning nonprofit sector whose services are both needed and expected by society. President Bush's recent creation of the Points of Light Foundation is a government initiative specifically designed to garner more private support for unmet public needs.

Overview of the Contents

The three sectors that make up American society—government, business, and nonprofits—have a mutual interest in the well-being of society at large. Part One discusses this three-way partnership, how it developed, how it operates today, and how it contributes to the common good.

In Chapter One, James A. Joseph makes the case that for-profit corporations have both the duty and the opportunity to use their varied resources for the building of strong, humane, cohesive communities at every level of society.

In Chapter Two, Barry D. Karl describes the development, from colonial times to the present, of the distinctively American business practice of using corporate resources to address high-priority unmet public needs. Karl's chapter is particularly helpful in its description of the cultural, economic, and legal forces by which corporate grantmaking has come to its present active and vigorous role.

In Chapter Three, Brian O'Connell draws on his comprehensive knowledge of this sector to describe its size, diversity, recent growth, and increasing importance as a key agent in the equitable allocation of human and financial resources. O'Connell's view of the nonprofit sector as an integral element in the private enterprise system is really an organizing idea for the balance of this book. This concept deserves to be understood, particularly in the business community, much more widely than it is.

Chapter Four, by Sanford Cloud, Jr., calls attention to recent dramatic changes in the impact that government at every level has on both the nonprofit and the business sectors. Until recently, the three levels of government have been essentially contributors to the nonprofit sector. However, the size of the federal debt, limited financial resources at the state level, and the burgeoning social service budgets at the local level have, in effect, turned all three levels of government, which once were grantmakers, into grantseekers.

Part Two describes different ways in which a business can enhance its position of community leadership by means of its contributions program. In Chapter Five, David Stanley candidly tells his fellow CEOs that in addition to their corporate duties they also have a duty to play an active role in society and influence legislation and public policy on issues like poverty and homelessness. He gives the twin social questions of poverty and homelessness a high priority for CEOs who are ready to exercise community leadership.

Chapter Six, by Lance C. Buhl, turns on the thesis that the

success of any corporate giving program depends on its officers' ability to build trust and support equally within their company and among the constituencies they seek to serve. Buhl sees the corporate contributions officer as a "marginal" agent who builds trust within two very different constituencies by being loyal to the company and candid and fair with the agencies seeking corporate support. The concept that corporate contributions officers have comparable responsibilities to several constituencies is cited often by other authors in this book.

Chapter Seven, by Peter C. Hutchinson, sets high standards for corporations that seek to be perceived as leaders in their communities. Hutchinson admits that it is always hard to define what we mean by community. In his view, corporations must learn to do a better job of sensing and responding to changes in the dynamic society that surrounds them. His eight rules for corporate leadership on community issues reflect the time and effort he and the Dayton Hudson Company have spent to perfect this art form.

In Chapter Eight, Mary Stewart Hall describes the delicate process whereby a corporation builds and rebuilds its culture while it monitors and evaluates the dynamics and the expectations of the different communities and constituencies it seeks to serve. Her specific examples of companies that have found the proper balance between these different, if not conflicting, values give readers helpful benchmarks for evaluating their own programs.

In Part Three, four grants officers and one chief executive offer some wise counsel to help grantmakers distinguish problems from opportunities in the handling of five key issues that are likely to confront them.

In Chapter Nine, Jack A. MacAllister structures his view about corporate grantmaking in the form of a memorandum to a new CEO. MacAllister's suggestions present clear and precise counsel from an executive who knows why and how his company earned its reputation as a good corporate citizen. He speaks with what Robert Greenleaf would call "the authority of service."

Drawing on her experience as a grantmaker and on her current role as a senior consultant to the Council on Foundations, Judith K. Healey in Chapter Ten provides the list of questions corporations must answer to determine the range and focus for their contributions program. The answers to these questions vary from company to company and even from time to time within a company. Healey's list of "dangers and opportunities" offers grantmakers reliable counsel on how to set the generic categories and the specific limits for their contributions programs.

Ever since American Express coined and registered the term *cause-related marketing,* the technique of tying corporate grantmaking to a company's marketing strategy has been a hot topic. Cynthia D. Giroud masterfully generates much light and little heat in her deft handling of this volatile topic in Chapter Eleven. By granting early on in her chapter that cause-related marketing can have a variety of risks, she proceeds to illustrate admirably the many ways in which it can be done to benefit both the contributing company and its nonprofit beneficiaries.

By this point, readers have likely discovered that *The Corporate Contributions Handbook* does not lobby would-be donors to give money to any specific charities. But in Chapter Twelve, Mary E. Pickard explores the expanding field of federated giving campaigns. Since its inception after World War I, the United Way has become the beneficiary of more corporate dollars than any other recipient agency in the country. Within the past two decades, a host of other federated giving programs have come of age, and they pose a challenge for corporations that until now have allowed only the United Way entrée to their payroll deduction system. Pickard's extensive experience with many United Way programs and with other federated giving programs gives her chapter on this broad field a valuable range of insights on how corporate contributions officers can best address the changing needs of the United Way and the proliferation of other federated giving campaigns.

One of the most difficult questions in the field of corporate grantmaking is how to manage a contributions program in a company undergoing voluntary or involuntary restructuring. In Chapter Thirteen, Lizabeth G. Sode shares the wisdom she has garnered after guiding the Beatrice Foundation through four successive restructurings. Sode avoids the trap of trying to settle the question of whether mergers, acquisitions, and takeovers are good or bad for the future of corporate contributions, and she wisely limits her counsel to a set of issues that every corporate grants officer must be prepared to face once a corporate restructuring is clearly underway.

In Part Four, experienced corporate officers talk about managing specific aspects of a corporate contributions program. Although their chapters do not cover completely every element of day-to-day grants administration, they do offer a comprehensive review of several large categories of structuring, managing, and overseeing comprehensive corporate grants programs.

In Chapter Fourteen, George M. Collins draws on his career as director of the Boston Globe Foundation to take new grants officers on a step-by-step tour of the duties that come with their assignments. In an approachable style, Collins recounts his own unexpected transition from the writing staff of the *Globe* to the director's chair of the company foundation and offers some sound advice to other corporate employees who suddenly find themselves making a similar adjustment.

John A. Edie lays out in Chapter Fifteen the legal standards against which corporate foundations and corporate giving programs are measured. It would be difficult to find in any other publication a more succinct but comprehensive study of this all-important topic. With Congress, state legislators, and attorneys general monitoring closely all aspects of philanthropy, grants officers must know the law governing their field. Edie's chapter will be a much-used reference of any corporate employee who has administrative responsibility for all or part of a company's grants program.

Jon Pratt's Chapter Sixteen tells corporate grants officers some of the things they should know about the legitimate expectations of today's grantseekers. As the founder and first executive director of the Minnesota Council on Nonprofits, Pratt has many insights to share on how grantmakers could perform more effectively. He has some hard things to say about shortcomings he has observed among us, but he writes with civility, courtesy, and forcefulness. His criticism is friendly but serious.

In Chapter Seventeen, Robin Reiter-Faragalli offers grants officers guidelines for selecting programs to support. She gives information on evaluating funding requests through questions for the grantmaker and the grantseeker.

One of the perennial topics for discussion and review at any

meeting of corporate grantmakers is that of changes in their handling of corporate gift-matching programs. In Chapter Eighteen,
Earl L. Gadbery and Helen L. Adamasko draw on their experience
in directing the widely recognized Alcoa Foundation's educational
gift-matching program. They describe both its structure and its flexibility as a guide for corporate grantmakers just entering this field
or for those contemplating enlarging their existing gift-matching
program.

     Probably the most challenging area for grantmakers today is
the management of giving programs in small companies. Typically, these companies have strong local community interest, modest contributions budgets, and a single (often part-time) employee
responsible for the whole program. An expert in this expanding
area is Iris J. Krieg, who oversees the contributions programs of six
companies under the aegis of the Field Corporation Fund in Chicago. In Chapter Nineteen, Krieg presents a knowledgeable and
detailed description of both why and how a smaller company can
mount a credible and effective giving program within those communities where it has a significant presence.

     The single most difficult task facing any grantmaker, corpo-
rate or otherwise, is that of monitoring and evaluating the ultimate
effectiveness of the giving program. Some large endowed foundations spend great amounts of money to evaluate and measure the
results of their grants program. Unfortunately, most grantmakers
lack the staff and the money to mount such a costly review process.
As president of the Metropolitan Life Foundation, Sibyl Jacobson
addresses this complex problem in Chapter Twenty. Any reader
who has grappled with the complexity of the amorphous process of
evaluation will find a wealth of useful insights and new hope in
Jacobson's excellent chapter.

     In Part Five, several authors take their cameras to a higher
level to focus on issues wider than the traditional concept of corporate contributions as donations of money only.

     In Chapter Twenty-One, Alex J. Plinio and Joanne B. Scan-
lan, who have previously written widely and well about the full
range of corporate giving of money, products, equipment, and services, return to this topic with new insights about the creative leveraging of corporate contributions and with a host of specific

illustrations on how this process can and should work. At the heart of this challenging chapter, corporate grantmakers will find an attractive invitation to locate and utilize many talents and resources within their companies to enlarge and enhance the effect of their program on the several constituencies and communities they wish to help. Total resource leveraging and matching as presented by Plinio and Scanlan offers corporate grantmakers a new way to think about corporate citizenship.

In Chapter Twenty-Two, Donna L. Cummings pulls together many threads from earlier chapters to emphasize that a cordial bond of mutual personal respect between grantmakers and grantseekers is essential if their joint ventures are to be successful. Some experienced donors and grants officers do not agree that grantmakers and grantseekers are indeed peers. It is, however, the consistent position of this book that donors and donees are equal and should deal with each other accordingly. Cummings's extensive experience as the manager of corporate grantmaking for a Fortune 500 company over a span of twelve years gives her the vantage point and the evidence to say forcefully that the grantmaking enterprise works best when grantors and grantees see and treat each other as equal partners in ventures they both hope will be successful.

Throughout this book, the authors have been asked to refrain from using their chapters as show-and-tell pieces about the giving programs in their own companies. Chapter Twenty-Three deliberately moves away from this standard and includes detailed descriptions by Sheryl Wiley Solomon (Ralston Purina), Barbara O. Ragland (Federal Express), Eugene R. Wilson and Myrna Plost (ARCO) of corporate volunteer programs they manage. The variety of employee volunteer programs is so great that a single chapter that would try to describe this vast range of corporate activity could not do justice either to its range or to its diversity. Hence, four managers of outstanding volunteer programs describe specifically how their programs work, leaving it to the readers to discern which of the elements discussed here are portable and useful in other companies.

Robert H. Dunn and Judith Babbitts bring to Chapter Twenty-Four well-honed skills and unusual sensitivity to the several ethical dimensions of the grantmaking process. It would be a salutary experience for persons engaged in this line of work to re-

read this chapter every six months. Doing so would remind them
that grantmaking is a high calling, and that the standards for doing
it responsibly can only be enforced voluntarily from within by its
practitioners.

In Chapter Twenty-Five, the concluding chapter, I list and
emphasize selected themes that have been cited most often by the
authors of earlier chapters. I also position these themes as necessary
elements in corporate contributions programs concerned about facing the serious problems and grasping the attractive opportunities
in the last decade of this century and into the twenty-first century.

The resources reprint four highly respected sets of standards
for effective grantmaking. They are "Standards for Charitable Solicitations," published by the Council of Better Business Bureaus,
Inc.; "Principles and Practices for Effective Grantmaking," by the
Council on Foundations; "Profiles of Effective Corporate Giving
Programs," written by E. B. Knauft and published by INDEPEN-
DENT SECTOR; and "Standards in Philanthropy," published by
the National Charities Information Bureau, Inc. The address of
each of these nonprofit agencies is printed in each Resource section
to enable our readers to write for additional information on recommended standards for effective charitable contributions.

The authors of this book see themselves positioned midway
between the global strategists and the corporate donors interested
primarily in small-scale local charities. Hence, when they speak of
corporate contributions, they are speaking principally of cash gifts,
gifts in-kind, employee voluntarism, and a broad range of services
that American corporations customarily donate locally and nationally. We found early on that we could not accommodate in this
single volume an adequate treatment of how to organize and manage
overseas grants programs. In light of the political and economic
changes now underway in Europe, Africa, Pacific Rim countries,
and Latin America, it is clearly imperative that multinational corporations have in place comprehensive strategies for doing business
worldwide. We trust that persons responsible for managing such
programs will find much good counsel and many replicable models
in this book, even though it does not purport to be a guidebook on
global contributions programs.

Terminology

The material assembled here is a series of discrete essays by both
hands-on corporate grantmakers and specialists in ancillary fields.
Each chapter synthesizes the views and the experience of its author
or authors on a particular theme. No rigid effort has been made to
integrate the vocabulary or the content of these chapters. For example, some of the authors prefer to speak of *corporate grantmaking,*
while others favor the term *corporate contributions.* Still others use
these terms interchangeably. We expect that our readers, already
aware that much of what happens in the nonprofit sector is untidy,
will not find these shifts in terminology burdensome.

Discerning readers will find instances of implicit differences
of opinion between and among our authors. No editorial attempt
has been made to reconcile these differences. Acting on the premise
that a good corporate contributions program is essentially a mosaic
and not an equation, we leave it to our readers to select the elements
that fit best into the contributions mosaic they are fashioning for
their companies.

A word is in order here about the various meanings conveyed
by the term *corporate contributions.* At one end of the spectrum,
multinational companies use this term to describe the full range of
corporate resources that they commit to the grand strategy of their
company's worldwide program. At the other end of the spectrum,
small privately held companies often use this term to describe what
is in essence a petty cash fund to underwrite the purchase of tickets
to the annual firefighter's picnic.

Acknowledgments

A book of this kind is the result of counsel given by good friends
and wise advisers too numerous to list. But a select list of these
mentors would include the following: Special appreciation must go
to our thirty authors, who gave generously of their talent, time, and
training to create this book. Early on when the book was only a
concept, Lynn D. W. Luckow, Richard Magat, Bernard J. Nolan,
Robert L. Payton, and Paul N. Ylvisaker graciously helped me and
the Council on Foundations' Committee on Corporate Grantmak-

ing define the reach and contents of this book. Over a span of more than a year, Alice C. Buhl, Maureen McGowan, and Leanna Mullins have quietly marshaled the resources of the Council to guide this project at every stage. The person who has given more time, talent, and concern to this publication than any other is Ruth Shannon. Without her as my partner, adviser, and patient best friend, this book would still be only a concept.

Wayzata, Minnesota   James P. Shannon
January 1991

Reference

Giving USA: The Annual Report on Philanthropy. New York: American Association of Fund-Raising Counsel, 1989.

CONTRIBUTORS

Helen L. Adamasko is program assistant for Educational Gift Matching, Alcoa Foundation, in Pittsburgh, Pennsylvania.

Judith Babbitts is a foundation consultant in San Francisco, California.

Lance C. Buhl is director of corporate contributions for BP America, Inc., in Cleveland, Ohio. Besides managing the grantmaking function at BP America, Buhl is grants officer for the company's grantmaking and social investment programs in urban development and neighborhood renewal.

Sanford Cloud, Jr., is vice president and executive director of the Aetna Foundation, Inc., in Hartford, Connecticut.

George M. Collins is a director of the Boston Globe Foundation in Boston, Massachusetts.

Donna L. Cummings is an independent consultant and meeting and conference planner. She was formerly the manager of the TRW Foundation in Cleveland, Ohio.

Robert H. Dunn is vice president, corporate communications and community affairs, and executive vice president of the Levi Strauss Foundation in San Francisco, California.

John A. Edie is vice president and general counsel of the Council on Foundations in Washington, D.C.

Earl L. Gadbery is president of the Alcoa Foundation in Pittsburgh, Pennsylvania.

Cynthia D. Giroud is manager of corporate social investment for the Scott Paper Company Foundation in Philadelphia, Pennsylvania.

Mary Stewart Hall is president and trustee of the Weyerhaeuser Company Foundation and vice president, corporate contributions, for the Weyerhaeuser Company in Tacoma, Washington.

Judith K. Healey is principal, Judith K. Healey Executive Consulting in Minneapolis, Minnesota, consultant to corporate giving programs and private foundations, and a senior consultant to the Council on Foundations in Washington, D.C.

Peter C. Hutchinson was commissioner of finance of the State of Minnesota. From 1980 to 1989 he served as chair of the Dayton Hudson Foundation and vice president, external affairs, for the Dayton Hudson Corporation in Minneapolis, Minnesota.

Sibyl Jacobson is president and chief executive officer of the Metropolitan Life Foundation and vice president of the Metropolitan Life Insurance Company in New York, New York.

James A. Joseph is president and chief executive officer of the Council on Foundations in Washington, D.C. From 1977 to 1981 he was

Under Secretary of the Interior. He was formerly vice president of the Cummins Engine Company.

Barry D. Karl is Norman and Edna Freehling Professor of History at The University of Chicago.

Iris J. Krieg is executive director of the Field Corporation Fund in Chicago, Illinois.

Jack A. MacAllister is chairman and chief executive officer of U S WEST, Englewood, Colorado.

Brian O'Connell is president of INDEPENDENT SECTOR in Washington, D.C.

Mary E. Pickard is community affairs officer of the St. Paul Companies in St. Paul, Minnesota.

Alex J. Plinio is vice president, market development division, of the Prudential Insurance Company in Newark, New Jersey.

Myrna Plost is director of public education and volunteer programs at the ARCO Foundation in Los Angeles, California.

Jon Pratt is executive director of the Minnesota Council on Nonprofits in St. Paul, Minnesota.

Barbara O. Ragland is director of the capital fund campaign for Rust College in Holly Springs, Mississippi. She was formerly manager of grants and community services for Federal Express Corporation in Memphis, Tennessee.

Robin Reiter-Faragalli is vice president, corporate community involvement, for Southeast Banking Corporation and executive director of the Southeast Banking Corporation Foundation in Miami, Florida.

Joanne B. Scanlan is director, community foundation services, for the Council on Foundations in Washington, D.C.

James P. Shannon is a senior consultant for the Council on Foundations. He was executive director of the General Mills Foundation from 1980 to 1988.

Lizabeth G. Sode was vice president, corporate relations, for the Beatrice Company and president of the Beatrice Foundation in Chicago, Illinois.

Sheryl Wiley Solomon is manager of community programs for the Ralston Purina Company in St. Louis, Missouri.

David Stanley is chairman of the board and chief executive officer of Payless Cashways, Inc., in Kansas City, Missouri.

Eugene R. Wilson is president of the ARCO Foundation in Los Angeles, California.

THE CORPORATE
CONTRIBUTIONS
HANDBOOK

PART ONE

The Vital Role
of Corporate Contributions
in Society

Chapter One

The Corporate Stake
in Community Involvement:
Has Business Lost
Its Social Conscience?

James A. Joseph

Many American corporations have a history of making a difference in their communities in both good and bad times. But within the last decade, many of the chief executive officers (CEOs) who were most visibly identified with corporate public involvement retired. They have been succeeded by a generation of corporate leaders whose views on corporate philanthropy and the social role of business are largely unknown. Some observers of business trends argue that business has lost its social conscience. Others argue that business has simply lost its public face.

In truth, philanthropy is now a part of the corporate culture of many businesses. The critical issue is not so much whether the philanthropic tradition will continue, but how it will continue. Will it be a marginal activity on the periphery of corporations, or will it play a mainstream role, contributing to the vitality of both corporations and their communities?

In 1988, the Council on Foundations undertook a major research effort to address a number of questions about corporate philanthropy, including: What role does corporate giving play in corporate life today? Has CEO support for corporate giving diminished? How does the next generation of CEOs, today's division presidents, chief financial and operating officers, and the like, view corporate giving? The survey, conducted by the Daniel Yankelovich Group, found corporate leaders deeply committed to corporate charitable giving (Council on Foundations, 1988). The leaders surveyed felt that businesses can and should address community needs, but they were concerned about the amount of corporate cash likely to be available because of flat markets, increased competition, and other changes in the economic environment. The one notion that permeated the survey was the growing emphasis by CEOs on the importance of the health of their communities to the health of their businesses.

Corporate philanthropy is, by its nature, destined to be at the center of tension between two very different cultures: one civic and one corporate, one driven by benevolence and the ballot and the other driven by productivity and profit. But the corporation that is likely to be the most effective in coping with a changing work force, changing communities, and changing public expectations will be the one that best understands the civic culture.

Corporate Contributions: A Corporate View

The present generation of businesspeople has a variety of ways of thinking about the relationship between business and society. Robert Haas, the chief executive officer of Levi Strauss & Company, spoke for many when he said in a speech at Columbia University in 1984 that "however small or large our enterprise, we cannot isolate our business from the society around us. Nor can we function without its goodwill. We may need the goodwill of a neighborhood to enlarge a corner store. We may need well-funded institutions of higher learning to turn out the skilled technical employees we require. We may need adequate community health care to curb absenteeism in our plants. Or we may need fair tax treatment for an industry to be able to compete in the world economy."

Haas is convinced that if a corporation ignores the needs of its communities, it may actually be ignoring its own needs in the long run.

Richard Mahoney, the chairman and CEO of Monsanto Company, uses the language of civic stewardship to describe the corporate stake in community involvement: "We earn our right to operate by doing the right thing—whether the arena is the competitive marketplace, Wall Street, the workplace or the communities in which we do business. . . . Doing the right thing in our communities means accepting our responsibility to be a good citizen—a reliable neighbor who works to improve educational, cultural and civic vitality, while conducting our business in a responsible, forthright manner. We care about and share in the quality of life in every community where we do business" (Monsanto Company, 1988).

When we were primarily a nation of merchants and farmers, and the boss of each farm or store was the owner of the business, both the bosses and the publics with whom they dealt saw the primary responsibility of business as providing goods and services. The goods and services pleased customers, made profits for the owner, and, at the same time, provided the corporation with an inherent legitimacy.

Today, however, the corporation is something far different. It is a social institution with enormous impact on the well-being of society. Some corporations have revenues that are larger than the gross national product of nation-states. They may influence where we live, what we eat, what kind of air we breathe and water we drink, what kind of products we buy, and even how we feel about ourselves and our community.

It is no longer sufficient, therefore, for corporations to simply appeal to classical economic theory or the demands of a marketplace to justify their activities. As those who sell illegal drugs in our communities have demonstrated, meeting a market demand is not necessarily the same as delivering a social good. The same can also be said about maximizing profits; it is not in itself a socially desirable end—new investments do not necessarily produce jobs.

Changes in Public Expectations

People around the world are raising three basic questions about all of their institutions: (1) What social good do they serve? (2) How do they distribute their resources among those from whom they derive their legitimacy? (3) What standards are normative in distinguishing between public and private interests? These are all questions of corporate responsibility. They reflect a continuing expectation by most of the public that their institutions will assume some responsibility for the public good and operate in accordance with normative standards of public responsibility.

The new transnational corporations with headquarters in Japan and other nations with a different tradition of corporate responsibility than found in the United States are also taking note of public expectations. They want to know why American corporations are not satisfied with simply producing a product or providing a service that pleases customers, providing jobs that please employees, and providing profits that please shareholders. Why, in other words, are American businesses using a portion of their profits to promote the general welfare?

How ironic it is that while many businesses in the United States debate the art of Japanese management and analyze the reasons for Japanese success in the marketplace, Japanese businesses have a growing interest in the American notion of corporate citizenship. As representatives of a new economic superpower, Japanese businesspeople are trying to understand the full implication of operating in political cultures and economic systems in which the public expects all of its institutions, public and private, to contribute to the public good. Japan has no tradition of private philanthropy as practiced in the United States and Europe. Japanese philanthropy is primarily corporate, most of it a response to public expectations outside of Japan. This acceptance of corporate giving as part of the way of doing business has led the Japanese government to consider tax incentives for corporate gifts made in the United States by Japanese corporations.

Many Americans expect corporations to make philanthropic contributions. But the manager who makes a social investment in the quality of life of the communities in which the company operates must also deal with critics. Some are social utopians, who want business to do more, economic isolationists, who want business to do less, and reformers, who seek to make business behave better.

Businesses using a portion of their profits for the pursuit of objectives that are not directly identified with economic goals have always been criticized by people who argue that a company's obligation to its shareholders is to pursue profits only. Critics maintain that the ultimate obligation of businesses to society at large is best served when producers of goods or services attempt to maximize profits. Economic isolationists like Milton Friedman, the Nobel laureate economist, categorically object to managers using corporate resources for community benefit on two grounds: our communities and their social needs are so complex that corporate executives will probably not know what course of action or project will achieve the desired results, and managers who involve their corporations in community issues are acting as unauthorized civil servants, taking independent action in areas more appropriately reserved for the elected representatives of the people (Andrews, 1989, pp. 152-153).

Kenneth E. Goodpaster and John B. Matthews responded to this line of criticism for many of their former students who now head business corporations when they wrote in a *Harvard Business Review* article that "the demands of moral responsibility are independent of the demands of political legitimacy. Neither private individuals nor private corporations that guide their conduct by ethical or social values beyond the demands of law should be constrained merely because they are not elected to do so" (Andrews, 1989, p. 163).

The social utopians present almost opposite views from the isolationists. They not only champion business involvement but they also argue that our economy can be revitalized, justice can be established, and a new stage of domestic tranquility can be realized through private-sector initiatives. The social utopians place the business corporation at the center of our national life. Many seek to limit the social role of government while increasing the social role of business. The expectations created by this new public philosophy are far more fundamental than anything envisioned when business was first called upon to help eliminate social inequities and to avoid polluting the environment.

A third group of critics are reformers who seek to make businesses behave better through government regulations or who seek to increase the social involvement of businesses through government incentives. In their ranks can be found consumer groups, environmental groups, community development groups, and stockholder activists who seek to get shareholders concerned about corporate behavior.

Critics of business can no longer be divided along conservative and liberal lines. Some conservative populists rail against big business as emotionally as any radical in the sixties, and some liberals argue that transnational institutions are in many instances the most efficient way to cope with a global economy. Although public expectations of business vary, most Americans continue to believe that a good society depends as much on the goodness of private individuals and private institutions as it does on the soundness of government and the fairness of laws.

Changes in Corporate Response

The new generation of corporate leaders appeals to social as well as economic philosophy in making the case for the importance of corporate public involvement. They usually emphasize one or more of the following themes.

The Idea of Stakeholder Obligation. The conventional notion of *stakeholders* (a play on the word *stockholders*) expresses the view that a corporation has responsibilities to a wide group of constituencies with a stake in its operation. Corporations have long considered the responsibility to shareholders a primary obligation. But they increasingly recognize that they have parallel (sometimes competing) responsibilities to a wide variety of other groups with a stake in their operation, including customers, creditors, communities, employees, suppliers, governments, and nation-states as well as stockholders.

J. Irwin Miller, the former chairman of Cummins Engine Company and preeminent corporate statesmen of the fifties and sixties, did much to focus attention on the idea of stakeholder obligation. For him, the responsibility of business to society begins with the decision to conduct business. The responsible corporation selects a site responsibly, builds a facility responsibly, chooses a work force responsibly, manufactures a product or provides a service responsibly, sets prices responsibly, distributes the return on the investment responsibly, and takes action in the public sector responsibly.

The Idea of Civic Duty. Some businesspeople argue that businesses are corporate citizens, with the rights and duties of citizenship. Some even argue that the corporate charter makes corporations trustees of the public good. Corporations are not simply economic institutions engaged in the business of making a profit but also are social institutions that have an impact on people and their communities. Corporate philanthropy, loaned executives, and corporate leadership of local charity drives reflect a larger commitment to being a good corporate citizen.

The Idea of Enlightened Self-Interest. Some businesspeople see their company's involvement in the community as enlightened self-interest, helping the company and the community at the same time. John H. Bryan (1988), chairman and chief executive officer of the Sara Lee Corporation, argues that altruism is one of the highest virtues for the corporation. In his judgment, it is altogether proper for this motive to stand alongside another motive—enlightened self-interest.

Other corporate executives like Henry Schacht, Irwin Miller's successor at Cummins Engine Company, point out that (1) the existence of a corporation is dependent upon the consent of the various individuals and groups whose lives the corporation affects, (2) a corporation is a social organization formed to produce goods and services in a competitive environment and gets the right to produce these from the consent of those individuals and groups it affects, (3) those who have a stake in a business corporation will make claims on it, and (4) the long-term, self-interest of even the shareholder depends on a corporation's ability to satisfy the claims of other stakeholders.

The Idea of Competitive Advantage. Public acts of social responsibility are sometimes used to enhance a company's image or promote a company's product and goals. *Cause-related marketing,* a phrase coined by American Express in 1981, is a highly visible effort by a corporation to earn a direct return for corporate charitable donations. The term refers to charitable efforts in which the company ties contributions to sales or the specific use of products and services. While some executives argue that this is simply a form of enlightened self-interest, critics call it "phony philanthropy," exploiting philanthropic causes for financial benefit. They make a distinction between enlightened self-interest, which seeks a congruence between public and private interest, and selfish interest, which begins and ends with the corporate interest.

These four ideas reflect differences in emphasis rather than totally independent rationales. The corporate executive defending the company's community involvement may make no distinction between enlightened self-interest and stakeholder obligation or between the idea of competitive advantage and civic duty.

In addition to changes in the concept of corporate giving, important changes are occurring in the content of corporate giving.

Changing Priorities. In 1978, 37 percent of all corporate giving by U.S. businesses went to health and human services organizations, as compared to 27 percent ten years later (AAFRC Trust for Philanthropy, 1989). The percentage of corporate giving that goes to education has remained almost exactly the same for the last ten years, but the mix within the educational category has changed dramatically. Corporate philanthropy increasingly emphasizes precollegiate education, and many companies are seeking to find ways to intervene effectively in the educational process. As the American economy comes to depend more on a well-trained work force, American businesses are investing more in education and training—starting sometimes before kindergarten.

Even higher education grants are changing as more corporate grants to colleges and universities are restricted to specific projects. Corporate giving for art and culture has remained largely unchanged, around 10 percent for the last decade. Corporate giving for civic and community projects has increased significantly.

Changing Leaders in Corporate Giving. The petroleum and manufacturing industries have traditionally been the leaders in corporate giving, but structural and other changes throughout business have led to structural changes in corporate grantmaking. The original corporate leaders now find that their numbers are smaller, their employees are fewer, and their overall ability to make a difference is less.

In an era of mergers and acquisitions, many nonprofit organizations accustomed to being beneficiaries of corporate support are now concerned that when two corporations merge, one plus one does not necessarily equal two. If the two merging corporations originally gave $100,000 in support of the same project, the merger is not likely to result in a $200,000 gift.

Few Role Models. It was not too long ago that talk of corporate ethics and public responsibility flooded boardrooms and consumed the agendas of many business organizations. Five percent and 2 percent giving clubs were formed, and companies like Dayton Hudson, Cummins, Atlantic Richfield, and Levi Strauss were the leaders in creative and effective corporate giving. While new companies have joined or surpassed these companies in effectiveness, the new generation of leaders in corporate giving is not as well known.

Slowdown in Growth of Giving. From 1975 to 1985, corporate giving grew at an annual average rate of more than 10 percent. A revised estimate of giving in 1986 and 1987 shows corporate giving increased by an extraordinary 15 percent in 1986 and declined by about 10 percent in 1987, suggesting that the 1986 Tax Reform Act appears to have had the same impact on corporate giving that it had on individual giving. Giving increased to take advantage of the higher incentives of the old tax law before the new law took effect, but in reality corporate giving was, for the first time in a decade, stabilizing into a pattern of slower growth. The growth from 1988 to 1989 was 4.2 percent, from $4.8 billion to $5 billion.

Thus, anxiety about the future of corporate giving on the part of some nonprofit groups is understandable. Not only are they having to cope with a reduction in the social role of government, but the demand side of philanthropy is increasing at a much faster rate than the supply side.

A Rapidly Changing Society: New Challenges

More and more corporate executives are focusing their giving programs on plant and facility communities. But if these giving programs are to be effective, executives will need to understand several key changes taking place in their communities. The first is the changing boundaries of community—a paradigm shift from the notion of a network of neighbors to the metaphor of a company of strangers. The second is the continuing barriers to community—the resurgence of racism, nativism, and a distorted form of nationalism. The third is the changing blueprint for community—creating community by design.

Changing Community Boundaries. We in the United States are prone to romanticizing the good old days when neighbors came together to build each other's barns, a time when communities were smaller and social cohesion and civic solidarity came from a common race, religion, or culture. But as Parker Palmer points out in his book, *The Company of Strangers* (1981), community in the years ahead is likely to involve a dynamic process in which strangers meet, discover their commonality, deal with their conflicts, and celebrate their unity while still remaining strangers. The strangers with an impact on the future well-being of business are the new immigrants and the minority groups in the United States, who will soon comprise the majority of the labor pool from which business will draw its work force.

Thus, the boundaries of community are not only changing conceptually and demographically but functionally as well. In the past, we saw our communities as divided functionally between three sectors: a public sector driven by the ballot, a private sector driven by profit, and a voluntary sector driven by compassion. But these boundaries are increasingly ambiguous, with the private sector engaged in the delivery of social services for a profit and voluntary organizations turning to profit-making measures to make up for the loss in government revenues. The impact of entrepreneurial activities on nonprofit organizations that are need driven and the capacity for compassion among social service providers that are market driven is often questioned.

The functional problems of plant and facility communities can be examined on another level as well. The so-called independent sector so widely celebrated in the United States and the United Kingdom is in many ways both interdependent and dependent. Many people are surprised to learn that government both in the United States and the United Kingdom is, and has been for some time, the single most important source of the voluntary sector's income. Business executives who are involved with their communities will almost certainly find themselves involved with government, either directly or indirectly. The new emphasis on business-government partnerships has produced what Peter Drucker describes as the fourth sector of public-private partnerships.

These partnerships can in many instances maximize the impact of the charitable dollar. But the intertwining of corporate contributions with local government revenues can also lead to problems if caution is not exercised. It would be a mistake for corporate philanthropy to be used primarily to bail out institutions endangered by the reduction of government support. Many of these institutions are important and should survive, but each corporation should carefully consider whether it wants to set its own agenda or simply respond to the agenda set by others.

The boundaries of community are also changing geographically. In a report on the evolving federal-state relationship, the Education Commission of the States points out that many cities are spilling into multistate jurisdictions. Forty percent of the residents of the metropolitan St. Louis area, for example, actually live in the state of Illinois, 30 percent of the residents of the metropolitan Memphis area live across the state border in Arkansas, and many of the people in the metropolitan Omaha area actually reside in Iowa (Peirce, 1989).

The same changes are occurring across the national boundaries in which business operates. The changing boundaries of community in the Eastern European Bloc, the European Economic Community, and the Pacific Rim; the pressure for new boundaries in the Middle East and Africa; and the migration of population groups across old boundaries challenge our notion of community as defined by geography. Communications technology, education, and travel have created groups that identify with others far beyond their geographical boundaries. Thus, the commitment to community philanthropy raises some major questions about what a corporation's community is.

Continuing Barriers to Community. Business executives who seek to understand the social context of their philanthropy must also understand how the continuing barriers to community are likely to influence their ability to invest their charitable dollars wisely. The first, and in some ways most fundamental, of these barriers is the resurgence of racism. Race is an issue that businesspeople, like politicians, go to great pains to avoid discussing publicly. But privately, it lingers in the consciousness of many of our citizens and manifests itself in many community practices. The constant drumbeat of racial explosions seems to suggest that something has happened in the eighties to make racism acceptable again. Racism is, for the moment, one of the single most critical threats to the coherence people need to act and feel like a community.

The resurgence of racism is accompanied by the resurgence of nativism, the fear or disdain for those who are not native born. Nativism raised its ugly head with the wave of immigrants in other periods of American history, but we are seeing its rebirth in Europe and Asia as well as in the United States as the movement of populations across the old boundaries threatens old centers of meaning and belonging.

The 1980s also ushered in new forms of nationalism that distorted patriotism into parochialism. It is only natural that human beings feel some affinity with their corner of the globe and with those who share a common history within national boundaries. But transnational community will require transnational philanthropy that respects national differences and cultural uniqueness while it promotes the kind of coherence people need to act as caring communities.

Probably nothing threatens the stability of American communities as much as poverty. The 1988 figures released by the Census Bureau brought bad news. The gap between rich and poor

Americans was the highest in the forty years that it has been measured. The social deficit that now exists alongside the federal budget deficit and international trade deficit may be more ominous for the United States than most businesspeople realize. We are the only industrial country in which children constitute the largest category of the poor. An editorial in the *Washington Post* described our national predicament: "The society is less equal than it ought to be and than it used to be; too many people, too many children are in need of help."

Changing Blueprint for Community. The greatest challenge facing the managers of corporations in the years ahead may be in helping to build social cohesion and civic solidarity in the midst of the many changes that are now occurring in cities, neighborhoods, and other forms of local community. As was evident in the aftermath of the 1989 earthquake in San Francisco, it is easy to build community when there is a crisis, but it is difficult to sustain the sense of community once the crisis is over. We need to learn to build community by design, to identify the elements of a strong and resilient civic infrastructure to match the sound physical infrastructure successful communities require.

The National Civic League, a very respected American citizens' organization begun by Teddy Roosevelt and other social reformers in the 1890s, has developed a civic index that it believes can be used to help design, develop, or sustain healthy communities. Neal Peirce (1989), a columnist and authority on urban issues, describes the elements of the index as the ingredients necessary for communities to "coalesce and function more cohesively." The principal components of the civic index provide excellent guidelines for community philanthropy aimed at building viable communities that can support and maintain viable businesses. They include:

1. Citizen participation. As Peirce reminds us, a city without strong citizen participation is not so much a community as it is a shell that people inhabit.
2. Community leadership. Strong communities have strong leaders, not simply the Lone Ranger variety of yesterday but leaders

who share leadership and reflect the diversity of the community in microcosm.

3. Government performance. Those who run the machineries of government must not only perform well, but in an age when perception is sometimes more important than reality, they must be perceived to be performing well.

4. Philanthropy and voluntarism. Not enough charitable dollars are available to meet basic human needs or to maintain failing infrastructures. But philanthropy can be to communities what the research and development budget is to business corporations, providing the money to think before acting, to take the long view, and to consider alternative policy options.

5. Intergroup relations. The multiethnic, multiracial complexion of our future requires new ways of resolving conflicts, new appreciation for cultural differences, and new ways of responding to increased diversity in schools, the workplace, and the many social groups that provide meaning and belonging.

Professionalization of Corporate Contributions Programs

Among the many considerations confronting the executive who wishes to establish a corporate contributions program that can respond effectively to the changing social context of business, few are as important as who will set priorities and provide direction. It is ironic that many business executives who would never make a decision about marketing or manufacturing without the best advice available are quite willing to make decisions about corporate philanthropy without the benefit of advice and counsel of equal competence or stature.

Although private philanthropy is generally regarded as more art than science, corporate contributions programs can be enhanced by planning, evaluation, needs assessment, and the techniques of good management. Some companies are turning to professional staff for their giving programs. Others who feel that their grantmaking programs are not large enough to justify staff may find it useful to use existing resources in the communities in which they do business.

A business might, for example, link up with a community

foundation, utilizing it for assessment of community needs and even processing of grants. In other situations, indigenous groups or community leaders who are familiar with the full spectrum of community needs and issues can be very helpful. Regardless of the approach used, the social needs of communities are far too complex to lend themselves to affective rather than cognitive responses. Many good grants may be made on the basis of intuition, but over the long term it is best to apply the techniques of objective analysis and careful planning to grantmaking.

This professionalism should not be confused with *credentialism*, the delegation of responsibility to people who assume a monopoly on expertise based on training or credentials. Actually, the word that best describes the qualities I have found to be most needed in running a contributions program comes directly out of the lexicon of business—*entrepreneurialism*. This word emphasizes flexibility and risk taking as well as judgment and wisdom.

But the tension between entrepreneurialism and credentialism in the larger society is also to be found in corporate giving programs. We romanticize daring and the lack of rigidity, but we reward order, stability, and that ever-present euphemism, a track record.

More and more corporate giving programs have become professionalized within the last decade, operating with contributions committees, using outside resources, or employing staff. This focus on the craft of grantmaking is likely to be even more important in the future, as demographic and other changes make it more difficult to discern how best to ensure the maximum return on the charitable investment. Professional staff not only provide special insight into community needs and philanthropic opportunities but they also serve as intermediaries for the busy executive—doing research, interviewing applicants, evaluating proposals, and ensuring that management is kept apprised of changing needs and trends in society.

Corporate giving officers are a unique resource to their companies in areas that go far beyond the formal contributions program. At a time in which societies around the world are having to cope with the ambiguities between the public and private sectors, many corporate giving officers have already mastered this art. What they have learned and what they are learning every day make them a very special resource for dealing with changing communities and changing public expectations.

This may seem like an unduly romantic and overly optimistic view of a position that is not only ambiguous itself but is in many places marginal. Yet, I offer this observation not as the idle hopes of an outsider but as the view of an insider who participated in the transformation of the corporate giving program of one company from a program concerned exclusively with charitable giving to one at the hub of corporate responsibility.

The responsibilities of the corporate giving officer may only include corporate contributions or may include other forms of public engagement, but, in either case, this person is strategically positioned to provide assistance to management in a variety of areas, including corporate values. Almost everyone agrees that honesty, fairness, respect, tolerance, and compassion are primary moral virtues, but the corporate giving officer is often prepared to go one step further, helping management to make good ethical decisions by looking at each pending decision and asking, Will someone get hurt, will someone be helped, and who will benefit?

Sometimes self-interest in its most narrow form—selfish interest—is assumed to be the primary or the proper motivational force of the corporation. This assumption has its own corporate theology, paraphrasing Thomas Aquinas's assertion that "every man desires his own good" to state that "every institution seeks its own good." Its economic philosophy is, of course, patterned on Adam Smith's declaration that the primal human instinct is self-love.

Even Thomas Hobbes would be pleased. But "self-serving" values are not effective without "other-serving" values as well. To stand at the point of intersection between the corporate and civic cultures is to stand both for a prudence that looks inward and a benevolence that looks outward. Corporate philanthropy begins as a voluntary ethic, but those who successfully bridge the gap between the two cultures have insights and experiences that can help transform it into a corporate ethic that combines the imperatives of business with the imperatives of a civil society in ways that serve the common good of both.

References

AAFRC Trust for Philanthropy. *Giving USA, 1989*. New York: AAFRC Trust for Philanthropy, 1989.

Andrews, K. R. *Ethics in Practice*. Boston: Harvard Business School Press, 1989.

Bryan, J. H. Speech made to the Arthur Andersen Partners' Breakfast, Chicago, Ill., Dec. 19, 1988.

Council on Foundations. *The Climate for Giving: The Outlook of Current and Future CEOs*. Washington, D.C.: Council on Foundations, 1988.

Monsanto Company. *A Commitment to Greatness*. The Monsanto Company, 1988.

Palmer, P. *The Company of Strangers*. New York: Crossroad, 1981.

Peirce, N. Remarks made at Community Foundation Conference sponsored by Council on Foundations in Philadelphia, Penn., Oct. 24, 1989.

Chapter Two

The Evolution of Corporate
Grantmaking in America

Barry D. Karl

Modern corporate philanthropy is, in a sense, an outgrowth of the tradition of benevolence practiced by wealthy individuals in the early days of agrarian and industrial capitalism. Although we can easily romanticize that tradition, it was generally understood at the time that wise, self-interested owners of plantations and factories would accept responsibility for providing at least minimal services for their laborers and the communities in which they lived.

A school of thought that can be traced back to the Puritans argued that corporations had inherent responsibilities that stemmed from their dependence on the moral fundamentals of human settlement, ranging from the protections provided them by the state to the moral injunctions placed on all economic activity by the requirements of religious institutions. That viewpoint did not stop Puritan investors in their comfortable places of business in England from responding to their fellow religionists' descriptions of the hardships they were suffering in the New World with their own complaints about the low return on their investments. The New World's capital was land and land that took more labor than trading companies had assumed it would take.

More than two centuries later, Henry George (1979 [1879]) argued that land got its value from the ways communities determined their practices of settlement, not from any value inherent in the land itself. The community, therefore, had rights in land that it encouraged others to develop, and the developers of land had responsibilities to the community that went beyond profits. Thorstein Veblen (1979 [1899]) castigated the "captains of industry" not for making money but for withdrawing it from the economic system to decorate themselves and their lives with what he called "conspicuous consumption."

The long history of efforts to make wealthy people responsible extends back at least as far as the practice of tithing that required religious contribution and the legal definitions of usury that can be found in both Christian and Moslem condemnations of the use of money to create more money rather than to contribute to the community's need for livelihood. Traditionally, the relationship between private enterprise and the various governments that make public policy in the United States has been debated through the issue of taxation. Simply put, the services the public wanted from government were funded by collecting taxes from the citizenry, which originally included property owners and corporations. The proportion of tax paid by each and the question of what the actual tax would be levied on have always been subjects of debate, some of it acrimonious. But, again in simple terms, the government decided how that money would be used to provide services. As historians are always quick to tell us, nothing is ever so simple as to be summarized in one brief sentence, so I am forced to add that the periodic resolutions of debates over taxes have always been temporary and ultimately unsatisfactory to all participants. Our habit of speaking of taxes and death in the same breath suggests both the simplicity and the profundity of the problem.

Historically, American governments have tended to expand the services they provide to the public. Our politics have required this expansion, and our election campaigns have traditionally been litanies of promises. But taxpayer rebellions have a history that cuts across any lines of economic class. The demand for services and the willingness to pay the taxes that provide these services might as well be creeds from two diametrically opposed religions. Taxing corporations to help finance services is the established and traditional way of viewing the corporation's responsibility to the public. In that way the public retains control over the way corporations influence public policy, it is assumed, because government decides how the tax money is to be spent.

In a very important sense, corporate giving is based on the idea that corporations ought to have a way of influencing public policy directly through the power to decide how their contributions to public well-being will be spent rather than leaving such decisions to political negotiations. The history of the disputes over corporate philanthropy rests on the problems generated by differing attitudes toward the potential power presumed to be hidden behind such gifts. Those attitudes range from the belief that the corporation has only two public contributions to make beyond its productive enterprise—its profits to its stockholders and its taxes to the community—to the belief that powerful corporations can endanger the public's right to make policy for itself. The former argument questions the appropriateness of corporate intervention in the social order. The latter raises complex issues of corporate responsibility or irresponsibility. In an odd way, taxation serves as the uneasy link between corporations and the public welfare—never enough money to satisfy those who demand more corporate contributions to the public and more than enough money to anger those who resent the way government spends the taxes it collects from them.

The courts tried to resolve the debates over corporate philanthropy and facilitate compromise by allowing corporations to give to projects that somehow reflected their particular self-interest. The definition of *direct benefit* became the battleground of dispute until relatively recently when the demand for a broadening of the concept appeared to succeed in transforming it entirely. The stage for modern corporate giving was set, but, if history has any meaning at all, the disputants themselves were likely to be transformed, not obliterated. A closer look at the background of corporate philanthropy might therefore be useful.

Nineteenth-Century Corporate Philanthropy

Nineteenth-century philanthropists were businessmen who gave a portion of their business profits to causes they deemed worthy. It was their money and their decision. They also paid taxes to support institutions for the care of the poor and the indigent sick whether or not they approved of these goals.

By the end of the eighteenth century, and increasingly in the nineteenth, however, economists and social theorists questioned the utility of charity as a method of coping with the ever-present problem of poverty. Supporting the poor in their poverty only kept them in that condition, they argued. And while some economists and social theorists were beginning to suggest that philanthropy could fund sciences to search out the root causes of poverty, to end it once and for all, others believed that the use of profits to expand production and thereby to provide jobs for the unemployed was the only appropriate way for businessmen to affect social problems. By the end of the nineteenth century, the various doctrines that were lumped together to produce what historians have called Social Darwinism combined elements of both beliefs: that only the demonstrably fit deserved to survive and that some of those who appeared unfit could be improved by science.

Contradictory though the ideas may sometimes have seemed, together they sustained the growing belief that the role of business in social matters was properly limited to the things business did best—produce profits and employment. Charity was antithetical to that aim. At the same time, the growth of the large corporation and the diversification of its ownership raised a new range of social and political issues. The fear of such economic entities and the political debates over the supposedly threatening influence of trusts on national economic policy generated an atmosphere of popular opinion that scarcely inclined anyone to believe that corporations were instruments for doing good. Even people unwilling to accept the idea that corporations were insidious monsters bent on destroying the well-being of the man in the street still looked on them as potentially ungovernable animals in need of regulatory control.

A beneficent mind in the boardroom ran counter to even the best images of a captain of industry, whose ruthlessness and dominance were virtues to be admired. Neither stockholders nor their Marxist revolutionary critics expected industrial leaders to do anything but lead. Their function was to guide the ship, not nurse the crew. Utopians in both the conservative and revolutionary camps based their predictions of the future on that conviction. Yet the urge to philanthropy among many industrial leaders was part of a practical reality that reflected an old and continuing interest in the business community, an interest based on the belief that community philanthropy was an expression of self-interest and good business.

Although gift giving by business corporations is a special species of beneficence, it faces all the problems of traditional philanthropy. Corporations give because they believe that it is in their interest to do so. In the early nineteenth century, that interest was relatively easy to define. Owners of businesses were also members of the communities in which they did business. As both owners and managers, they could expect appeals from organizations run by people like themselves, fellow business leaders and their wives who volunteered their time to help citizens in need. They also could expect to solicit donations from time to time, and they gave with an awareness of what the entire process meant. Christmastime benevolence, unusually hard winters, recurrent epidemics, and periods of economic hard times joined the routine search for funds by the almshouses, orphanages, and hospitals as reminders to the fortunate that their blessings might depend on higher powers who had to be propitiated. Theories of stewardship of wealth defined such responsibility for giving. Providence, it could be argued, determined who would receive and control the community's wealth; those who had benefited from the selection were required to care for those who had not.

Less theological interpretations of self-interest also affected the process of giving. Urban leaders were well aware of their own needs. A contented labor force and a buying public were essential parts of the community in which business expected to operate. The poor, the unemployed, the sick, and the uneducated were not equipped to work or to buy. Their existence and their persistence damaged the stability of the system and, at the same time, represented the failure of the community to achieve the minimum standards of well-being that were increasingly part of the promise of political progress. It was thus easy to see the relation between the business climate of a stable urban community and the self-interest of the businessman and his gifts.

Narrow definitions of self-interest contributed to the development of American corporate philanthropy in its early years. Railroads spanned a continental wilderness between the settlements of the trans-Mississippi West and California. Railroads were willing to contribute to the establishment of Young Men's Christian Associations as hostels for the work force needed to build and run the rapidly growing rail system and as anchors for the social communities required for the expansion of American civilization westward. Yet, even then, more sophisticated conceptions of community planning were subject to debate. The need for thriving communities along the rail lines to produce goods for the railroads to carry and to serve as markets for goods produced elsewhere stimulated only a few of the more enlightened railroad managers to attempt to extend their responsibilities from the housing of a work force to the creation of new communities. James J. Hill of the Great Northern Railroad, a line that ran through some of the most uninhabited and uninhabitable part of the great West, was a model of such a responsible manager, partly because he stood so singularly alone.

Railroad car builder George Pullman was forced to face the issue squarely and painfully when he created a model town for his workers near his plant site south of Chicago. Elaborate and attractive public buildings, as well as planned housing facilities, were part of a carefully constructed plan that drew worldwide attention. But when the panic of 1893 and the depression that followed forced wage cuts and layoffs, Pullman was not willing to be forgiving of his workers' rent and utility bills. Pullman was not in a position to argue company policy on such matters on his own, if he indeed considered the idea. He had already convinced doubtful colleagues that the profits of the expanding industry could be used for building communities for workers. Increasingly, industrial managers who wanted to put company money into worker benefits were going to face the criticism of directors and fellow investors who thought such benefits a form of charity that had no place in the operation of a profit-making business.

Twentieth-Century Corporate Philanthropy

Pullman's problems were destined to characterize the next twenty-five years of judicial and legislative debate over the benefits managers could offer employees without incurring the wrath of stockholders who considered such benefits an assault on their rights to receive dividends fully reflecting the company's profits. Henry Ford's efforts not only to follow Pullman but to outdo him in benefits for his workers were destined to establish the legal practices that made such benevolence—if *benevolence* is the right word—clearly impossible.

Labor disputes of the period, of which the Pullman strike was one of the more dramatic, had brought labor conditions under public scrutiny, but it was the role of labor in the First World War that laid the groundwork for new understandings between industrial managers and the labor force. Wartime boards spoke of such standards as "a living wage" and rejected the idea that labor was nothing more than a commodity to be priced and traded as some fantasy image of a worker's market. By 1921, Internal Revenue Service policy accepted the idea that business donations to charitable, medical, or educational institutions were legitimate if such institutions served the needs of the firm's employees. This change in policy reflected a limited broadening of the idea that corporate philanthropy could be justified only where direct benefit to the company could be demonstrated.

The ideas that led to the creation of the concept of direct benefit are generally traced to a famous statement of England's Lord Justice Bowen in the *Hutton* case of 1883 (Hutton *v.* West Cork Railway Co., 23 L.R. Ch. Div., 1883, p. 654): "Charity has no business sitting at the board of directors, qua charity," a richly quotable British assertion that had little to do with the issue of philanthropy. The company in question was going out of business and the stockholders had authorized gratuities to be paid to the retiring directors. Such gifts, the lord justice ruled, were not "reasonably incidental to the carrying on of the company's business for the company's benefit." As is sometimes the case in judicial history, however, the words served a wider purpose than the situation to which they had originally been directed. A judicial aside constituting a critical attack on a highly questionable practice became a noble doctrine designed to measure all corporate behavior. The fact that the concept of direct benefit was used until 1953 suggests perhaps the need for such a doctrine to limit and define practices that had yet to find their place in the growth of the modern corporation.

The historical conditions that reshaped the idea of direct benefit were dramatic events that could not have been predicted. World War I occasioned the transformation, as it did for so many other national attitudes and practices. The actions taken during the war were intended only to meet unprecedented war needs. The possibility that they might become part of the public policy was scarcely a worry.

The rapidly escalating demands the war placed on one of the nation's oldest national philanthropies, the Red Cross, had raised the issue of corporate giving. The Red Cross first faced the task of aiding civilian populations of war-torn Europe. After the United States declared war on Germany and its allies in April 1917, the Red Cross quickly took over the role of serving the needs of Americans in Europe. Although newly formed philanthropic organizations like the Rockefeller Foundation quickly stepped in to help (and on a hitherto unprecedented scale), the responsibilities of the Red Cross seemed literally to explode and were well beyond the resources of any single organization operating on an older charitable model. The solicitation of contributions from individuals began, again with new methods and with a much enlarged program, but even that was not sufficient. Fund raisers needed to tap corporate resources and to tap them fast.

If Justice Bowen's words were heard in corporate boardrooms and in the offices of corporate legal advisers, they were muted, as indeed many dissenting sentiments were muted, by the sense of wartime emergency and the government's assertion of the need for unquestioning national patriotism to defeat the Hun. Businesses were still cautious on the legal issues involved, and they used a shrewd device that placed on the potentially irate stockholder the responsibility for vetoing the corporation's actions. "The Red Cross dividend" enabled companies to request authorization from stockholders for a special dividend to be contributed to the Red Cross.

Individual stockholders could refuse to serve the nation in its time of troubles—if they dared to, that is.

Wartime legislation in the states of Texas and New York permitted gifts by corporations, although it was clear that permission for such gifts was stimulated by and possibly limited to the war effort. Over the next decades, however, states were increasingly inclined to include such gifts among the powers of corporations—but Congress was not so inclined where income tax policy was concerned. Congress raised the issue of tax deductions for corporate gifts in its debates over the Revenue Act of 1919 and explicitly rejected the idea. The survival of the wartime method of philanthropy was not altogether assured, to say the least, but the wartime experience was a persistent reminder to the growing number of community organizations in need of funds. Reform legislation over the previous three decades had placed increasing responsibility on state and local governments to provide modernized services in education, medical care, social welfare, and professional urban management. Such services, once the province of voluntary associations of citizen amateurs, were costly and a strain on the tax bases of many of the nation's growing metropolitan regions. Throughout the 1920s, traditional philanthropic organizations joined with the expanding service agencies to form central funding groups and single fund drives. Community Chests and United Ways, under various local names, proliferated on a national scale, and with the wartime Red Cross drives as a model, they sought to adapt in peacetime an effective method of operation learned in the war. Herbert Hoover was one of the architects of the new method of raising funds. As secretary of commerce, he attempted to persuade industry to fund university research and training. As president, he moved quickly, once the Depression had started, to marshal the nation's charitable and philanthropic resources to deal with what he presumed to be a short-term emergency.

Despite Hoover's efforts, the Depression rapidly taxed charitable and philanthropic resources to the breaking point. Although no one wanted to admit it, the war had generated jobs and profits. The Depression, certainly, generated neither. Unwilling to accept the idea that government would have to intervene, Hoover launched a heroic campaign, gathering together business leaders and radio and movie entertainers to persuade the public to give, but the legal status of corporate charity remained unclear. Corporate legal advisers still believed that the only safe philanthropy would be benefits to workers and, stretching themselves cautiously, services in the communities in which the workers lived. The principle of direct benefit excluded everything else. Winning the war had been a direct benefit, but the war was over. Would aiding the poor and the unemployed qualify?

By 1934, the Depression was still at its depths, despite initial advances made by the New Deal, and the question called for resolution. The Old Mission Portland Cement Company found itself testing the point in the courts. It had claimed that its contributions to the San Francisco Community Chest were of direct benefit to its business interests because they improved the company's standing among its customers. The Supreme Court, citing what it knew to have been congressional intent in excluding charitable deductions for corporations in 1919, said no. Although the decision did not attack the principle or the action of Congress as such, it did threaten the future of corporate philanthropy. The Community Chests organized an effective lobbying effort that resulted in amendments to the Internal Revenue Code of 1936 permitting charitable contributions by corporations if they did not exceed "five percentum of the taxpayer's net income as computed without the benefit of this subsection" (Internal Revenue Code, Section 170).

What the Supreme Court's decision and Congress's response to it did was to blur the issue of direct benefit. If the Court had allowed for a broadening of the definition to include charitable service to the community, companies would not have been limited in their gifts except by their capacity to see such gifts as legitimate business expenses and to deduct them accordingly as costs of doing business. Congress effectively created the distinction between a charitable gift and a business deduction, a distinction destined to prove as troublesome as the problem it appeared, for the time, to resolve. To be sure, companies were prohibited from claiming both charitable and business deductions for the same gift, but making the distinction between the two deductions was not always going to be easy. The fate of the concept of direct benefit was not at all obvious, and legal advisers of corporations were inclined to look on it as a dead bee whose sting could still hurt.

The urge to limit corporate charity was part of the antibusiness rhetoric of the New Deal era, but it was also a concern that stretched back to the Populist and Progressive era debates over the power of large corporations. Most people believed that business acting in its own interest, defined as narrowly as possible, was safer than business acting on the basis of some broadly conceived public or charitable interest. While the term once applied to John D. Rockefeller's charitable contributions—*tainted*—does not appear to have been raised, it clearly was implied. Naked self-interest was acceptable; self-interest concealed under the cloak of charity was dangerous.

Transformations in tax policy during World War II both complicated and extended the definition of corporate contributions. The groundwork for business donations to war-related charitable activities had already been laid. The Excess Profits Tax, combined with restrictions on consumer goods to be advertised and sold, led to increased corporate funding of cultural events as institutional advertising. Yet, even at the height of wartime affluence, people remained concerned for the future and were scarcely reassured by the debate over whether or not government intervention had in fact ended the Depression. Although most economists remained convinced that the temporary full employment created by World War II would lead once again into a major postwar depression, government support of benefit for veterans seemed to be staving off the predicted collapse. By 1950 the issue faded. The Cold War and its explosion in the Korean War shifted the focus completely. Periods of relative economic stability, interspersed with periods of economic manipulation by government that seemed to work, made it possible for most Americans to forget that some Americans still lived in conditions of intractable poverty.

At the same time, fears among managers of the nation's private institutions of higher education mounted as the G.I. Bill, which had helped them weather the war and pull out of the twelve years of prewar depression, threatened to come to an end. Corporations could certainly continue to contribute to research programs that benefited their interests, but the question of general budget

support and contributions to capital funding remained unanswered. The change in the New Deal tax policies remained to be
tested by stockholder suits. When the A. P. Smith Manufacturing
Company gave $1,000 to Princeton University, the stage was set for
the debate.

In upholding the company's action in Smith *vs*. Barlow, the
Supreme Court of New Jersey not only overturned the direct benefits rule but also repudiated the need for permissive legislation to
make such donations possible. "And since in our view," the court
states, "the corporate power to make reasonable charitable contributions exists under modern conditions, even apart from express
statutory provision, its enactments simply constitute helpful and
confirmatory declarations of such power, accompanied by limiting
safeguards." The court went on to justify its overturning of the
direct benefit concept by arguing the social responsibility of corporations as members of larger communities (A.P. Smith Manufacturing Co. *v*. Barlow, et al., 13 N.J. 145, 98 A. 2d 551, 1953).
Philanthropy thus was not only permissible within the range of
corporate enterprise but quite possibly a condition of public
responsibility.

The court's appeal to historic change presented the issue
clearly. "When the wealth of the nation was primarily in the hands
of individuals, they discharged their responsibilities as citizens by
donating freely for charitable purposes. With the transfer of wealth
to corporate hands and the imposition of heavy burdens of individual taxation, they have been unable to keep pace with increased
philanthropic needs. They have therefore, with justification, turned
to corporations to assume the modern obligations of good citizenship in the same manner as humans do."

Philanthropic Foundations

To argue that corporate philanthropy came of age in *Smith* vs.
Barlow is tempting, but exaggerated. Corporate philanthropy still
does not come close to the 5 percent of income permitted under the
provisions established in 1935. Whether recent urgings, some of

them based on a case more than thirty years old, are going to make a significant difference remains to be seen. But some issues worth considering are apparent in the history of the foundation as a form of government-enabled philanthropy.

First, replacing the rule of direct benefit with doctrines of public responsibility may not be as easy as it sounds. All of us are expected to figure out what will be directly beneficial to our interests and needs. We do not have common doctrines of social responsibility that empower us to determine what someone else's interests and needs might be. Foundations have learned the hard way that their efforts to influence the public interest have not gained them friends in every camp. They have grown accustomed to living with public criticisms of what they do and how they do it. Their social and cultural experiments have drawn mixed reviews even from experts, and their efforts to reform other parts of the country than their own, let alone the world, have been sharply attacked by people who consider their interests endangered by reform. Direct benefit may seem to be a selfish standard, but it is safe. Being "socially responsible" is not going to be any easier for corporations to define than it is for individuals.

Second, foundations and their donors have learned that the world that receives their largesse may not bless them for it. As a public relations ploy, the business of giving away money has limits even John D. Rockefeller had to accept. He got better press from the dimes he distributed than from the dollars, and even that was not very good. The public relations effects of philanthropy are mixed at best. Being publicly responsible has never been a dependable source of approval.

A reading of the *Smith* case makes it clear that the Court saw a definite purpose in corporate giving, a purpose that broadened self-interest but by no means discarded it. Previous to the *Smith* case, foundations had expressed their purpose as in concert with the idea of general welfare for all of mankind. *Smith* vs. *Barlow* specified support for the American way of life, the defense not only of democracy but of free enterprise against attack by foreign ideology. Support for corporate capitalism is, after all, part of corporate self-interest. Nonetheless, the ideological underpinnings of the case are clearer now than they ever have been for foundations and their purposes.

Third, foundations know that their relations with American politics are complex and dangerous. The lines that separate philanthropic behavior from political action are sensitive trip wires that, if crossed, will trigger an attack on foundations for using their money to obtain political ends. In a society like ours, in which everything is a potential subject of political debate, separating philanthropic and political contributions has not been easy. Congress has persistently tried to forbid foundations from involving themselves in political matters, and foundations have just as persistently argued their right to do good as they see it. Even in an earlier era, when it was easier to draw lines between what government did and what people did for themselves, the distinction between philanthropic and political contributions was tricky. Nonetheless, philanthropists have always had to learn that money, even generously and sweetly given, is still power.

Finally, there is a sense in which foundations have always been uncomfortable with doctrines of "general purpose" and the "welfare of mankind." Their search for definition and specificity has taken the form of anxiety about "program," as most of them have come to put it. If, like some kind of perverse oyster, they have sometimes turned the pearls they were initially given back into grains of sand, they nonetheless found the irritations of specificity more satisfying than the uncertainties of their initial license and, therefore, less troublesome in the long run.

Corporate philanthropists may find themselves facing that problem in reverse. The concepts of self-interest and direct benefit may have been restrictive, but they served as the lodestones that have made justification possible, if not always easy. The search for new directions without such guidance will provoke discomfort, at least, and, at worst . . . ? We will undoubtedly see. The power of large corporations has long been one of the bugbears of American politics, but most doubts about corporations have always rested on the belief that their power was a power to do harm. What we must now cope with is their power to do good.

References

George, H. *Progress and Poverty*. New York: Penguin, 1979. (Originally published 1879.)

Veblen, T. *Theory of the Leisure Class*. New York: Penguin, 1979. (Originally published 1899.)

Chapter Three

The Strategic Links Between
Business and the Nonprofit Sector

Brian O'Connell

Freedom and the Private Enterprise System

One of the unanticipated roles of the organization INDEPEN-
DENT SECTOR, with which I am involved, has turned out to be
serving as a resource to representatives from other countries who are
eager to learn more about what makes America tick, including our
philanthropy and voluntarism. These people are not necessarily
unhappy with their political structures, but they are keenly aware
that a very real aspect of freedom is missing when multiple opportunities to exercise ability and influence are not available. At best,
they find this lack of opportunity restrictive and at worst, oppressive
when there is only one governmental system and the country has no
tradition of independent markets and criticism.

In 1989, I served as chairman of a Salzburg Seminar that
attempted to ascertain the state of pluralism in various countries
and cultures. For two weeks and through advance study of resource

material, fifty participants compared views and experiences about private initiative in their very different countries. Though our focus was on voluntary initiative as expressed by private philanthropy and community service, it was obvious that the larger interest was pluralistic opportunities of every form, including free enterprise. Intense interest in and encouraging signs of multiple outlets for creativity and influence were evident in the nations of Eastern Europe, such as Hungary and Poland; underdeveloped countries, such as Uganda and India; and the developed countries, such as Japan and Germany.

The very notion of pluralism, upon which the voluntary sector rests, can be seen in the variety of forms of free expression we now see emerging in many countries. Factors encouraging free expression vary by country and culture but include:

- Pressure from the people for change, power, and improved services
- Pressure from within the government to tap the self-interest, time, talent, and money of the people to develop or maintain services
- Pressure from the outside by bodies such as the World Bank, foundations, corporations, international private voluntary organizations (PVOs), and religious groups to accelerate development
- Growing awareness by people and governments of the practical limitations of big government, whatever its form or ideology

When people from Senegal or Thailand discuss opportunities for creativity and influence, they are equally interested in commercial and voluntary endeavors, and they recognize that the common denominator of both is the freedom of individuals to pursue their own ideas. The same freedom that allows a would-be entrepreneur to incorporate a new for-profit business allows any other citizen to form a nonprofit corporation. In the American system of private enterprise, for-profit and nonprofit groups are partners in their mutual and freely pursued efforts to determine the needs of a dynamic society and to find creative and efficient ways of meeting these needs.

The specialness of the American commercial and voluntary

sectors is often recognized more clearly by people from other countries. If we accept that our patterns and levels of participation and generosity make important contributions to our national life, it is important for us to understand and nurture all of the roots that give rise to such pluralism.

Many perceptive American businesspeople understand that our voluntary and commercial opportunities are inescapably linked under the banner of private enterprise and are mutually dependent on our rights to freely engage in such private initiatives. Randall Meyers, former president of Exxon, USA, says that what is at stake in both voluntary and commercial opportunities is "freedom, whether it is expressed in the freedom to state one's beliefs, to teach different philosophies, to form social or labor organizations, or to pursue a business opportunity." He concludes "that all private institutions are harmed when the ability of any one to pursue its legitimate role in society is impaired" (Meyers, 1979).

In an article entitled "We Must Help Each Other," Elvis Stahr, who has had the benefit of viewing the American scene from many different perspectives—Audubon Society president, corporate director, secretary of the army, and university president—says that the profit and nonprofit spheres "must help each other if we expect to attain the independence and freedom that mean so much to us all" (Stahr, 1979).

John D. Rockefeller III, in the article "America's Threatened Third Sector," says that it is essential that all three sectors of our society remain strong. "As long as each sector is healthy, we will preserve our uniqueness, our diversity, the source of much of our strength and creativity—and our best hope for a promising future." He continues, "Two of the sectors are recognizable to everyone: business and government. But the third, the private nonprofit sector, is so little understood that I am tempted to call it 'the invisible sector' " (Rockefeller, 1978).

The Breadth of the Nonprofit Sector

The voluntary side of America is little understood because our unusual levels of generosity and participation have seemed natural, and there appeared to be no need to study them. Recently, however, signs have shown us that we should not assume that these behaviors will go on indefinitely, at least not without some clear understanding and encouragement of them. Research is beginning to produce a body of knowledge about what the independent, or voluntary, sector is and what it contributes to our way of life.

Though the size of the voluntary sector is smaller than most people assume and far smaller than business and government, it is impressive nevertheless. Approximately 900,000 exempt organizations are officially registered with the Internal Revenue Service, but that number does not include religious congregations or the local affiliates of many national organizations such as the Boy Scouts and the American Cancer Society. When these and all the less formal neighborhood and community groups are added in, the figure is something over two million.

A 1988 report from INDEPENDENT SECTOR, "Giving and Volunteering in the United States" (Hodgkinson and Weitzman, 1988), points out that individuals account for approximately 90 percent of all charitable contributions. Corporate giving, as important as it is, only represents 5 percent of all contributions, as does foundation giving. Three-fourths of American families make contributions to the causes of their choice, giving an average of $790 a year. Approximately half of all adult Americans are active volunteers, and they give an average of 4.7 hours a week. Twenty million Americans give 5 percent or more of their income to charity, and 23 million volunteer five or more hours a week. Contributions to voluntary organizations exceeded $100 billion in 1988, and 80 million people volunteered a total of 14.9 billion hours, which, conservatively estimated, is worth another $150 billion.

These "thousand points of light," as President Bush refers to them, include the neighborhood improvement societies, Catholic Charities, overseas relief organizations, American Association of Museum Volunteers, private schools and colleges, United Way, corporate foundations and public service programs, United Negro College Fund, fraternal benevolent societies, National Association of Neighborhoods, conservation and preservation groups, Council of Jewish Women, community foundations, National Public Radio, and millions, not thousands, of other groups. Whether our interest is wildflowers or civil rights, arthritis or clean air, Asian art or literacy, the dying or the unborn, organizations are already at work, and if they do not suit our passion, we can start our own organizations.

We need not go back in American history to find examples of this voluntarism. A far larger proportion and many more parts of the population are involved in community activities today than at any other time in our history. Americans organize to influence every conceivable aspect of the human condition, and they are willing to stand up and be counted on almost any public issue. In recent times, Americans have successfully organized to deal with a vast array of human needs and aspirations, including rights of women, learning disabilities, conflict resolution, culture and rights of Hispanics, problems of the aged, voter registration, culture and rights of Native Americans, experimental theatre, international understanding, drunken driving, population control, consumerism, and on and on. Our interests and impact extend from neighborhoods to the ozone layer and beyond.

It is important to recognize what these opportunities for involvement and pluralistic problem solving mean to the kind of people we are. This voluntary participation strengthens us as a nation, strengthens our communities, and strengthens and fulfills us as individual human beings. The historian Merle Curti says (1958), "Emphasis on voluntary initiative has helped give America her national character."

For the book *America's Voluntary Spirit,* Ann O'Connell and I (1983) reviewed a great many of the major reform movements in the United States. Clearly, these movements contribute not just to social change but also to the spirit, empowerment, and freedom of our people and country. When people care and contribute, not only are causes and other people helped but something very special happens for the giver, and the community and the nation take on a spirit of compassion, comradeship, and confidence. Through work on the companion books *Philanthropy in Action* and *Volunteers in Action* Ann and I (1987, 1989) found thousands of examples of grants and people who have made overwhelming differences in almost every field of human endeavor. These books further illustrate that philanthropy and voluntary action, operating at their best, add an enormous extra dimension to almost everything we want to accomplish.

Beyond helping the urgent causes and crusades, the independent sector simply provides more of us a chance to be different and a bit freer. In his book *The Endangered Sector,* Waldemar Nielsen (1979) summarizes the wonderful variety of interests that Americans freely pursue through our voluntary organizations.

If your interest is people, you can help the elderly by a contribution to the Grey Panthers' or teenagers through the Jean Teen Scene of Chicago; or young children through your local nursery school; or *everyone* by giving to the Rock of All Ages in Philadelphia.

If your interest is animals, there is the ASPCA and Adopt-a-Pet; if fishes, the Izaak Walton League; if birds, the American Homing Pigeon Institute or the Eastern Bird Banding Association.

If you are a WASP, there is the English Speaking Union and the Mayflower Descendants Association; if you have a still older association with the country, there is the Redcliff Chippewa Fund or the Museum of the American Indian.

If your vision is local, there is the Cook County Special Bail Project and Clean Up the Ghetto in Philadelphia; if national, there is America the Beautiful; if global, there is the United Nations Association; if celestial, there are the Sidewalk Astronomers of San Francisco.

If you are interested in tradition and social continuity, there is the society for the Preservation of Historic Landmarks and the Portland Friends of Cast Iron Architecture; if social change is your passion there is Common Cause; and, if that seems too sober for you, there is the Union of Radical Political Economists or perhaps the Theatre for Revolutionary Satire.

If your pleasure is music, there is a supermarket of choices—from Vocal Jazz to the Philharmonic Society to the American Guild of English Hand Bellringers.

If you don't know quite what you want, there is Get Your Head Together, Inc. of Glen Ridge, New Jersey. If your interests are contradictory, there is the Great Silence Broadcasting Foundation of California. If they are ambiguous, there is the Tombstone Health Service of Arizona.

I am constantly aware of how much of the country's pattern of community service and advocacy relates to the earliest activities of churches and to the initial and continuing protections of freedom of religion. Despite how obvious this is, people tend to set aside this half of the voluntary sector as though it does not really belong, as though it relates largely to salvation. But, if we look at what the conscience, the meeting ground, and the organized neighborliness represented by religious congregations mean to the kind of society America is, religion takes on a different and larger significance.

The Nonprofit Sector's Relationship
to Government and Business

Although research and the growing body of literature are helping to clarify the unique role and functions of voluntary activity, a great deal of confusion about what voluntary organizations can and should do remains. For example, the line between voluntary and commercial activity is blurred in the debates about unfair competition and the unrelated business income of voluntary groups, and the line between voluntary and governmental functions was blurred by President Reagan's efforts to transfer government responsibilities to nonprofits.

Philanthropy and voluntary effort fulfill many roles, but their central value is the extra dimension they provide for people to do and see things differently. They cannot take the place of business or government, but they do provide additional ways to address our needs, pursue our hopes, and help keep government responsive and effective.

Commerce generates 79 percent of our national income (NI); government, 15 percent; and the whole of the independent sector, only 6 percent. Philanthropy alone, including all giving by foundations, corporations, and individuals, accounts for just 2 percent of NI. If individual contributions are subtracted from this figure, the proportion for foundations and corporations is 2 percent of the national income.

The comparison becomes even starker when the philanthropic dollars of foundations and corporations are measured against the expenditures of government. As large and important as foundation and corporate giving are, they are not nearly as large as most people think. These two sources of philanthropy represent total annual expenditures of about $10 billion, while the combined annual expenditures of the three levels of government are about $2.5 trillion. Even the expenditures of the entire independent sector, $250 billion annually, are only about 10 percent of government expenditures.

Clearly, the efforts of the small independent sector must be targeted uniquely, or they will not be worth very much to society's needs and goals. The sector's funds can be spent in ways that make a difference far beyond the relative size of the expenditures, but if not targeted carefully, they will add an incidental rather than an extra dimension to the efforts to address our major needs and aspirations.

A few years ago, I attended a Ditchley Foundation conference in England that had the ambitious title The Future of Philanthropy in the Western World, and I learned that for other countries, such as England, the total funds of the independent sector are minuscule compared to government funds. In England, the funds of the total sector are about 2 percent of government funds. Nevertheless, representatives from other countries argued that however small the percentage of the funds is, the sector provides absolutely vital elements of flexibility, innovation, creativity, and the capacity for criticism and reform, and, therefore, must be preserved.

One issue participants discussed at that meeting was whether or not philanthropic dollars should be used to supplement government expenditures, particularly at a time of government cutbacks. At that time, both Prime Minister Thatcher and President Reagan were arguing that private philanthropy should be used to make up for some government retrenchment. Many U.S. mayors were also urging foundations and corporations to help government keep schools, libraries, and parks open and to maintain other public services. During the discussion and subsequently, it became clear that although philanthropy has a responsibility to deal with emergency matters, particularly those involving human suffering, in the long run, philanthropic funds must be reserved for unique purposes. If they are not, philanthropic expenditures will not represent anything different from government expenditures and might not be worth preserving.

At the heart of the uniqueness of the voluntary sector is its relative independence and freedom to contribute to innovation, advocacy, criticism, and where necessary, reform. With this freedom, the sector has provided an enormously important extra dimension in our pursuit of happiness and protection of inalienable rights. Its impact is clear in just about every field of endeavor, including fields as different as architecture, health, human rights, historic preservation, international understanding, the arts, neighborhood improvement, empowerment, patriotism, agriculture, rocketry, physics, aid for the homeless, and astronomy. Most of the great movements of our society have had their origins in the independent sector: abolition of slavery, clarification and protection of civil rights, creation of public libraries, care and opportunities for the handicapped, and on and on. Some of the leaders of these efforts were viewed as unpopular, troublesome, rabble-rousing, and perhaps even dangerous. One of the hallmarks of the sector is its offers of support to unpopular people and ideas and its protection of their freedom.

Henry Allen Moe, long-time head of the John Simon Guggenheim Memorial Foundation, delivered the Founders Day Address at Johns Hopkins University in 1951 and gave it the appropriate title "The Power of Freedom." He spoke of the genius of America—its freedom as a society and the freedom it allows individuals and institutions. He quoted Elihu Root: "Freedom is the supreme treasure of our country." And he quoted Detlev Bronk: "Freedom is the grand ingredient of the great adventures of the human mind."

Occasionally, philanthropic support of unpopular ideas has led government officials and others to question the relative value of the voluntary sector's independence versus the need for public control over private expenditure of tax-free dollars. In 1953, the House Select Committee to Investigate Foundations and Other Organizations, popularly known as the Reece Committee, held hearings on the use of foundation grants "for subversive purposes or for active political propaganda." During those hearings, the *Christian Century* (1954) published an editorial that presented a convincing argument for preserving philanthropy's independence and in the course of it used the apt phrase "They uphold and practice freedom of enterprise." The editorial says, "The central issue then is freedom. The foundations are not prepared to surrender to government the exclusive right to be concerned over the health, the education, the prosperity or even the safety of the people. They should be supported in their liberty to explore social questions. They uphold and practice freedom of enterprise in humanitarian concern for welfare, in intellectual concern for study and research. Having no faith in ignorance as a servant of democracy, they encourage independent inquiry and publication in politics and economics. Knowing that the more important issues, including survival, depend on right national and international relationships, they dig for and disseminate knowledge in these bitterly contested fields."

Speaking of the special role that the sector plays and of the freedom it requires, John W. Gardner, one of the founders of INDEPENDENT SECTOR, observes:

Perhaps the most striking feature of the sector is its relative freedom from constraints and its resulting pluralism. Within the bounds of the law, all kinds of people can pursue any idea or program they wish. Unlike government, an independent sector group need not ascertain that its idea or philosophy is supported by some large constituency, and unlike the business sector, they do not need to pursue only those ideas which will be profitable. If a handful of people want to back a new idea, they need seek no larger consensus.

Americans have always believed in pluralism—the idea that a free nation should be hospitable to many sources of initiative, many kinds of institutions, many conflicting beliefs, and many competing economic units. Our pluralism allows individuals and groups to pursue goals that they themselves formulate, and out of that pluralism has come virtually all of our creativity.

Institutions of the nonprofit sector are in a position to serve as the guardians of intellectual and artistic freedom. Both the commercial and political marketplaces are subject to leveling forces that may threaten standards of excellence. In the nonprofit sector, the fiercest champions of excellence may have their say. So may the champions of liberty and justice [Gardner, 1979].

Unique Characteristics of Nonprofit Organizations

If voluntary organizations are an integral part of private enterprise, why are they not more like business? In my thirty-five years with voluntary organizations, one of the greatest challenges has been to capitalize on the interest and ability of corporate executives without letting the many different characteristics of voluntary organizations get in the way of the enthusiasm and effectiveness of these executives. The greatest frustration for businesspeople working with nonprofits is the difficulty in defining and measuring the success of nonprofit enterprises. Voluntary organizations do not simply measure success by the bottom line. Many businesspeople who serve with voluntary groups want desperately for the organizations to mirror what they know best, and they are extremely impatient with their nonprofit counterparts. They may assume and claim that voluntary organizations generally are inefficient and poorly managed. I have routinely heard businesspeople make observations such as "These do-gooders just don't know how to manage" or "If we could just get more management discipline into these cause-oriented organizations, they would be far more effective."

My own observation is that these perceptions are often inaccurate and unfair. Voluntary organizations, like businesses and other human institutions, vary in their effectiveness. About one-third of businesses and voluntary organizations are models of excellence, another third are good to fair, and the lower third are poorly managed and generally ineffective. To determine if a nonprofit organizations is effective, it is important for businesspeople to have a clear understanding of what is unique about these organizations, both in the social role they fulfill and in the ways they operate. If we simply apply bottom-line efficiency as the standard, we fail to distinguish the special characteristics of dynamic voluntary organizations.

Many attempts to identify the unique profile of nonprofits tend toward quantification, such as determining number of board meetings held, dollars raised, or number of clients served, and omit any analysis of such factors as social impact or influence on quality of life that are often the true measure of the effectiveness of these groups.

I have worked on evaluation teams with business leaders looking at voluntary organizations and have often been surprised that my corporate counterparts will present a very negative appraisal compared to mine. They might even say that the organization is the epitome of poor management and point out the organization's failure to have adequate bylaws, minutes, a planning process, or an annual report. On the other hand, I will give high marks to the same break-all-the rules group because I will see evidence of real influence on the community toward improving schools, mass transit, or other public services or providing humane services to vulnerable populations that no one else has discovered— such as elderly patients who can stay in their homes if someone will just provide repairs. A great many voluntary organizations are both dynamic and efficient, and all should strive for both. But if I have to settle for one characteristic, it will be dynamism.

Cecily Cannan Selby (1978), former national director of the Girl Scouts, called for nonprofit organizations to be more effective but not always with the business model in mind: "In using the term nonprofit, which refers to a financial balance sheet only, perhaps we obscure the essence of this sector of our society, which is indeed to be profitable to citizens, business and government—to benefit its constituents, its clients and its employees. This sector has found, and one hopes will continue to find, new and better ways to preserve and enhance pluralism, voluntarism, and the distinctiveness of art, intellect and charity."

Businesspeople may be impressed by the results nonprofit organizations achieve measured against costs. In Peter Drucker's recent article, "What Business Can Learn from Nonprofits" (1989), he underscores how much voluntary groups accomplish with the combination of maximum caring and minimum cost. He admires their effective utilization of volunteers and boards and their ability to stretch a dollar so much farther than business. He says for example, "As a rule, nonprofits are more money-conscious than business enterprises are. They talk and worry about money much of the time because it is so hard to raise and because they always have so much less of it than they need."

Recently, I was comparing business and voluntary organizations with Andrew Heiskell, former CEO of Time, who has probably had as much exposure to both types of organization as anyone. Heiskell said, in a personal conversation with me, that he has come to believe that "voluntary organizations demand much more of themselves than most businesses, and they get much more out of their boards, staff and dollars."

Even in large nonprofit organizations, businesspeople tend to overlook unique factors of effectiveness. When I was national director of the Mental Health Association, new board members with corporate backgrounds would invariably state that the board of fifty-one was too large, that there were too few administrative staff members, or that, for efficiency, we should consider merging with the Retardation Association. They did not understand the need to involve as many people as feasible and to keep citizens mobilized around causes they care passionately about.

Businesspeople know little about keeping volunteers involved, enthusiastic, and effective. Volunteers are unpaid, even more independent than employees, and there are far more volunteers per staff supervisor than employees. Voluntary groups are quite different from business because of: the need to constantly achieve maximum community involvement, fund raising, dual board roles of policy making and policy implementing, lack of advertising budgets, and far lower salaries. In the March/April 1989 issue of *Across the Board,* published by the Conference Board, several former business executives indicated that they thought their transfer to full-time roles on the voluntary side would be "a piece of cake," but all of them had retreated to the corporate ranks as a result of the dizzying complexity of working with artists, faculty, independent-minded boards, fund-raising groups, and staff and resources totally inadequate to meet obligations. Voluntary organizations can learn a great deal from business about good management, staff development, planning, evaluation of results, and much more, but these are often not the primary ingredients contributing to their effectiveness and the fulfillment of their unique role in American society.

Although there are very real differences between for-profit and nonprofit organizations, both types of organizations are nevertheless parts of America's distinctive private enterprise system. In concluding his piece on the third sector, Rockefeller says (1978), "If voluntary giving lags, we will be well on our way toward a two-sector system. Opportunities and incentives for individual initiative will disappear, and the vaunted pluralism of American society will gradually give way to a monolithic system."

Both the for-profit and nonprofit sides of private enterprise are faced with growing domination by government. The nonprofit side seems to be the weaker in dealing with what Senator Daniel Patrick Moynihan (1980) calls "the growing monopoly of government." He and many others point out that if this so-called third sector becomes further dominated by government, we will in fact have only two sectors and, inevitably, one sector. In the long run, the vitality of all private initiative depends upon it truly being free enterprise.

References

Christian Century, July 28, 1954, pp. 894–895.

Curti, M. E. "American Philanthropy and the National Character." *American Quarterly*, *10* (Winter 1958), 420–437.

Drucker, P. "What Business Can Learn from Nonprofits." *Harvard Business Review* (July-Aug. 1989), 88–93.

Gardner, J. W. "Preserving the Independent Sector." Remarks delivered at the Council on Foundations thirtieth annual conference, May 16, 1979, Seattle, Wash.

Hodgkinson, V. A., and Weitzman, M. *Giving and Volunteering in the United States.* Washington, D.C.: INDEPENDENT SECTOR, 1988.

Meyers, R. *Exxon USA*, special edition, 1979.

Moynihan, D. P. Remarks at Charter Meeting of INDEPENDENT SECTOR, Mar. 5, 1980, Washington, D.C.

Nielsen, W. A. *The Endangered Sector.* New York: Columbia University Press, 1979.

O'Connell, B. *America's Voluntary Spirit.* New York: Foundation Center, 1983.

O'Connell, B. *Philanthropy in Action.* New York: Foundation Center, 1987.

O'Connell, B. *Volunteers in Action.* New York: Foundation Center, 1989.

Rockefeller, J. D., III. "America's Threatened Third Sector." *Across the Board,* Mar. 1978.

Selby, C. C. "Better Performance from Nonprofits." *Harvard Business Review* (Sept.-Oct. 1978), 77–83.

Stahr, E. *Exxon USA,* special edition, 1979.

Chapter Four

The Changing Role of Government
and Its Impact on the
Nonprofit and Business Sectors

Sanford Cloud, Jr.

The American public has witnessed a dramatic reallocation of responsibility for social welfare programs from the government to the private sector. Sociological, economic, and political developments from the 1960s to the 1980s, in particular, have resulted in a shift in financial accountability from the public to the private and voluntary domains.

In *The Shadow State: Government and the Voluntary Sector in Transition,* researcher Jennifer Wolch (1990) describes the paradoxical nature of this shift: the contrasting ideological rationales yet similar conclusions put forth by the political right, the political left, and the pragmatists. Policymakers on the right claim that private-sector involvement and ownership of social welfare programs "forestalls state monopoly over service provision and [prevents] the

Note: The author appreciates the assistance of Patricia A. Sheeran, senior program officer at the Aetna Foundation, in writing this chapter.

destruction of private initiative and responsibility." Those on the left, conversely, believe grass-roots participation of community leadership and greater self-determination occur when the private sector has greater involvement, thereby preventing excessive government control. And the pragmatists argue that the private sector can promote more cost-effective and efficient service delivery, increase available services without a commensurate increase in government bureaucracy, and incorporate new constituencies into the political system.

President George Bush began his term in office by reaffirming his predecessor's goal to transfer an increasing share of responsibility for social welfare programs to the voluntary sector. Bush's plan, described as the "thousand points of light" initiative, not only called for the private commercial sector to shoulder a larger share of the burden but also challenged individuals to recognize and fulfill their personal obligations to aid those less fortunate than themselves.

Perhaps reflecting the sociological phenomenon in which the self-centered values of the 1980s, the "me decade," became more compassionate and humanistic in the 1990s, President Bush made a strong case for private-sector and individual community involvement and leadership. In effect, he proposed a new norm for good citizenship. Said Bush, "From now on in America, any definition of a successful life must include serving others." This statement advocates not only a new set of institutional values but also new individual values. Bush also states: "These problems were long in coming and cannot be solved overnight. But if each American citizen and each American institution responds to the President's call to engage 'one-to-one' in the life of another person in need, this initiative will be the most comprehensive and inclusive movement of our time. This movement can dramatically reverse negative trends on many fronts and ensure the fulfillment of America's promise" (White House, 1989).

The tone set in 1989 by President Bush was an encouraging shift in policy from prior administrations. It was positive and based on reality, and it called upon all Americans to assume a fair share in underwriting the solutions to America's socioeconomic problems. However, this policy shift raises an important question: What are the proper roles and responsibilities for the public and private sectors and the community in addressing social problems? To appreciate what those roles should be, a historical perspective on their evolution over the last twenty-five to thirty years is helpful.

Historical Perspective

Traditionally, the federal government has provided for the national security, protected civil rights and liberties, accommodated basic needs within the social welfare system, ensured public education, and generated tax revenues. During the decades of the sixties to the eighties, depending on the political and personal agenda of the incumbent president and the mood of the populace, federal programs have ranged from aggressive social activism, such as the Great Society programs of the 1960s and early 1970s, to attitudes of benign neglect and virtual disdain toward those in poverty for much of the 1980s.

It was during Lyndon Johnson's administration that the federal deficit first became a major concern—a concern that plagues us today. Although the causes of the deficit are exceedingly complex, some social observers attribute it to Johnson's "guns and butter" approach, which pursued both the Great Society initiatives and the Vietnam War, a combination of federal expense too extreme for the national budget to accommodate without incurring debt. Judgment of this era is best left to historians; however, there is no question that Johnson's program to rid America of poverty was a noble and activist effort. During the 1960s and early 1970s, the federal government was the major funder for community-based agencies. In many cases it granted funds directly to local grass-roots groups, bypassing state and local governments except as pro forma signatories to the funding process. The federal government was the primary experimenter in attempting to reduce social ills and poverty.

The private sector, specifically major business enterprises, remained on the sidelines until the civil disturbances of the late 1960s and early 1970s. Business traditionally supported only organizations such as the United Way, college and university capital campaigns, and hospital construction projects. Corporate leaders watched with interest what Johnson was doing, but were skeptical of the long-term impact of his approach. After the riots of the 1960s, business leaders realized they could no longer simply concern themselves with making profits for shareholders while the nation's social infrastructure was threatened by major urban unrest. What today is termed the *public-private partnership* evolved from the early initiatives started jointly by business and government in the late 1960s.

Early Public-Private Partnerships. The Two Billion Dollar Urban Investment Program of the life insurance industry was one of the significant early public-private partnerships. This program, started with $1 billion in late 1967, received the full encouragement and support of President Johnson and his administration. The newly created Department of Housing and Urban Development (HUD) was the insurance industry's primary partner in providing loan guarantees for over 100,000 housing units constructed during the next several years. When the life insurers pledged an additional $1 billion in 1969, President Nixon sustained federal support for the effort by continuing loan guarantees and other government incentives for investment. In addition to supporting housing, the Two Billion Dollar program created small businesses, financed minority owned and operated financial institutions, and developed thousands of new jobs.

Although the Two Billion Dollar Investment Program did not achieve all of its objectives, it still illustrated the depth and capacity of the private sector and its potential, in partnership with government, to substantively address the nation's socioeconomic problems. This program was a major factor in encouraging other businesses to increase their grantmaking and investments to address broader community problems.

President Nixon retained many Great Society programs and played a major role in fostering public-sector leadership in minority business development through the Office of Minority Business Enterprise within the Department of Commerce. Although this effort had the support of the private sector, federal leadership and funding were crucial catalysts that encouraged the private sector to participate. President Ford's tenure in office was not long enough to allow him to craft his own innovations, but he sustained many initiatives started under the Nixon administration.

The Carter administration represented a maturation of public-private-community partnerships. Carter's Department of Housing and Urban Development, specifically the Office of Neighborhoods and Urban Development Action Grant programs, became a model for an expanded public-private partnership centered around community revitalization and development. A partnership involving HUD, Aetna Life & Casualty, and the National Training and Information Center (NTIC), headquartered in Chicago, illustrates the success of the Carter administration's approach. HUD provided grant seed money to assist several local neighborhood organizations in New York, Philadelphia, Chicago, and Cleveland in increasing their capacity to organize and operate a housing development organization. NTIC offered technical assistance to train the local organizations, and Aetna provided grant and investment dollars to the project.

Over ten years, residential and commercial mortgage loans through this program totaling $25 million allowed community development organizations to produce affordable housing units in thirteen cities across the nation. Together, HUD, Aetna, and NTIC raised another $65 million and encouraged local financial institutions to increase their mortgage lending to neighborhoods once thought to be abandoned. State and local government agencies joined this effort. Families and neighborhoods were saved; once destitute communities became positive living environments. Each of the three partners was comfortable with the role it played.

During the Nixon, Ford, and Carter eras, the concept of balanced roles for government and the private sector flourished. The federal government involved state government both in design and financing of programs. Grass-roots community organizations could secure funds from several levels of government. They could look to the private sector for assistance as well.

Effects of "Reaganomics." President Reagan changed the tone of federal involvement to such an extent that some critics claim he abdicated government's responsibility in dealing with social needs, particularly for those in poverty. At the same time, he required state governments to solve their problems mostly on their own. Reagan also required the private sector to provide resources to address basic human service needs formerly filled by the government.

Ironically, state and local governments were thus transformed from grantors to grantees, and they looked to the private sector for funding. Community organizations, now cut off from federal resources, also looked increasingly to the private sector for support. Reagan's reluctance to deal affirmatively with the disadvantaged multiplied the number of poor, placing further demand on strained local public and private-sector resources.

Reagan's policies severely altered the demographic and economic profile of the nation's underprivileged. According to the Institute for Educational Leadership, 40 percent of the nation's poor are children and 23 percent of all young children under the age of five are poor (Hodgkinson, 1989). Eight million low-income renters compete for four million housing units because the federal government discontinued support for subsidized housing. More than 2.5 million Americans were homeless as of 1988, and over 50 percent of the homeless were families. Most of these families were headed by women with two or three children under the age of five. Many of these children will experience serious developmental problems caused by poor health and bad living conditions.

As Reagan altered the rules of the game, the private sector began questioning the appropriateness of its role. The public-private partnership increasingly took on the look of sole proprietorship by the private sector.

Growing Gaps in Funding

According to a major *New York Times* article, between 1980 and 1988, the federal government's share of financial aid to philanthropic causes decreased from 82 to 70 percent of the total resources going to these causes, and the private sector's share increased from 18 to 30 percent (Bloom, 1989). Although the decrease in spending by the federal government is discouraging and the increase in spending by the private sector is encouraging, this trend points to a widening gap between resources and needs. Also, certain private-sector support of philanthropic causes has reached a plateau. Ac-

cording to a study published in the *New York Times*, "Corporate
contributions, adjusted for inflation, have fallen by 7% since 1985,
to 4.8 billion in 1988" (Bloom, 1989). The same article notes that
"the use of cash draining mergers and [acquisitions], the stock
market crash in 1987, increased foreign competition and a reduced
tax incentive" are the reasons for the decline. Private sector leaders
are concerned that the public sector is abdicating its responsibilities
in addressing social programs. The private sector is willing to pay
its share but cannot fill the gap left by federal resource reduction.

With the growing number of nonprofit service providers, the
financial demands on private-sector resources continue unabated.
Nonprofit organizations dealing with child and spouse abuse, drug
and alcohol abuse, the homeless, and AIDS are dotting the map
across America. These organizations fulfill vital needs for many
segments of the population. The federal government's response to
assisting these organizations has been limited. The private sector
has tried to nurture these organizations with its limited resources
but lacks the capacity to fulfill every demand. Meanwhile, state and
local government often must call on the private sector to help when
their resources fall short.

Principles and Guidelines for Corporate Giving

The Bush administration restructured roles for public-private partnerships and for individual action by all Americans. Keeping in
mind this new tone and the lack of significant growth in public-
sector resources, what principles and guidelines should a corporate
grantmaker follow to ensure success in dealing with publicly and
privately funded projects?

First, and most important, a company should clearly focus
its grantmaking. An organization's effectiveness is limited if its
grantmaking is scattered, that is, if it attempts to fund a small
portion of every good proposal that it receives.

Second, an organization should decide whether it is going to
be primarily a "first-in, middle-in, or last-in" organization; will it
provide start-up funds, wait until there is a track record or experience before providing funds, or provide ongoing funds once an
initiative is mature and successful? Grantmakers can play a role at

each phase. It is unlikely that an organization with a clearly articulated focus will participate in all three phases.

Third, the corporation should be sure that it can bring something special to the table; that is, can it offer resources, expertise, or other support critical to the project's or program's success that otherwise would be unavailable from public or nonprofit sources?

Fourth, a team, including representatives from both the public and private sectors, should track the grant. The team will be able to monitor program progress at any given time as the nonprofit group works to accomplish its goals and objectives.

Fifth, private-sector participants working with their public-sector counterparts must have flexibility and patience. Many more people and layers of government bureaucracy are involved in the public sector than in the private sector. Public-sector representatives should be from the highest level possible in order to reduce the decision-making time, which may have an impact on the project.

Sixth, the corporation must be prepared to fund a nonprofit group longer than originally anticipated, assuming good progress is being made. Sometimes an extension of funds is required when a group has legitimate reasons for missing an original deadline. A grantmaking organization must also be prepared to cease funding when sufficient progress is not made and prospects are not promising.

Seventh, when a private-sector organization is involved in a project that also receives government funds, the project and the organization are likely to attract press and media attention. An organization must be willing and prepared to handle this attention.

In the past, corporate grantmakers often would underwrite substantially all the needs of an organization for a particular project in order to claim ownership and have that project clearly identified with the corporation. In such a case, the business has more than a grantmaking role to play. It must encourage other grantmakers and foundations to participate.

Collaboration and Leverage. Although "single project ownership" grantmaking still goes on today, it is less frequent. This type of grantmaking usually cannot meet the needs of community organizations, which continue to increase dramatically because of federal aid reductions and expanding caseload. If corporate grantmakers are truly concerned with addressing socioeconomic problems, pooling and leveraging of resources by many organizations must occur. Examples of this kind of grantmaking include a partnership by several major corporate grantmakers and a community foundation to fund a five-year program to reduce infant mortality in certain segments of the community; another is the joint effort of the corporate grantmaking community, a community foundation, and the church community to initiate and fund the Local Initiative Support Corporation for housing development. As long as corporate egos can be controlled, every organization can share in the credit of a joint project and give the project a better opportunity to succeed.

Businesses should pursue additional resources by collaborating with local community foundations. In many cases, community foundation leaders have a better understanding and relationship with local agencies than the corporate grantmaking staff has and, therefore, should be viewed as valuable and viable partners.

Public Policy Advocacy. Corporate grantmakers today also function as public policy advocates, both internally and, where appropriate, externally. Corporations must define the parameters of the public and private roles necessary to address and solve the country's socioeconomic problems. They must also challenge whether government is playing an adequate role in providing education and housing, and preventing drug abuse and hunger. If they do not, they have no right to criticize government's reduction of its role on any of these issues.

The chief executive officers, chief operating officers, and other senior officers of American businesses should understand that the federal government's role in certain issues is out of balance. Corporations are being asked to shoulder more than their fair share in addressing some of our socioeconomic problems. The pendulum must begin to swing the other way; and government's commitment to education, housing, and related issues, must be restored to break the cycle of poverty for a growing number of citizens.

These issues must be incorporated into the corporate legislative and political agendas along with tax and deficit issues be-

cause they have a similiar impact on the long-term health and
prosperity of the corporation. With support from the corporate
leadership, the company's governmental relations staff must include these additional issues as they lobby on behalf of the corporation. And corporate grantmakers, therefore, must be able to
provide the information and staffing so that this lobbying can be
done effectively. In addition, businesses should support and endorse
regional associations and national associations, such as INDE-
PENDENT SECTOR and the Council on Foundations, increasing
their involvement in public policy development advocacy.

Business Leadership and Stake in Society

Private-sector leaders should encourage their own industries to
place these broader socioeconomic issues on their business and industry trade association agendas. In informal remarks to an internal
task force on AIDS in November 1987, Aetna Life and Casualty
chairman James T. Lynn commented: "It's a three legged stool. We
must be concerned about the economic and financial impact on the
industry; we must be concerned about the legislative and regulatory
climate as we conduct our business; and we must deal with the
corporate public involvement concerns in dealing with AIDS." To
an extent, corporate grantmaking becomes a business issue. As long
as the grantmaking program maintains its integrity and independence while sustaining a proper balance of business interests and
the broader societal interests, that is fine.

To successfully solve society's most pressing problems, as so
well articulated by President Bush, a better balance must be found
between public- and private-sector roles. Corporate America must
exert greater leadership in this arena, just as it has done in the tax,
trade, and budget deficit issues. A community short on healthy,
educated, and well-trained people will not be able to nurture and
maintain prosperous businesses and industries. Business has a legitimate stake in the changing role of government in addressing our
socioeconomic problems. And corporate grantmakers can play a
critical part in balancing these roles to better serve both the private
sector and the broader public good.

References

Bloom, C. "What's New in the Nonprofit Sector?" *New York Times,* Oct. 29, 1989.

Hodgkinson, H. *The Same Client: The Demographics of Education and Service Delivery Systems.* Washington, D.C.: Center for Demographic Policy, Institute for Educational Leadership, 1989.

White House, Office of the Press Secretary. "Fact Sheet—Points of Light Initiative." June 22, 1989.

Wolch, J. R. *The Shadow State.* New York: Foundation Center, 1990.

PART TWO

Effective Leadership:
The Key to Successful
Corporate Philanthropy

Chapter Five

To Make a Difference:
The Challenge to Corporate Leaders

David Stanley

The corporate chief executive officer is uniquely positioned in American society to influence the choice of which issues society will address, how it will conduct the discussion, how it will decide what to do, what it will decide to do, who will take action, and how society will pay for what it decides to do. As a chief executive officer, I believe that CEOs can influence the way this nation addresses socioeconomic issues and that the vigorous exercise of this influence is the proper leadership role of the CEO.

Five basic beliefs shape my view of the leadership role of the corporate chief executive officer in philanthropy.

1. The largest problem facing the United States is poverty. It lies at, or near, the root of many of our other ailments.
2. The United States is not helpless in the face of poverty. We know many things that will work and have worked; we are not doing enough of what we know how to do.

3. A major redistribution of resources will be required to deal with poverty and its consequences, including new or increased taxes and a restructuring of the Social Security system.

4. Conventional corporate philanthropy devotes too much money to subsidizing the life-styles and preferences of the nonpoor and not enough to addressing the problems of the poor. But conventional corporate philanthropy, even if redirected, simply does not involve enough money to make much difference. In addition, corporate philanthropy is under bottom-line pressure in this age of the takeover, the leveraged buyout, restructuring, and big corporate debt. Growth in philanthropy, if any, will be slow. The socially concerned chief executive officer—and most of them are socially concerned—should focus the corporation's philanthropic efforts on the community's most pressing needs in a way that promises to make a difference.

5. The real power of CEOs lies not in their corporation's philanthropic program but in their circles of influence—the people they know and have worked with, their ability to create linkages toward a common purpose, their skill at mobilizing people and money, and their political access. CEOs have clout, and they should use it.

The Problem of Poverty

To designate poverty as the nation's leading problem may seem to be scrawling with a rather blunt crayon. After all, poverty in its simplest definition is nothing more than being poor. And being poor, as people used to say, is no disgrace, just damned inconvenient.

Today, for millions of the poor, being poor is more than an inconvenience. It is a sentence to a way of life and a state of mind devoid of hope and opportunity. It is a sentence that grandmother, mother, and grandchild may serve at the same time in the same prison. It is a rotten way of life where bad things never get any better.

We have trouble discriminating between the causes and effects of poverty. Is a young man poor because he dropped out of high school, or did he drop out of high school because he grew up in poverty? Is a teenaged unwed mother poor because she is young, a mother, and unwed, or is it the other way around? Unable or unwilling to deal directly with poverty, we have concentrated our remedial efforts on its visible manifestations.

But poverty, writes Lisbeth Schorr (1988) in her compelling book *Within Our Reach,* is the "greatest risk factor of all" in producing what she calls "rotten outcomes." (She attributes the phrase to Mary Jo Bane of the Kennedy School of Government.) Family poverty, Schorr adds, is "relentlessly correlated with high rates of school-age childbearing, school failure and violent crime" (p. xxii). Moreover, she continues, virtually all the other risk factors that make for rotten outcomes are also more likely to be found disproportionately among poor children.

Schorr cites an Urban Institute study of 1980 census data that identified every census tract with unusually high proportions of high school dropouts, welfare recipients, female heads of household, and working-age males not regularly attached to the labor force. The study found 880 tracts with all four characteristics. If a fifth characteristic—that at least 20 percent of the people in the tract had incomes below the poverty line—were added, only six of the tracts would be eliminated. Correlation does not establish cause, but it is enlightening.

The link between poverty and rotten outcomes is also cited in the Committee for Economic Development's (CED) 1987 report titled *Children in Need: Investment Strategies for the Educationally Disadvantaged.* The report states: "Poor students are three times more likely to become dropouts than students from more economically advantaged homes. Schools with higher concentrations of poor students have significantly higher dropout rates than schools with fewer poor children. . . . (C)hildren of the poor suffer more frequently from almost every form of childhood deficiency, including infant mortality, gross malnutrition, recurrent and untreated health problems, psychological and physical stress, child abuse and learning disabilities" (p. 8).

We Know What to Do. As Schorr notes in her introduction to *Within Our Reach,* many Americans, including corporate philanthropists, have soured on "throwing money" at problems that seem to keep getting worse anyway: "They are not hard-hearted, but don't want to be soft-headed either." But, says Schorr, in one of the most important messages of our time, "the knowledge necessary to reduce the growing toll of damaged lives is now available" (p. xvii). The CED's 1987 study says something similar: "Ironically, we know how to save about half of the young people who fall prey to illiteracy, unemployment and teenage pregnancy. Twenty years of research on preschool education has demonstrated the effectiveness of early protection" (p. 19).

My family has chuckled for years over a city dweller who visited us on our farm during World War II and who expressed great concern about the farmers being called into military service. How would the cattle get fed? The city dweller came up with an answer: Why not, she suggested, dry grass in the summer and feed it to cattle in the winter?

She had invented hay.

We do not need to invent the basics in our fight against poverty. We do not know everything, but we know some things, enough to get moving. We cannot expect to improve the lives of all at-risk people, but we can improve the lives of many of them.

We know that teenage pregnancies can be reduced. We know that prenatal care produces healthier babies and mothers. We know that Head Start is successful. We know that low-income housing is successful in many places. We know how to cut the dropout rate. We know how to make education meet the needs of the disadvantaged. We know something about family counseling. We know how to build neighborhoods. We know the benefits of nutrition programs. We know how to retrain people for jobs. We know something about treatment for drug addiction and alcoholism.

Yes, it would be costly to address these many poverty-related issues. But it would not be throwing away money.

Redistributing Resources. Being poor is not just a little bit worse than not being poor; it is a lot worse. The slightly more than 85 percent of us in the United States who are not poor use about 65 percent of the gross national product (GNP) for consumption and health care. The slightly less than 15 percent of us who are poor use between 2 percent and 3 percent for consumption and health care (Stein, 1988). That means that consumption by persons who are not poor is almost four times as great as consumption by those who are poor.

Even if we could set aside the effects of poverty—and we cannot—the imbalance between the resources of the poor and the nonpoor is too great, from the standpoint of both Judeo-Christian ethics and sound economics. Yet, in this free-market society, the share of the GNP the poor now receive is more or less in line with the value of their economic contribution. It is what they earn. They are not very productive as a group; that is why they are poor. But what they earn is not what they need. Having a large part of the population so relatively unproductive creates a considerable drag on the economy.

As a nation, we are less productive than we must be, as our trade deficit illustrates. There is a tragic incongruity between the need for skilled workers in the United States and the lack of skills of the poor. If we are to deal with our nation's lack of productivity, we must commit ourselves to programs that have proved they can increase the productivity of people who are at high risk of being unproductive. The proper objective of government is to reduce the economic distance between the poor and the nonpoor and to decrease the percentage of the population that lives in poverty. And it is the obligation of government to raise the needed resources and direct them toward that objective.

The Ford Foundation Project on Social Welfare and the American Future (1989) estimated that it would cost about $29 billion annually to implement the recommendations in its report, *The Common Good: Social Welfare and the American Future.* Those recommendations include a broadened Head Start program, improved access to prenatal care, more funding for the Women, Infants, and Children special supplemental food program, federal child-care subsidies for low-income families, funding for child welfare programs, expanded Medicaid, more funding for drug-addiction treatment, new job training outlays, a public-sector jobs program, and a package of increases for senior citizens.

The Ford report recommends financing its proposals through full taxation of the Social Security benefits that exceed what recipients contributed during their lifetime of work. The report says that the Congressional Budget Office estimated revenues from the tax would grow to about $26 billion a year within five years. This tax may not be the best way, and it certainly is not the only way, to finance the cost of programs to fight poverty, but the tax would raise close to the $29 billion needed to implement the Ford Foundation's recommendations.

Another way to fund programs—and one that appeals to me in light of the great gap between spending by the poor and the nonpoor—would be a tax on consumption. The trade deficit suggests that we are consuming too much. A tax that would dampen consumption while providing funds to increase the long-term economic contribution of poor Americans has many positive points. Restructuring of the Social Security program also makes sense in light of the relative affluence of the elderly in comparison with the nation's young. We should not forget that while 5 percent of the elderly population in our nation live below the poverty line, 20 percent of our nation's children live in poverty (*Forbes,* 1988).

The political problems in raising taxes or restructuring Social Security require the reshaping of the American conscience so that we will want to do what is right and the economic education of Americans so that we will know a prudent investment when we see one. Our political leaders are unwilling to attempt these tasks. President Bush has said no new taxes, and Congress seems unwilling to address poverty seriously or to confront well-organized Social Security recipients.

The Limits of Corporate Philanthropy

Corporate philanthropy is small in terms of its total funds and in relationship to the size of the problems we face as a nation. The nation's corporations and corporate foundations donated an estimated $4.75 billion to nonprofit organizations in 1988, up from $4.5 billion a year earlier. The $4.75 billion represented 4.5 percent of all giving in the nation during 1988—a drop from 4.8 percent in 1987. In contrast, the government spent roughly $33 billion in 1985 just on the Aid to Families with Dependent Children (AFDC) program and on food stamps and Medicaid for AFDC families.

These figures do not imply that corporations should give up on their philanthropic programs. However, the figures point out that we cannot look to corporations for the financial answer to the problems of poverty and productivity. The money corporations do spend on philanthropy must be targeted to the areas of greatest need and areas in which some realistic hope exists of making a difference.

Education is the largest recipient of corporate philanthropic funds, receiving approximately 43 percent of the total funds given. Higher education receives most of that money, but corporations have shown a growing and refreshing interest in contributing to elementary and secondary education, which are more likely to address the problems of the poor. Human services—not more specifically defined in the report but certainly including the United Way—is the second largest recipient of funds at 24 percent of the total. The category of "Arts, Culture & Humanities" receives about 12 percent, and "Public/Society Benefit" receives 13 percent of the funds (AAFRC Trust for Philanthropy, 1987).

Corporate contributions have leveled off in part because of the rapid growth of contributions in preceding years, which made further increases difficult to achieve. Contributions have also been affected by serious economic difficulties experienced in some key industrial sectors, as well as mergers, friendly and unfriendly acquisitions, leveraged buyouts, growing debt, and an increased emphasis on short-term performance in many corporations.

Most CEOs and CEOs-in-waiting, according to a survey conducted by Daniel Yankelovich Group for the Council on Foundations in 1988, believe in corporate philanthropy. The survey states, "The CEOs' deep personal commitments, stemming from a sense of ethics, moral obligation and company tradition are still powerful motivators" (p. 6). So, too, is a concept of "enlightened self-interest" (p. 36). And, although many respondents believe that business should not take on the burdens that the federal government has backed away from, "There appears to be a growing recognition that business can and should help to address these needs" (p. 37).

According to the survey, 67 percent of the executives said corporate giving is a moral obligation. The same percentage cited a personal sense of ethics as a reason for their involvement, and 72 percent said they have a personal desire to contribute to a worthy organization.

Those are reassuring numbers; however, about 30 percent of

the respondents apparently did not feel any such obligations to make contributions. As one of this minority told the interviewer, "This isn't something a company should do much of. It's what we've got charities for and all that government spending" (Yankelovich, p. 14). This attitude defines the corporation as something separate and distinct from the society in which it operates, which, of course, the corporation is not. A corporation is, albeit artificially, a citizen. And, like other citizens, it finds its opportunities constrained or enhanced by the society around it. Ethical considerations aside, a corporate CEO should not leave the shaping of society to the government and nonprofit groups, both of which the average CEO tends to suspect anyway.

The survey also found some uneasiness among CEOs about the current and future effect of the business climate—mergers, acquisitions, competition, debt, and emphasis on short-term profits—on philanthropic programs. Although most CEOs still support corporate philanthropy for ethical and moral reasons, some CEOs have or are finding other reasons for giving. Sixty-two percent of respondents said a company's philanthropic program will help attract good people to the company and community; 52 percent said giving is good for public relations; 49 percent felt it enhances the company's image with customers, stockholders, and others; 39 percent said it enhances the climate for doing business; and 39 percent said it helps sell products. Only 13 percent said giving will actually contribute directly to profits, and they are probably wrong (Yankelovich, p. 45).

Sixty-nine percent of the CEOs surveyed said they agree with the statement that "enlightened self-interest must guide giving." And 71 percent said they agree that the "company has to determine benefits to the company of each cause it supports." The problem for corporations and society will come as corporations seek to determine whether a program dealing with family violence or early childhood development, for example, is in the company's self-interest or how it benefits the company. And the problem will intensify if the corporation becomes a takeover target or is acquired or has a few bad quarters.

The days of the truly "sweet" corporation seem to be numbered—the sort of corporation that grew up in the town where it was founded, is run by the descendants of the founders, sponsors everything from softball teams to a float in the big parade, has a wing in the hospital and a humanities chair at the local college named after it, and gives all employees a day off on their birthday. The size of a corporation's philanthropic effort has a limit, and a wise CEO will develop a sense of what that limit is.

Within that limit of giving, corporations should address specific societal needs with programs that demonstrate some promise of working and work through agencies with some reasonable prospect of success. At my company, Payless Cashways, Inc., for example, we have chosen to emphasize human services, particularly programs addressing neighborhood redevelopment and family violence.

The philanthropic program should run like any other part of the company, with goals and objectives. It does not have to report to the CEO directly, although it can. It should not be run by—how to say this politely?—well-intentioned individuals without the training to make them peers of the other leaders in the corporation. A philanthropic program should be run by professionals trained in the business of philanthropy who know what is needed and who can solicit proposals, evaluate grant applications, oversee grants, evaluate results, and who know when to sustain programs and when to drop them. It should be run in a fashion that permits employees to participate, and their community interests should, if possible, be reinforced and their involvement encouraged.

The roles of CEOs in all of this are not materially different from their roles in running the rest of the company, except that they more often may need to defend what will seem, at least to some critics, to be unwarranted spending on unrelated purposes. Possibly, too, some CEOs may find it necessary, in order to pass judgment on the philanthropic mission, to learn something about a previously unfamiliar subject—young gangs or child abuse or job training. This does not seem too high a price to pay.

The CEO's Power to Help Reshape the United States

The corporate philanthropic program can be targeted to those problems most troubling to the United States. And CEOs can have an impact on those problems by virtue of the power they hold over philanthropic programs.

But, as noted, the amount of money available for corporate philanthropic programs is small, and demand far exceeds supply. We also have seen that the people who have access to the large sums of money that societal change requires—the politicians—either lack the philosophical conviction that government should do anything about our society's problems or, if they have the conviction, lack the necessary courage.

Business leaders are not universally admired, but they do get attention. When they speak, the media, mayors and council members, legislators and governors, members of Congress, and, indeed, the president listen. They are sometimes perceived by virtue of their positions as having special knowledge and understanding, maybe even wisdom. They have clout.

My company does business in twenty-six states, and our name is well known in forty or fifty congressional districts. I personally know many city council members, a number of mayors, a number of legislators, several governors, five or six senators, and eight or ten members of the House. They take my phone calls or, more commonly, return them. People who run bigger, more prominent companies know bigger, more prominent political leaders and more of them.

When business leaders take major public roles in connection with public issues, the results can be remarkable. Owen "Brad" Butler presents a good example of personal activism. As CEO of Procter & Gamble Company, he led the Committee for Economic Development's research on the condition of children in America and then took to the road traveling across the nation spreading the word of the need for and importance of business and community involvement in the education system. In great part because of his personal efforts, businesses are now ultimately involved in supporting improvement of public education systems in cities and towns everywhere. In 1988, a U.S. Department of Education suvery of 1,495 school districts showed that 25 percent had one or more active school-business partnerships.

When business leaders act together, they can be more effective still. My company is an investor—not a charitable contributor—in the National Equity Fund, and, along with other corporations, we have raised $140 million for equity investments in affordable housing for low-income families across America. Cleveland has risen from its own ashes through the efforts of business-led Cleveland Tomorrow. Business leaders in Minnesota and in South Carolina have shown the way to major improvements in the educational system. In South Carolina, money was raised in part by increasing the state sales tax. Other examples of business leadership in education include the Boston Compact, the Atlanta Partnership of Business and Education, Invest Indianapolis Compact, the California Regional and Occupational Centers and Programs, the New Horizons programs in Richmond, Virginia, and Philadelphia High School Academies.

The Committee for Economic Development, through its research and advocacy, has consistently been a leader on issues of societal reform, most recently with its *Children in Need* report. That report states: "As a strong community force, business can help bring together a wide variety of interested parties—schools, parents, community groups, and government agencies—to explore opportunities for creating new partnerships or strengthening those that already exist. Corporations can also help guide the use of public and private resources in directions that represent sound investment strategies. Most of all, business leaders can become a persuasive voice for the millions of disadvantaged children who lack advocates in the political process. Business leaders must speak out on behalf of the educationally disadvantaged because these children cannot speak out for themselves."

The challenge is both flattering and frightening. Most CEOs did not seek this kind of influence. It is a marvelous and miraculous gift that has come to us through some mixture of good fortune and hard work. We are derelict in our responsibility if we do not use it to good purpose. And we are also damned fools if we do not make every reasonable effort to improve this society in which we conduct business. A corporation's role, its purpose, is to create value, and improving our society is one important way to do that.

If business leaders believe, as I do, that it is a high priority for this nation to intervene in the lives of the poor, that we must implement proven programs to increase the likelihood that the poor will become productive members of our society and cease to be poor, that this intervention is the proper function of government, and that its massive cost should be borne by the entire population through the federal revenue-raising system, then we ought to say so, loudly and vigorously, to everyone we know. We ought to use our leadership positions to inspire the conscience of the nation, to change the behavior of our elected leaders, and to get on with the job of changing our society.

References

AAFRC Trust for Philanthropy. *Giving USA, 1987.* New York: AAFRC Trust for Philantropy, 1987.

Committee for Economic Development. *Children in Need: Investment Strategies for the Educationally Disadvantaged.* Committee for Economic Development, 1987.

Forbes, Nov. 14, 1988, p. 223.

Ford Foundation. *The Common Good: Social Welfare and the American Future.* New York: Ford Foundation Project on Social Welfare and the American Future, 1989.

Schorr, L. B., with Schorr, D. *Within Our Reach: Breaking the Cycle of Disadvantage.* New York: Doubleday, 1988.

Stein, H. "Tax the Rich—They Consume Too Much." New York *Times,* Aug. 23, 1988.

Daniel Yankelovich Group. *The Climate for Giving: The Outlook of Current and Future CEO's.* Washington, D.C.: Council on Foundations, 1988.

Chapter Six

Leadership Opportunities for Grants Officers

Lance C. Buhl

One definition of leadership is: making it look like you are leading a parade when in reality you are being chased by a lynch mob. Actually, this is not the sort of leadership I want to talk about at all. But the leadership role of grants officers could look like that if three interdependent truths that are central to the nature of corporate grantmaking positions are not honored.

First, the function of grants officers is marginal. Second, we are power brokers and must be ever mindful of power's ethical and unethical uses. Third, leadership entails direct, personal, active engagement. We will explore each of these notions before considering some do's and don't's for effective personal leadership as grantmakers.

Marginality and Leadership

"Marginal employees," argue Daniel Oran and Jay M. Shafritz (1983, p. 255), "are those members of an organization who contribute least to the organization's mission because of . . . the inherent nature of their duties." By definition, corporate grantmakers hold marginal positions. We give money away, scraping against every grain of the corporate ethos, which is to make money for owners. It should not be surprising that we are often looked at by others in companies as oddities or that, when hard times hit, our jobs are deemed expendable.

Recruitment patterns for grants officers tend to reinforce the perception of the position's marginality. A fair number of corporate grantmakers spend most of their careers in other fields. Many companies assign responsibility for grantmaking to personnel who, rightly or wrongly, are evaluated as over-the-hill or without promising career potential. Certainly, most outsiders soon learn and honor the folkways of the companies that hire them and thus get known as insiders; similarly, most grants officers refuse to be typecast as losers and increasingly are acknowledged as operating for their companies. These ameliorating tendencies do not, however, change the fact that the grantmaking function itself is marginal.

Also, and more important, consider how we do our jobs. We work the margins or fringes between our corporations and our communities. We reconnoiter social conditions and company interests. We explain company to community and community to company. Our task is to discover the intersections of needs, interests, and mutual values that bind our employers and the civic cultures of which they are a part.

But what, you may ask, has marginality to do with leadership? The short answer is, a lot—so long as both marginality and leadership are properly understood and practiced. Although our positions are marginal in the scheme of corporate life, as human beings and professionals, we need not be marginal. As professionals, we should, in essence, persuade Oran and Shafritz to alter their definition so that they describe "marginal positions," rather than "marginal employees." And we should be exploring the potential benefits that working in the margins confers. This is more productive than feeling sorry for ourselves about not being at the center of corporate life, and it leads to some important conclusions about the relationship between marginality and leadership.

For example, in my judgment, marginality is a source of

strength. It gives our work integrity. Who else in the corporation is paid to worry and care—to express corporate philanthropic concern—about society's ills, misalignments, and dysfunctions? Who else has the primary responsibility for surveying critical issues and making key recommendations about whether and how our companies will play roles in education, economic progress, medical and human services, access to recreational activities, and public problem solving?

Marginality of this sort is both an essential and necessary aspect of effective grantmaking and of the leadership that corporate grantmakers can choose to take. Our employers, large or small, are powerful in their own right, certainly relative to most other individuals and institutions in American life. They can and often do open doors for us to powerful situations and afford us seats at key decision-making tables both inside and outside the corporation. In that sense, our marginality makes us power brokers, occasionally even power wielders. Power confers on its holders higher than average influence over others and over the direction and pace of events.

Also, marginality confers a benefit few others in corporate life enjoy. We serve the good of our employers and the communities in which they operate. We must know and explain both corporate and community interests, needs, and values—indeed be the conscience of our employers with respect to social need—and thus we have a unique and advantaged position from which to see how power works. This privileged perspective creates the ethical context in which corporate grants officers operate. Effective leaders are those who use power ethically.

This perspective does not automatically make us ethical leaders. In working at being ethical leaders, we should be guided by the relationship between power and leadership that leading psychologists and political theorists have postulated (McCelland, 1975; Burns, 1978). Their central concept is that the leadership necessary for a pluralistic, constitutional, and democratic society and its many institutional expressions, including corporations, is "servant" or "transforming" leadership. Leadership is most powerful—most able to achieve an organization's goals over the long term—when it empowers people. A leader, according to this viewpoint, acts on the seemingly paradoxical axiom that to be powerful you must share power.

The usual definitions of powerful leadership emphasize concentration of authority, positional privilege, and the top-down action and decisiveness of the person or small group in authority. Empowering leadership is concerned primarily with assisting people affected by power to do those things that are necessary for their own and the system's welfare and growth. Empowerment, of course, is the essential purpose of philanthropy.

At a minimum, this definition implies that the corporate grantmaker who would be a leader ought to treat grantseekers with the utmost respect for what they do and who they are. Grantmakers, especially those who would take leadership, must not shield themselves behind the trappings of position, perceived as powerful by most who come to them. We must do no interpersonal harm. More positively, the concept of empowering leadership suggests that corporate grantmakers should try to ensure that philanthropic resources are used in significant part to empower one or more of those groups of people who are most at risk—the ill, the elderly, the poor of all ages, the disfranchised, the illiterate.

Leadership is less the directive actions of one or a few individuals than a set of functions that need to be carried out. The essence of empowering leadership is engaging as a full partner with others in problem solving. The empowering leader allows, indeed encourages, others to carry out one or more of the leadership functions—essential responsibilities like convening, initiating, listening, summarizing, negotiating, fact finding, planning, deciding, implementing, and constituency building.

Ethical, effective leadership at its best is the sum of many instrumental acts undertaken by any number of people. Corporate grantseekers are at their best when they serve as maître d's of resource development and allocation tables, when they help ensure that many interest groups, especially those most affected by philanthropic decisions, are intimately and equally involved in philanthropic programs. Power is thus shared appropriately along the continuum of decision making, from initial identification of a significant societal problem through implementation of some corrective action to resolve it.

No corporation or corporate grantmaker can deal with just any, much less all, significant societal problems without dissipating power and resources. The key to effective, empowering leadership in corporate grantmaking is "focused activism."

To focus, of course, is to decide what is worth paying attention to—to be strategic, to organize resources to achieve some purpose or hit some target. In the business context, having a focus seems too obvious to dwell on. However, many companies, as evident from a reading of their annual contributions reports, have no discernible grantmaking strategy and seem not to have given any consideration to the relationship between corporate responsibility and the plight of less-fortunate citizens.

Grants officers, in essence, help corporations determine where institutional self-interests and community needs meet and, on that basis, construct one or more grantmaking programs that are likely to make a difference in the targeted areas. No correct templates for effective grantmaking programs exist, and grant dollars will most likely be spread across the categorical map of concerns (education, health and human services, civic and community issues, culture and the arts) at the end of the year. But we ought to be able to give a coherent rationale for our choices. And it hardly seems likely that a corporate grantmaking program that bears no relationship at all to at least one of today's social or human ills can legitimately claim to satisfy the requirements of responsible citizenship. The impact of a philanthropic budget, large or small, is a function of focusing the resources.

The reader may have guessed that my use of the word *activism* instead of *action* was a matter of deliberate choice. Sometimes leadership calls for, instead of assertiveness, quiet reflection, forbearance, listening, recording, or what may seem to be menial service roles required to move a process along. These aspects of leadership, although not action filled, require active, attentive involvement in the process of social problem solving. Certainly, reconnoitering the margins in order to become an informed participant is an act requiring great and focused energy.

If I am right about marginality, effective power brokering, and focused activism, then the chief ethical pitfalls we must avoid if we aim to be effective grants officers and leaders are obvious. We must avoid

1. Assuming that we are at the center and doing the business of business, that is, making bottom-line contributions to our company's profit and loss statements or, alternatively, assuming that we are the central actors in nonprofit affairs in the community. Both keep us from taking advantage of marginality's perspective on power.

2. Amassing the attributes of power for purposes other than serving the well-being of the company, the community, those with legitimate needs, and individuals who seek enablement through our influence. Amassing power for purposes other than these all but obviates the possibility that leadership will empower anybody, including ourselves.

3. Indulging in delusions of adequacy by assuming that our individual acts of leadership are sufficient to meet the problems at hand. Such delusions limit the possibility that our leadership can effect enduring change; that is, no one will be empowered by our leadership.

4. Indulging in inaction, disengagement, complacency, and other stances of arrogance and omission. These are forms of action, but are of the least appropriate sort, contravening the spirit and letter both of philanthropy and of leadership.

With this backdrop and these sins in plain view, I move on to promised do's and don't's. I will not give you a checklist of things to do to become a leader. Many courses tout surefire recipes for achieving that end (though I do not recommend them). The do's and don't's I will describe relate to realizing the potential for leadership in ourselves and, especially, in others. My assumption is that effective grantmaking and empowering leadership are basically the same thing.

Leadership

Knowing the Territory. The corporate grantmakers I most admire are those who strive simultaneously to understand their corporate base; learn a great deal about the community's critical problems and those actors who can be instrumental in addressing them; and discover where and how the company can make a real, and even lasting, contribution to the community's finding solutions to one or more of those problems. Understanding these three areas is the test of true leadership in corporate grantmaking, much more so than presiding over a large grants budget, being next to the great and the powerful, or being particularly adept at media relations. These latter activities may be very helpful and call upon special talents, but they do not, alone or in combination, amount to leadership where it counts—in the margins where community and business interests intersect.

Knowing Your Business. It is nearly impossible to imagine how corporate grants officers, whatever the nature or size of the business, can be effective and exert leadership unless they know and are perceived as knowing their home base—its culture and its key people. Spending time learning (and relearning) these matters pays off handsomely.

The culture of a corporation is in significant degree a function of what business the company perceives itself to be in and what markets it serves. That most businesses value their good names is a given. A consumer-oriented company, however, is much more likely to exhibit sensitivity to what people on the streets think (each person, after all, is a potential customer) than is a business that makes its money primarily in capital markets or resources extraction. Decision makers in the latter corporations are not necessarily less conscious of the company's responsibilities as a corporate citizen. But, when corporate grantmaking programs are defined or reaffirmed, these decisions makers will probably be less concerned about the immediate effects of grantmaking decisions on popular opinion. This relative insulation is neither good nor bad in itself but may influence a company's judgment of the risks it will take in grantmaking.

The nature of the business tends to have other effects on the corporation's culture and what is considered valuable and acceptable in grantmaking. A company dominated by engineers is likely to prize support for projects that produce quantifiable, even tangible, results. A bank with a large portfolio of home mortgages is more likely than an industrial firm to understand the inner workings of financing for low-income housing and could thus be receptive to a grants program in the area of housing. The company whose base is direct retailing may be looking for direct and legitimate connections between key product lines and problems faced by groups of present or potential customers.

Of course, a company's culture is greatly influenced by its persistent historical themes and myths. What, for instance, is the company's historical pattern of citizenship and involvement in the community? And, equally important, how do things happen inside the company? When someone within the company says, "This is how we do things around here; it's always been done this way, so here's what you need to do to get things done," pay attention. Knowing these informal rules is almost as important as knowing the formal bureaucratic requirements for handling information, making decisions, and securing resources.

The corporate grants officer, especially one who wants to establish a base of leadership within the corporation as well as outside of it, is well advised to respect, indeed take advantage of, the power of cultural norms. The grantmaker also must look for corporate norms that violate larger societal norms about ethical behavior or promise to undercut the grantmaking function. But be highly selective in deciding which norms to break and when to break them. Prudence suggests the importance of demonstrating that we have honored salient norms—or have made principled objections to dysfunctional ones—when we approach key people for grantmaking decisions.

Executive decision makers, who determine the fate of a company's cultural system, are worth knowing. Who are they? They may not all be at the top. How do they operate? How do they, individually and collectively, relate to the system's behavioral norms? How is each involved in the community, and how does each tend to think about corporate social responsibility? What do they look for and respect in argumentation and presentation? Who is most influential with senior management and with the chief executive officer? Is it possible to make friends and allies among the company's influential decision makers?

Employees of all levels and responsibilties influence, as well as reflect, the corporate culture. They live in the community and have time, talent, ideas, and money that are worth cultivating. What do they value? To what extent are they engaged in the community or are willing to be tapped for the community's good?

Learning as much as possible about the company's culture, employees, and decision makers will not automatically give the grants officer the correct grantmaking profile because no one profile is correct. Rather, these data form the clay out of which we help to sculpt plausible, coherent, even elegant, statements of a firm's interests, values, needs, and interpretations of its social responsibilities. And, from this information, we can fashion reasonably consistent grantmaking programs. Knowing how the company works and who its players are is essential to making sure that definitions of grantmaking programs, priorities, and rules are translated into action with some integrity.

Securing Home Base. Corporate grants officers must work to secure as well as to understand their base of operations. A secure base is essential for grantmakers to take advantage of leadership opportunities and make a convincing case for the philanthropic program. Securing the base calls for four kinds of activity—taking care of business, being businesslike, thinking strategically, and telling the truth (and associated risk taking).

Taking care of business involves attending to the tasks, on time and within rules, that satisfy the basic requirements of sound management. Grants officers may not have managerial responsibilities per se; however, their effectiveness is at risk if their department's management is not efficient. A reputation for sound management of budgets, people, and corporate processes on the part of the grantmaking department or foundation is an advantage for the grantmaking program and its officers.

Taking care of business also requires continual circuit riding within the company—regularly touching base with key decision makers. And, of course, it means making timely, informed responses to senior management's requests for counsel about community situations and appropriate corporate responses. If a grantmaker fails to cultivate senior management, the grantmaking program loses credibility.

Being businesslike involves using the language and the techniques of business and being a faithful witness to the firm's values and interests as we make and manage grants. Business language and techniques essentially reflect the corporation's legitimate concern about the efficient use of resources. Whether we analyze grantseeking agencies' budgets in their terms or in the company's version of standard economic analysis is probably not important, but it is useful to have a working knowledge of the company's assumptions and routines. However, grantmakers must analyze proposals and their economics systematically and diligently. We cannot eliminate risk, but we can understand it and portray it clearly.

Thinking strategically in developing grantmaking programs is much like thinking strategically in the business context. What are the outcomes—nonquantifiable as well as quantifiable—that can be expected? What are the milestones along the way of development? Which grantmaking opportunities add value, and which should be rejected? How do grants fit together and create goal-achieving synergies? What projects need sunset provisions?

One of the corporate grantmaker's primary ethical requirements is to tell the truth—principally in the form of making the case for grantmaking, and, especially, the community interest. James MacGregor Burns, in his seminal study *Leadership* (1978), argues that what gives leadership a transforming character is the leaders' ability to move their system to, and hopefully through, the next higher level of moral concern and decision. This view suggests that corporate grants officers have a stewardship responsibility, not only to ensure that funds are effectively employed but also to see that each grant program expands to meet key challenges of fairness, equity, and justice.

Fairness, equity, and justice may, to some, be strange concepts to associate with business, but I think not. Enlightened self-interest alone supports the contention that business shares responsibility for, and is one beneficiary of, a society that includes an increasing number of its citizens in the educational and economic mainstream. Clearly, companies pay a heavy toll and face a heavier one in the future for illiteracy, poverty, and social disorganization.

Translating these truths into the fabric of grantmaking may entail risks. For example, the suggestion to expand funding for the arts to support a nonprofessional minority dance group or a community theater in a poor neighborhood may not be well received by corporate decision makers. But the corporate grantmaker ought to build strong cases for grants that serve broader social purposes than the conventional grants do.

Although one of our most important roles is that of advocate, we must also be skilled in presenting decision-making risks (as perceived by us and by senior management) that can be accepted. Thus, we must attend to the educative sides of our roles. We are part journalists—portraying reality with accuracy and some depth through successive background papers and grant recommendations—and part teachers—establishing conditions and timing for decision making that reflect senior management's broadening understanding of the social stakes and corporate responsibility.

Telling the truth also involves explaining accurately to the community the interests, values, and constraints that define our company's approach to the external world. If our firm's stance is less than optimum, we may hope that it broadens and evolves in healthy ways and, as suggested above, we have a duty to work toward such changes. But it is only fair to the company and to the community that the grantmaker be as clear as possible about the company's present perspective on social responsibility. To misrepresent the company is dishonest and undercuts the possibilities for mutually empowering relationships in the community.

It is especially important for us to distinguish between what is philanthropic and what is not. Each grant and form of community support can be placed on a continuum between the poles of pure altruism and pure self-interest. This continuum represents "exchange values," or benefits that each side of the transaction hopes to achieve. Near the middle of the continuum, each corporate grants officer needs to draw a line between what is primarily in the community's interest and what is primarily in the company's or its officers' interest. If the exchange value seems clearly on the side of corporate interest, the grantmaker needs to argue against the transaction altogether or, more often than not, have another department handle the budgetary and monitoring responsibility for the exchange.

Determining that cause-related marketing is not corporate philanthropy is easy. If at least 50 percent of the rationale for and expected benefit from supporting a cause is cast in terms of a measurable increase in sales, the transaction properly belongs in the advertising or marketing budget. However, the call is much tougher and more risky, but fundamentally more important, when the values are less quantifiable and corporate history or one or more senior officers has a stake in the transaction. When do we tell ourselves and advise senior management that support of a certain nonprofit group does not really qualify as a philanthropic gift because it is so infused with corporate or executive self-interest that the community interest plays a distinctly secondary role? What about the gift to sponsor an event for which the company receives a public relations advantage but that has little philanthropic justification? How can we justify support of this or that college, human service organization, or performing arts group when the grant's principal motive is satisfying the social obligation of a senior officer?

To be leaders, we must make such calls honestly, although we may not always win. (Gorillas do sleep where they choose!) If we do not tell the truth, we deny our philanthropic function. We indulge in the false notion that grants are really investments and that we are really at the center, earning money for the company like everyone else.

Our function is philanthropic. At their margins, companies large and small can and do act with philanthropic intent to improve their communities without concern for bottom-line returns. Government encourages them to do so by providing tax breaks for contributions.

I am no Pollyanna; like most other corporate grants officers, I am very concerned about advancing my company's good name, and I work hard to make sure that the public knows about my company's support for its communities. But this function falls in its appropriate slot—second—after a decision to fund has been made based on careful examination of the community's need for the grant within the context of the grantmaking program.

To describe our function as anything but philanthropic—

particularly to describe it as business—erodes the very ground that gives us a special place to view and use power and to forge appropriate links between our company and the community. It takes us out of the marginal context that informs and guides moral and ethical reasoning essential to effective grantmaking and any claim we might make on leadership.

Exploring the Margins. Effective grantmaking and leadership are not possible unless you know the territory outside the company and particularly the boundary land in which company and community meet. Understanding this territory is as important and as demanding as understanding home base. This seems obvious, but how many corporate grantmakers actually explore their communities on a firsthand, personalized, and regular basis to discover strengths, weaknesses, and problems and to find out what nonprofit groups are doing and are not doing? Being there and being known for being there are prerequisite conditions for effective grantmaking and leadership.

We can define the parts of the community that we need to understand either geographically or categorically. A grants officer in a small company may need to understand only the immediate vicinity surrounding the plant or only those nonprofit groups in an area of interest to the CEO. In a large company, the grants officer may need to reconnoiter the entire community, at least in the early stages of defining where the company can make a difference. More often than not, the territory and agencies are confined to parts of the community relevant to already established grantmaking programs.

Visiting the community does not mean that new or increased funding or a flood of new proposals must follow. (On the other hand, do not overlook the value of receiving new proposals. After all, they are an important part of the job.) The grantmaker must be honest and not appear in the community under false pretenses. The main reason for being there is to listen, question, and discuss issues. If we are there for another purpose—grant monitoring, feedback about a grant request, concern about the organization's performance—we must be equally clear about that, too. In fact, it is best to separate routine circuit riding from grant discussion. Both activities are valid and ought not be confused.

Equally important, grants officers must not confuse their role as resource broker with that of expert in the field, no matter what their background. The action takes place in the community where nonprofit groups operate, not in the corporate grantmaker's office. We may have experience that is helpful in evaluating information and may be helpful to people in the field, but they are running the programs and their ideas should be given the most weight.

Think of working in the community as an exciting educational venture. In the early stages of program development, grants officers should find mentors, knowledgeable people who, with a reasonable degree of detachment, can chart the field and its current challenges, and give them entrée to its significant actors. Even as the program matures, mentors new and old are useful sounding boards.

The syllabus for routine circuit riding is a daunting list: discover new insights and confirm old ones, renew acquaintances with relevant actors and make new ones, expand the who's who list and include names of those who are real actors but are not necessarily the obvious ones, discover what continues to work and what the next promising approaches are, inform ourselves about the community's culture and the dominant ways in which planned change occurs, figure out the interconnections and possibilities for synergistic effects among grantees, and convey the current status of the program. Ultimately, two values accrue from knowing the community—credibility and trust in the community and enhanced credibility within the company. Knowledgeable argumentation lends credibility to the grantmaker in making a case for funding. Clearly, we cannot be so associated with the community that we lose perspective or senior management's faith in the integrity of our representations of corporate interests. But working from dated or inadequate information on grantseeking organizations, their missions, their capabilities, and their relationship to and likely impact on the community concerns they address corrodes linkages with internal and external constituencies very quickly and possibly permanently.

Building Community Alliances. It does not matter whether the grants officer represents a large, middle-sized, or small company, a manufacturer, retailer or bank; the plain fact is that few, if any, community concerns are satisfied by the action of a single corporate entity. No matter which problem we want to tackle—securing the future or even the operating budget of a single valued institution, strengthening the capabilities of several nonprofits, or making sure the field as a whole addresses fundamental issues of equity and justice—we need friends, allies, and partners.

The alternative—playing the Lone Ranger—is not likely to achieve a lot for the company, the grantmaker, or the grantmaking function. It probably is not even possible in the long run. Some short-term public relations advantage may be gained by acting alone and battling this or that emergency in the community, but acting alone does not win friends. Going it alone will probably not make a material difference in the life of the community. The predominance of the federated funding campaign in the nonprofit world is strong evidence that the Lone Ranger was never more than a figment of a fertile imagination.

Taking individual stands is sometimes necessary and important, but adopting the "heroic" perspective of leadership, in most situations, is less effective than adopting the "collaborative" view of that role. Leadership increasingly demands that the grantmaker become an active, constructive player at one or more tables of resource development. Indeed, very often grantmakers must help to fashion such tables where they have not existed before and to fill the seats around them with resourceful people. These requirements call on us to develop and use a special set of conflict resolution skills— negotiation and mediation in the public interest.

Sophisticated and practical literature on this sort of negotiation is readily available, and there is no need to review it here. Any grantmaker is well advised to master negotiation skills. I will touch on a few underlying attitudes that people with good negotiating skills commonly display.

The first is a commitment to inclusion. Typically we need as many people at the table as possible. This includes not only our counterparts in other companies and foundations but also representatives of other institutions and sectors who have something to bring to bear on the current problem. At a minimum, staff of affected nonprofit groups must be included. Depending on the nature of the problem, governmental officials, spokespersons for concerned religious organizations and educational institutions, and most particularly, representatives of the people targeted for assistance should be included. Each person at the table must be regarded as a full-fledged partner, an equal, in the discussion because each, through an institution or constituency, has one or more interests at stake and resources to contribute. Effective leaders often search for opportunities to set up community-wide dialogues.

People with good negotiating skills exhibit a willingness to share both the work and the credit for achievements. They think in terms of win/win strategies from the inception of the problem-solving process to its conclusion. This means, in part, that they work as hard as anyone else and play a variety of process and substantive roles as required by the situation and mix of abilities. Leadership, as defined earlier, is a set of functions. It involves finding ways for each partner to receive appropriate credit for success. This goal is not incompatible with meeting the needs of the grantmaker's company for positive public relations, but it does suggest sensitivity to similar needs of other actors engaged in the process.

Effective negotiators are committed to frank, open communication. They are clear about their own interests and willing to hear and acknowledge the interests of others. They work to open channels of communication when the process begins to bog down, and they make sure that information is shared equally among all parties. They maintain a commitment to the public good without sacrificing the essential interests of their own organization or those of others in the process. Fisher and Ury (1983) call this "principled" or nonpositional bargaining.

Conclusion

It is apt to end these musings just after a discussion of attitudes. Leadership and effectiveness in grantmaking seem to result from activity in the corporation and the community that is motivated and energized by empowering concerns as much as, probably more than, any specific push to get to the top of the heap or gain personal recognition. I do not denigrate the desire to influence people and events. Psychologists tell us that is a normal, even healthy, motivation. Rather, a consistent expression of this desire through focused activity on behalf of larger, morally valid ends—specifically, the integrity and growth of those with whom we interact and of those to whom we hope to lend a hand—sets the transforming leader apart.

Grantmakers must believe that humankind can achieve great, at the very least better, results; that empowered individuals and groups of people do build communities worth living in and caring for; that corporations, companies of people after all, can use their vast powers as partners for securing the commonweal. In short, the empowering corporate grantmaker has a motivating and sustaining vision of a more humane, just, effective, and achievable order of things. Those members of our profession whose vision is ennobling and whose actions are transforming point out to us that becoming leaders in our grantmaking roles is possible, and it is a worthy process.

References

Block, P. *The Empowered Manager: Positive Political Skills at Work*. San Francisco: Jossey-Bass, 1989.

Buhl, L. C. "Ethics at the Margins." *Foundation News*, July/Aug. 1989, pp. 53–55.

Burns, J. M. *Leadership*. New York: Harper & Row, 1978.

Carpenter, S. L., and Kennedy, W.J.D. *Managing Public Disputes*. San Francisco: Jossey-Bass, 1988.

Fisher, R., and Brown, S. *Getting Together: Building a Relationship that Gets to Yes*. Boston: Houghton Mifflin, 1988.

Fisher, R., and Ury, W. *Getting to Yes: Negotiations Without Giving In*. New York: Penguin, 1983.

Greenleaf, R. *Servant Leadership: A Journey into the Nature of Legitimate Power and Greatness*. New York: Paulist Press, 1977.

Lewicki, R. J., and Litterer, A. *Negotiation*. Homewood, Ill.: Irwin, 1985.

Lindquist, J. *Strategies for Change*. Berkeley, Calif.: Pacific Soundings Press, 1978.

McCelland, D. C. *Power: The Inner Experience*. New York: Irvington, 1975.

Oran, D., and Shafritz, J. M. *The MBA's Dictionary.* Reston, Va.:
  Reston Publishing, 1983.
Suskind, L., and Cruikshank, J. *Breaking The Impasse: Consensual
  Approaches to Resolving Public Disputes.* New York: Basic
  Books, 1987.

Chapter Seven

Providing Effective Leadership
in the Community

Peter C. Hutchinson

There was a time when we knew, without thinking much about it, what constituted our community and our community leaders. Our community was wherever we lived: the people around us were like us, and the institutions we created served our needs well. Our community leaders were a small group of people who were well known in town and took it upon themselves to deal with our community's problems. Typically, they were the leaders of commerce, government, religion, the media, and education. Together they worried about preserving our quality of life and community values.

A lot has changed. Now it is less clear what constitutes a community, and it is even less clear who our community leaders are.

Traditionally, we have thought of a community as a group of people held together and supported by what they had in common. Our communities were first formed by groups of people who shared a common heritage or set of experiences and who joined together to create a new place for themselves. Community also meant a group that banded together to survive against a harsh environment or difficult circumstances.

A good example of this form of community is the Twin Cities, where I live. Minneapolis and St. Paul are located at the head of navigation of the Mississippi River and at what was the end of the railroad—they were geographically isolated. Generally, the population that settled here was homogeneous, with similar backgrounds and experiences. Perhaps most importantly, they were people who needed one another to survive and to prosper.

Once formed, communities have been maintained by institutions created to serve the needs of the people. The institutions served as the "glue" holding people together. Institutions, by their very nature, incorporate the community's processes, rules, and rituals for turning aspirations into outcomes or results. Every community has a collection of institutions that grew up with the community—our churches, businesses, educational organizations, civic clubs, youth groups, and governing organizations. Each of these institutions has developed its own mechanism to fulfill the expectations of community members in return for their support and involvement. Most communities have created a common set of institutions—a city council, a museum or an orchestra, schools, a United Way, a chamber of commerce, a newspaper, a Rotary Club, and, of course, a collection of churches. Individual communities have also created unique institutions. For example, in the Twin Cities we have created:

- The 5% Club, to celebrate the civic contributions of those in the business community who contribute 2 or 5 percent of their taxable income to charitable causes
- The Citizens League, a nonprofit membership organization that has been a very creative participant in community problem solving
- The Minnesota Center for Corporate Responsibility and the Minnesota Business Partnership, which bring the business community together to confront community concerns in a unique way
- The Youth Trust, a partnership of businesses, schools, com-

munities, and the city to ensure that our young people have the skills and aspirations necessary to succeed

Changes in Communities

The things that have historically defined communities are changing and disappearing. The boundaries around communities have been broken down by spectacular increases in our ability to communicate and in our mobility. Isolation has given way to interconnectedness; domestic competition has given way to global competition; and homogeneity has given way to diversity of backgrounds, cultures, rituals, and life experiences. Probably no community in the country has not experienced a growing diversity in its population, either through major demographic changes or through immigration and migration.

One of the factors that has traditionally held people together as a community—their similarity to one another—has weakened. Increasingly, we see tensions developing in our communities about decision-making processes and about the allocation of resources. We also see a rapid change in the kinds of problems that demand attention in our communities—problems of single parenthood, drug abuse, non-English-speaking populations, and an aging population, for example.

As both the makeup of our communities and the problems and challenges that we face have changed, our problem-solving institutions seem less and less able to turn community aspirations into meaningful outcomes. Confidence in our community institutions has been falling. Opinion polls tell us that public confidence in institutions of all kinds—religious, educational, business, media, or government—is at an all-time low. People have become increasingly skeptical about the ability of large institutions to serve changing needs.

Institutions seem less and less able to hold communities together for two reasons. First, institutions, by their very nature, find it difficult to deal with the changing character of communities. Institutions that were originally set up to serve a certain kind of community and to confront certain kinds of challenges find it difficult to reapply themselves to new populations and new challenges. In fact, the very rules, regulations, and standard operating procedures that initially made some institutions, especially large businesses, successful often act as barriers to change and cause institutions to perform poorly today. The inertia and inflexibility that many argue limit the competitiveness of American corporations are manifest in our religious, governmental, media, and educational institutions as well. As a result, institutions are less able to serve their diverse customers, clients, and constituents.

Second, institutions are failing in their role as the glue holding us together because we have lost our personal connection with and responsibility for the outcomes they produce. As institutions succeed, we increasingly make the institutions themselves responsible for what they do rather than holding the community or those within the institutions responsible. For example, we say that government should take care of the disadvantaged rather than that we should. We say that the schools are responsible for educating our children rather than that we are. We talk about the ethics of corporations rather than about the ethics of those of us within corporations. Increasingly, employees (especially managers) within our institutions have become responsible for process—for doing things the right way—rather than for results—for doing the right things. In the end, no one seems responsible, and we are left unsatisfied with the results.

What difference does all of this make to businesses both large and small? We know that when our business institutions fail to respond to changing customers, suppliers, or competitors, we fail. We know that when an institution fails those it is supposed to serve, the institution has only two choices—to go out of business or to recreate itself as a more responsive and effective organization.

In general, those of us in business today are increasingly aware of the need to remain sensitive to our changing constituents and to change ourselves in response to their demands. In this sense, we are very well positioned to foster change within institutions in the context of community change.

Perhaps more important, if community institutions fail to change, the communities will suffer and so will we in business. Successful businesses are part, but only part, of successful communities. A terrific business located in a suffering community will itself suffer, while even an average business located in a prosperous setting will have enhanced prosperity. In many ways, the community is like a family unit in which an individual business is one of the family members. As such, businesses need to care about their own development, growth, and success but cannot ignore the impact that the success or failure of other family members will have on the family as a whole and on the businesses. The success of businesses makes the community successful and vice versa.

The prescription, then, for responding to the growing diversity of our communities is simple: be sure our businesses are changing and re-creating themselves as effectively as possible in response to the changing constituents they serve, while also challenging community institutions to change and re-create themselves in order to enhance the health of the community as a whole and each of its individual parts. Put another way, we need leadership within our organizations to make our organizations successful and we need leadership in our communities to assure that our mutual aspirations are achieved.

Where will this leadership come from? The first and most important thing to recognize is that the traditional leaders have retired from the scene or are in positions of diminishing influence. These were the "organization men" who came to their adulthood in the post-Depression, post–World War II era and are now retiring. They have passed the torch, in many cases, to a traditional generation made up of Korean War era managers, who are themselves in the process of passing leadership responsibility on to the baby boom generation. These transitions are rapid and ongoing and leave many with the impression that there is no leadership, that the leadership we need cannot be identified or does not exist.

At the same time, the changing structure of our communities has meant that a different kind of leadership is required. In business, the old U.S. Army model of organization, with strict hierarchies and multiple pyramids, has given way to a much flatter, more participatory structure. The same is true in our communities. Leadership has become more diverse as power and responsibility have become more decentralized in every institution. The processes of leadership and management have taken on wholly new forms that require participatory and consensus-building skills rather than only decision-making and analytic capabilities. We need to look for leadership in new places, and we need to encourage leadership that is increasingly responsive to the changing aspirations and needs of those who make up our communities.

The increasing value of pluralism in our communities gives those of us in business both an opportunity and a responsibility. The opportunity is based on the skills, experiences, and resources that we can make available. The responsibility emanates from the need in a pluralistic system for each of us to do at least part of the work if everyone is to benefit. Furthermore, in a pluralistic system, those not at the table take the risk of being left out. Perhaps more important, a pluralistic system creates a dynamic in which the whole can be greater than the sum of the parts. By focusing multiple perspectives on a common problem, a group can find a better solution and apply more energy to it than individuals working independently. What business leaders add to the problem-solving process enriches and broadens its scope; better answers that are more likely to work result.

Rules for Leadership

The problems our communities face today are too large and too numerous for one businessperson to participate, let alone lead, in solving them all. Businesspeople often express frustration when facing these problems: "It takes too much time." "Our first priority ought to be to run our businesses." "We don't really understand community problems and have a hard time feeling as though we have a legitimate place in the process." "Our company is not big enough to have influence or to make a difference." All of these statements are true, to some extent, but they need not paralyze any of us from responding to real community needs and concerns. A basic set of rules can help guide us as we think about when, how, where, and under what circumstances to play a leadership role.

Be a Leader on Something You Care About. Leadership is not a dispassionate activity—quite the opposite. To be a leader, you need to be committed and you need to care. A company should work on issues or concerns that are of direct and important strategic value to the company itself: for a publishing company that might mean literacy, for a drug manufacturer that might mean health care concerns, for employers of entry-level workers it may mean K–12 education reform, for a national company it may mean issues that have a national scope, and for an individual business proprietor it may mean concern for things in the immediate neighborhood.

This strategic linkage, however, is not sufficient by itself. Concern about the issue must also be manifest in the business leaders themselves. For example, the CEO of a major financial planning and services firm in the Midwest has a major concern about child care because his company employs so many young professionals. The fact that he is also the father of a young child adds an important dimension to his strategic passion about this important community concern. The combination of strategic linkage and personal concern is almost unbeatable.

Lead in Priority Matters for the Community. If you want to make a difference that counts, in addition to working on something that you care about or for which you have a strategic passion, you need to work on something that counts for the community. The areas in which the strategic concerns of your business and the concerns of the community overlap provide the most powerful leadership opportunities.

Within our Dayton Hudson family of companies (whose employees and customers include significant numbers of young families), two good examples can be given. Mervyn's, based in California, has identified child care as a major concern for the company, as well as a major concern in the community. Its child-care initiative combines those dual concerns into a major effort to increase the quantity and quality of child care in the communities they serve. Similarly, the Dayton Hudson Department Store Company has identified access to entry-level workers as a major company concern, which mirrors the concern of the communities in which the company operates for providing work opportunities for those who might otherwise fall back on public assistance. Through what the company calls the JobPlus program, it is able to join these common concerns into a remarkably effective program for pulling young, at-risk women into the permanent work force. The point is obvious—where the passion of the company and the energy of the community come together, effective things can and will happen.

Lead with Your Ears First. Our communities are filled with people eager to contribute who also have great knowledge of the community, its problems, and solutions that work. Effective leaders begin by listening, paying attention to these people, and giving them the opportunity to contribute their knowledge and insight, both in identifying problems and creating solutions. The stereotype of business leaders suggests that they spend time giving orders and pay little attention to those around them. The realities of effective leadership are quite different. Truly effective business leaders, or leaders in any institution, begin by paying attention, first to the people they serve and then to the people employed to provide the services. Receiving honest, candid, and useful feedback from clients, constituents, customers, and employees—in short, listening—is the leader's first imperative. Acting on what you hear must follow, but acting without listening is a mistake to be avoided.

Lead with Everything You Have. Our organizations, both large and small, have many resources that can be used in dealing with complex community problems. Our grantmaking programs obviously have money. Our grantmakers themselves have expertise acquired from researching and working in our fields of interest. Others in our companies also have important expertise, whether in human resources, management information, finances, production operations, or other areas. Also, we have access to enormous quantities of information about attitudes, orientations, behaviors, and new technologies because of the very nature of our businesses. Increasingly, information is the key resource for dealing with both business and community challenges. We in business have a unique opportunity to bring our information resources to bear on community problems.

Leaders who use all of their resources make their leadership matter. They look at problems multidimensionally and apply multiple resources to the challenges they face. They bring people into the process and let pluralism be a strength rather than a challenge.

In so doing, they gain the respect and support they need to be effective.

Make Others Part of the Action. Almost no community problem can be solved by a single organization or leader. A leader must focus multiple resources on complex problems. The most effective leaders are those who pull the entire community into the problem-solving process, make other people leaders in important areas, and make these leaders understand that their part is an important contribution to the whole. This kind of pluralistic leadership may seem to take more time initially, but it loses less time later in defending programs against attacks by those who were not involved in the first place. Pluralistic leadership may appear more chaotic, but out of such "chaos" comes creative and comprehensive responses that are attuned to the real nature of the challenges.

Leaders who make others part of the action reduce the overall burden on themselves and each of their partners. These are leaders that recognize that if several good people each do a little bit, together they can do a lot. These leaders increase the quantity, quality, and diversity of an increasingly diverse community's leadership resources.

Lead Where You Find Yourself. Leadership is needed in every organization, committee, task force, or group. Grantmakers lead by asking questions and pursuing concerns about organizational responsiveness to changing needs. Board members lead by being supportive and challenging in pursuing the affairs of the organization. Organizational re-creation in a time of changing community circumstances is not easy. Board members must be willing to challenge and support their board colleagues as well as management if the process of re-creation is to gain the legitimacy and energy it needs to be successful.

Leadership comes from serving on task forces as well as in elected positions. Leadership means raising your voice when those in the leadership positions do not see what you see and assuring that others have the chance to do the same thing when you are in the chairperson's role. Leadership means taking the initiative, whether on your block, in your local business association, through your service club, on a citywide task force, or in a legislative debate.

Finally, and most important, leadership means acting consistently in all of your roles as businessperson, citizen, neighbor, parent, friend, or sibling. If child care is important to you at home, it should be important to you at work. If concern for your neighbors' medical care brings you to their assistance, let that concern also take you into the debate over health care in your community. Leadership means that the commitment you make through your church to serving inner-city youth finds its way into your personal involvement as well as your company's involvement. In short, leadership means taking action wherever you find yourself and wherever you have the opportunity.

Encourage Others. Leadership is not one person's job; it is every person's job. Often, this is forgotten in the search for new leaders. How many times have we heard the question, Who will lead? when the most important question ought to be, How can I lead or support someone else's leadership? Encouraging others, seconding someone else's motion, can be a critical function in creating additional leadership resources within our communities.

Some very effective leaders go largely unrecognized. They plant ideas, nurture them along, and encourage others to take important steps. People recognized as leaders will tell you that an important part of their success was not just their own passion and commitment but the passion and commitment of those around them. The ability of leaders to create and nurture leadership capabilities in their followers is critical to success in the community.

Celebrate Your Successes. Community problem solving is hard work, and success will almost naturally come in small doses. An effective community leader must celebrate those small victories as they occur. Community leadership can be fostered by celebrating the successes of others as well. The 5% Club is one of the ways in which we in the Twin Cities celebrate the community involvement of people throughout the Twin Cities and Minnesota. Nothing is more likely to move people to continued commitment than recognition for the results of past efforts. Organizing the community to celebrate itself, its successes, and the achievements of its members is, then, an important leadership function and opportunity.

Leadership Outcomes

Leadership by our businesses will manifest itself locally, citywide, and at the state and national levels on a wide array of problems that confront our communities. It will emerge from people who have both a personal and organizational passion about a community problem and from a community prepared to come together to attack that problem.

If we are successful leaders, we will have better communities, measured in terms of their success in solving problems and, more important, measured in terms of their ability to re-create a sense of community, collective will, destiny, and mutual commitment. These communities will be healthy, vibrant, and exciting places to live, work, play, and grow.

As successful leaders we will also have better companies because the quality of communities and of companies reinforce one another. Our companies will be competitive and our personnel better trained and better prepared for the world of the future. Our companies will also be better positioned to take on the challenges of an international marketplace and their bottom-line performance will be better.

Successful leadership also generates individuals in our communities who are prepared to take the necessary moral responsibility for the character and the quality of our communities and the lives of the people within them. Moral responsibility may sound like a tricky concept, yet it is the essence of leadership. Leaders commit themselves to results; they care about outcomes. Managers, on the other hand, are typically more worried about process. Much of the anxiety about leadership, especially as it is expressed in our communities, is about finding people willing to take moral responsibility for the outcomes of our institutions. That is what leaders are supposed to do. When we in business accept our share of moral responsibility for what happens in our communities, we help enliven and enrich the quality of the communities, and we set an example that will be emulated by people throughout the community and thus will raise the level of moral responsibility within our communities while simultaneously increasing the number and raising the quality of those who act as leaders.

Communities are important. They provide the launching pad from which individual growth and achievement are possible. They are the reservoir of energy and creativity on which we, as businesses and individuals, draw to fuel our own success. They are the mechanism by which both our individual and our collective aspirations are turned into reality.

Being part of a community is not an option—it is a choice. We are part of a community, but what we choose to do as part of that community is our option. We can choose to make it a better place, more vital and with greater creative resources, or we can choose to ignore it and let it dissipate. From a bottom-line point of view, there is no choice. We would not let our business assets dissipate, our creative energies be sapped, and our wherewithal be drained. By the same token, we cannot and must not let this happen to our communities. By enriching our communities, we create a fertile environment in which all community members can grow and prosper, including ourselves and our businesses. This enrichment is in our self-interest, and it is in our collective interest. It is both our opportunity and our obligation.

Chapter Eight

Linking Corporate Culture
and Corporate Philanthropy

Mary Stewart Hall

One of Joseph Nolan's favorite stories about the culture of the
Weyerhaeuser Company is cited in *Commitment to Community:
The Story of the Weyerhaeuser Company Foundation*. Nolan tells
how chief executive J. P. "Phil" Weyerhaeuser, Jr. had struggled for
fifteen years to overcome his concerns about the appropriateness of
giving away stockholders' money. Even after this issue was resolved,
he delayed filing the Weyerhaeuser Foundation's articles of incorporation until the highly cyclical forest products company was in a
position to contribute at least $1 million to an initial endowment.
He told Nolan that the formation of the foundation should not be
announced until the foundation had sufficient resources to prove the
firm's ability to sustain an ongoing grants program. Nolan, who was
the company's general counsel and one of the foundation's first officers, said this combination of modesty, integrity, and stewardship
were major elements of the Weyerhaeuser values (Svicarovich).

A similar tale is told about Anthony "Tony" Lee Andersen, head of H. B. Fuller Company, a large adhesives manufacturer based in St. Paul, Minnesota. Craig Smith, publisher of *Corporate Philanthropy Report,* interviewed Andersen in 1988, and they met again on an airplane following the Council on Foundations' 1989 annual conference. Smith said he was a bit shocked to find Andersen in the plane's tourist section, but Andersen remarked that since employees were not permitted to travel first class, neither did he. This company, along with giving 5 percent of its income, is noted for its accessible management and the value it places on employees. It manifests these traits in several ways, such as having a broadly representative committee of employees appointed by its corporate foundation trustees to make most grant decisions. Smith commented later that Andersen's company presents an excellent example of how an entrepreneurial family has institutionalized its values in a corporation and that he should not really have been surprised to find the company's leader riding in the crowded tail of an airplane.

These two stories illustrate the unique culture of two companies. They point out the importance to that culture of what executives pay attention to, control, and reward and illustrate that the true measure of a corporation's culture is what people do and not necessarily what they say. The anecdotes also demonstrate that a firm's culture often manifests itself in community involvement activities.

The Importance of Corporate Culture

The literature on corporate culture began at least thirty years ago. But, it was not until 1981, with the publication of the blockbuster *The Art of Japanese Management* by Richard Pascale and Anthony Athos that the notion of corporate culture became widely discussed and accepted in American corporations. Financial manager Dennis Cross (1988) noted, "Corporate culture is the most important concept to come out of the 1980s. In good companies, it has been around for decades, but it is just now being identified and catalogued." Most definitions of corporate culture are similar to the one used here: a pattern of shared values, beliefs, assumptions, and behaviors that define an organization's view of itself and its environment and that are considered sufficiently valid, over time, to be taught to new members as the correct way to perceive, think, feel, and act.

Surprisingly, however, the literature has largely ignored the role of corporate philanthropy in corporate culture. This is unusual, not only because the charitable function is so dependent on a nurturing corporate environment but also because philanthropy, bridging as it does a firm's internal and external worlds, is an obvious way in which corporate cultures are manifest. For very practical reasons, the interdependence of corporate culture and corporate philanthropy should be given attention. The proper mesh between the culture of a business and its community involvement activities is probably the single most important determinant of how successful the latter (and those who manage these activities) will be. A bad fit between the corporate culture and the philanthropic program is also a significant reason for many of the problems that make up the folklore of corporate contributions staffs such as the difficulty of coping with drastic and overnight changes in philosophy and direction when corporate leadership changes.

The importance of a corporation's culture to its community involvement activities is even more compelling today given the increasing drive by most firms to cut overhead. The threat that this trend represents for corporate philanthropy has been stated boldly by Craig Smith (1989b): "The old notions of advocacy-arm-twisting, boosterism, goal setting—are out of touch with the new leverage points in corporate culture. Many companies cling to outmoded notions . . . that they must give out of a sense of obligation. Such obligatory giving must by necessity be increasingly marginal . . . without strong countervailing pressure from advocates for philanthropy, companies will surely move to sever ties to nonprofits which they quite mistakenly think to be nonessential."

As contributions managers struggle to rethink the case for their function, one of their new rationales is the role that community involvement programs can play in changing or embedding revised cultures in the entire organization. A firm that has capitalized on this potential is General Electric Company (GE). Struggling through the 1980s to instill a commitment to excellence as its core value, GE reinforced this message with some highly visible programs to reward quality in the nonprofit sector. One of these is their Angel Grants program, designed to recognize people who are entrepreneurs of volunteering and giving. Paul Ostergard, former president of General Electric's foundation, points out that the fundamental purpose of the program is to make role models of individuals who spot a problem in their communities and who go out and solve it. "This entrepreneurial spirit, focus on excellence, and empowering the individual to make a difference are all consistent with GE's new corporate culture," he notes. "We were consciously looking for ways to model these concepts in the Foundation's activities" (personal conversation with author, Jan. 1990).

A similar approach can be found at Levi Strauss & Company, with headquarters in San Francisco. Robert H. Dunn, vice president of community affairs and corporate communications, explained that his firm has initiated a series of employee activities that stress innovation and leadership, two characteristics essential to survival in the firm's highly competitive industry. "Employee teams are encouraged to tap both company and foundation resources to tackle tough and risky issues, such as AIDS and racism" (personal conversation with author, Dec. 1989).

The Elements of Corporate Culture

In what is undoubtedly a spirit of entrepreneurship, scholars have sought to coin their own particular labels for the elements that contribute most to the phenomenon of corporate culture. However, most focus on at least six common factors: philosophy and values, mission, strategy, structure, means, and style. An understanding of these factors, how they are manifest in a particular company, and how they can be applied in a philanthropic program is important to the savvy manager, whether in a large or small business.

Philosophy and Values. The philosophy and values of a firm have often been called the "soul" of a corporation's culture since they are composed of those collectively held beliefs and assumptions that define the unique spirit of the firm. Increasingly, businesses codify these beliefs in written statements. Weyerhaeuser's value statement, for example, says that the company believes how a profit is earned is just as important as profitability itself. It characterizes the company's core principles as integrity, stewardship, fairness, and balance. These values are also expressed in aspects of Weyerhaeuser's philanthropy. As illustration, its foundation has a two-pronged mission to address the needs of Weyerhaeuser's communities as well as the needs of its industry that was selected to reflect both the company's commitment to stewardship and the balance between short-term and long-term gains benefiting its various stakeholders. The often onerous practice of answering all charitable appeals with a clear rationale for decisions is in this case based on beliefs about integrity and fairness. This conscious effort to manage a fit between corporate culture and the firm's contributions is one reason why Weyerhaeuser's giving continued during the 1980s, when the forest products industry recorded near-Depression level earnings.

Mission. If philosophy and values are the "soul" of a corporation, its mission is the "guts" since the mission reflects the organization's primary business goals and its reason for existence. Corporate contributions managers have consistently focused on tying this element of corporate culture to their own activities. The field is replete with examples of grantmaking that reflect the nature of the firm's business. The Medtronic Company makes pacemakers and, understandably, has fashioned a corporate grantmaking program that favors aid to elderly people. Jostens makes class rings and pins, graduation caps and gowns, yearbooks, and diplomas. Thus, the Jostens Foundation gives grants to support schools, colleges, students, and recent graduates. SAFECO insurance companies give priority to grants in the health care field and have been particularly attentive to nonprofit initiatives on low-income health care, teenage pregnancy, AIDS, the nursing shortage, and home-based health care in its geographical areas of operations. Boeing, the world's largest airplane manufacturer, places an emphasis on technical education in its grants program.

The reason for these links is obvious. Publicly held companies that give away shareholders' money must be able to discern and communicate some legitimate benefit to the company as a result of its civic largesse.

Strategy. The rapid rise of the cause-related marketing movement can be viewed as a primary example of the alignment of firms' business strategies with their community involvement activities. *Corporate Philanthropy* newsletter points out that even the environment is benefiting from what is becoming a normal corporate practice: "If you purchase Burpee seeds, you will learn about the Nature Conservancy. Buy boots from REI, Inc. and you can join the World Wildlife Federation. An Eddie Bauer shirt will generate a donation to the Wilderness Society. Get a Patagonia jacket or L. L. Bean hiking shorts and as much as 10 percent of profits will go to a cross-section of conservation organizations" (Smith, 1989a).

Security Pacific Bank of Washington state decided many years ago to compete for new individual accounts by emphasizing how the firm helps its local community. The contributions and employee volunteer programs that Peter Broffman manages are thus not only tied to the firm's marketing strategy, they are also an essential ingredient in implementing this strategy.

Strategic ties are not limited just to the promotion of products and services. For the past twelve years, Weyerhaeuser has relied on its contributions program to help implement the strategic choice to remain largely self-sufficient for raw materials by owning its own timber-producing lands. This choice has led to grants and employee volunteer projects emphasizing the interdependence of the firm and the communities adjacent to its land holdings. Multifaceted grants programs have focused on environmental land-use issues. For example, Weyerhaeuser's foundation played a major role in creating a new nonprofit organization in Washington state that provides a forum and technical assistance on wildlife and land-management issues. The group has played a key role in the development of voluntary agreements between environmentalists, Native Americans, state agencies, and private forestland owners.

Chrysler has turned to its contributions program to help implement its strategy for upgrading the quality of its future work force. The firm has some 45,000 jobs that require a high school diploma and "recognizes it will win or lose the competitive battle on the shop floor," according to Lynn Feldhouse, manager of the Chrysler Corporation Fund (personal conversation with author, Nov. 1989). It has reallocated more than half of its charitable resources to initiatives to improve education and is also instituting techniques for involving its employees in school reform.

These strategic links can be even more subtle. GE chose to become more competitive through growth and subsequently faced the problem of how to emphasize the advantages of being a very large corporation. One way they decided to emphasize the advantages was to develop community involvement programs that were clearly in the nation's interests and could only be mounted by an organization with massive resources and a sophisticated work force. These programs led to inner-city public school improvement initiatives that drew heavily on the firm's formidable financial and human resources.

The overseas grantmaking activities of H. B. Fuller Company also help to illustrate the advantages of being a multinational corporation. Karen Muller, director of community affairs at Fuller, notes that each of the corporation's foreign-based subsidiaries is moving toward the goal of being a 5 percent donor. Each business is also launching grants programs directed by employee committees. This approach, which she calls "employee-run, management-supported," also helps reinforce some of the parent corporation's basic values (personal conversation with author, Oct. 1989).

Structure. Successful community involvement programs are designed to consciously attend to both the formal and informal organizational structures in the corporation. The Burlington Northern Foundation, for example, reinforces the message that it draws its income from several distinct operating companies by requiring that grantees list each of these businesses whenever credit is given for grants made by the foundation. GE has fostered distinct community initiatives by its thirteen operating firms. Its go-go plastics business, composed largely of a baby boomer work force, chose to rally employees to rehabilitate an inner-city YMCA in one day. The resulting publicity has fostered competition between other GE units to launch similar activities.

Many contributions managers have ensured that representatives from all levels in the organization, from corporate directors to unionized hourly employees, are involved in decision making about programs and in their implementation. However, they may have done a better job in reaching upper management than the rest of the work force. An informal survey for the Council of Foundations in 1988 revealed that while most managers surveyed felt their firms' contributions programs were "good to excellent," the majority of other employees rated the programs only "fair to poor" (Hall, 1988). Contributions managers obviously must pay more attention to building the case for corporate philanthrophy with the hourly and salaried work force.

      The informal structural norms of a company are also worth considering. Firms that have a highly developed history of using cross-unit task forces will be comfortable with community involvement programs that use this same approach. Such task forces are part of the Securiteam Program at Security Pacific Bank and the Elfun Society at GE, both mechanisms for recruiting and rewarding employee volunteer groups. Reinforcing corporate structural norms is a simple and effective way to gain acceptance for the contributions program while also conveying that the program's management fits in the mainstream of corporate practice.

      Delegation of authority in a firm's contributions department may not match the degree of delegation in other departments. In many companies, it is still true that while operating managers have authority to make multimillion-dollar decisions on all other aspects of the business, they must refer even small corporate donation requests to headquarters. In some cases, this is because the firm has chosen to use a corporate foundation for its major grantmaking mechanism, and the "arms-length" requirements result in final grant decisions being made by a small number of designated officers or trustees. But, all too frequently, corporations send signals that operating managers cannot be trusted to make sensible decisions when choosing to give money away. If contributions managers want their counterparts in the firm to pay the same degree of attention to community involvement activities as they do to other business decisions, these managers must ultimately reconcile this structural dilemma.

      Another challenge to a corporation's culture is restructuring, whether caused by mergers, acquisitions, divestitures, or shifts in leadership. These changes almost inevitably require modification in an organization's culture and are often first reflected in the firm's structure. A case in point is IMC Fertilizer Group, Inc., of suburban Chicago. According to Colleen Keast, IMC's manager of public affairs, the business has changed its focus from fertilizers and other commodities to that of a "business that consists of three separate enterprises" (personal conversation with author, Nov. 1989). Its product lines now include medical products, specialty chemicals, flavors, and animal health and nutrition products. At the same time, IMC is preparing for the retirement of its chairman, an individual very involved in community activities at the national and local level. An executive team has been formed to guide the management transition and to implement a strategy for maintaining as much flexibility in the nature of future business as is necessary to "maximize shareholder value." In addition, the firm has cut its corporate-level staffs by three-fourths.

Not surprisingly, these changes have had a major impact on IMC's community involvement programs. Keast must find a way to make the firm's foundation and contributions program responsive to both companywide and individual subsidiary needs. She must do this while maintaining sufficient flexibility to cope with resource levels that vary because of a new policy allotting 2 percent of the prior year's profit to charity. While maintaining uniform standards and expectations, she must also delegate an appropriate level of decision making to the subsidiaries. And, finally, she must establish a culture of social responsibility throughout the organization instead of relying primarily on leadership from the chairman.

Keast has been asked to frame a new philosophy and value statement for community social responsibility because IMC is aware of the demands being placed on its culture. "Getting clear on what we want IMC to stand for is really important when you are undergoing this much change," she says (personal conversation with author, Nov. 1989).

Means. A mismatch between the corporate philanthropy program and the rest of the corporation's culture can become acutely visible in the area of means, the standardized management processes and routines normally expected throughout the firm. When executives feel that their company's philanthropic program is poorly managed, the program is usually not overtly attending to some of the firm's most prized systems. These systems most often deal with planning, decision making, communications, personnel, financial controls and reporting, and performance evaluation.

Problems exist in the area of means for many reasons. In small businesses, the contributing program may be handled by a manager responsible for many other functions who may feel the program is too small or too unimportant to warrant the use of the systems expected elsewhere. Some corporate foundations employ their own staffs, who either do not have the inclination or the opportunity to use procedures similar to those of the parent company. In other businesses, managers seem to have decided that philanthropy is "too different" from the profit-making aspects of the organization to apply the same systems to it.

It is a challenging task to use for-profit management approaches in a nonprofit program, if only because of the difficulty of quantifying the bottom line. But most departments face the same difficulty. The trick is to identify and adapt useful business practices. Seafirst Bank of Seattle, for example, issues an annual report on its community involvement activities with a very similar format to the corporation's annual report to shareholders. Weyerhaeuser has used widely recognized photographs from its corporation's advertising as the cover for its foundation's reports. Dayton Hudson uses its corporation's issue-management process as a planning mechanism for charitable activities. An increasing number of firms follow the same financial reporting formats and tracking systems in both their for-profit and nonprofit units.

An even more explicit tie between corporate practice and a community involvement program can be found in the large forest products firm, Boise Cascade, with headquarters in Idaho. Elaine Nielsen, former manager of corporate contributions for the company, reports that every three years, the top company leaders make personal visits to each of the corporation's facilities, which number between 130 and 150. Meetings to discuss local needs and concerns are arranged with civic and business leaders as well as with employees. This process, of direct benefit in helping the firm sense emerging political and union issues, has also begun to play a direct role in shaping the agenda for future grantmaking and employee volunteer assignments (personal conversation with author, Oct. 1989).

Levi Strauss has recently evaluated its community involvement program in light of its management's increasing attention to improving performance measures throughout the firm. One interesting outcome of this analysis was the firm's decision to initiate the new Grants-Plus program. This program, in recognition that all of the company's grantees have organizational needs, allocates up to 15 percent of each Levi Strauss award for purposes such as employee training, team building, or management improvement. The firm is also devoting part of its employee volunteer resources to strengthening grantee capabilities.

Some contributions staff members are finding ways to compare their performance to that of their competitors, just as is done in the operating units. They are setting up objective benchmarks, which will, over time, allow performance evaluation and process-based cost analysis in comparison to the community activities of major business competitors. Few successful models exist yet for this complicated undertaking. Nevertheless, making the management processes of the contributions department compatible with those of the rest of the business is important to the internal reputation of those who lead the department and to the survival of the department itself.

Style. A corporation's style is seldom reduced to written statements or codified in employee handbooks. The only way to determine a particular firm's style is to look at the types of behaviors that are rewarded.

SAFECO's employees are highly prized volunteers in the Seattle community. Jill Ryan, the company's community relations manager, has hypothesized that this may be because of the firm's cultural style: a strong belief in efficiency, in doing things quickly but thoroughly (personal conversation with author, Oct. 1989). SAFECO employees have a reputation for being hardworking, serious, and responsible volunteers. They prefer assignments in difficult health and welfare settings, rather than more high-profile roles in arts organizations. Microsoft, of Redmond, Washington, one of the whiz kids of the high-technology industry, stresses a casual style that appeals to its bright, young, and somewhat eclectic work force. Microsoft has brought these characteristics to its contributions activities, most of which emphasize employee interests and involvement. A commitment to work force diversity is an aspect of corporate style at Security Pacific Bank that has been manifest in its growing program of minority student scholarships, employee mentoring, and internships. This emphasis on diversity is also found in many of the community involvement activities of the Seattle operation of U S WEST Communications, one of the Northwest's leaders in educational programs for minority youth.

Teamwork across boundaries, empowered people, innovation, entrepreneurism, and visionary managers are all obvious results of behavioral styles. What people in the organization do, rather than what they say they ought to be doing, is most important. Therefore, some corporate contributions managers have worked hard to get their firms to adopt employee volunteer recognition and reward programs (such as those at Borden) or to add community service as an element of managers' performance evaluation and compensation (such as at E. I. du Pont de Nemours & Company).

Assessing and then adapting to a corporation's style is perhaps most important to a new contributions manager. Personnel consultant Neil Macdougall (1987) has conducted research indicating that the lack of compatible styles between company and employee is the single most important reason for employee failure. He notes that an understanding of a company's behavioral expectations is particularly critical to employees in positions with responsibilities cutting across the whole organization and dealing with both internal and external audiences. Differences in style may create particularly acute problems for new contributions managers who have no prior business experience. Macdougall found that fitting in is doubly hard for those who enter firms from some other setting such as academe, government, or the nonprofit world.

Assessing the Match Between
Corporate Culture and Philanthropy

An easy way to begin evaluating the extent of the mesh between corporate contributions and corporate culture is to draw a chart similar to the one shown in Figure 8.1. Column two of the chart is filled in by listing the firm's characteristics, beliefs, and practices that best represent each of the six elements of corporate culture. These can then be correlated in column three to examples found in the community involvement program. Although elementary, this matrix does provide a useful framework for analysis.

Steps to improve the mesh between the corporate culture and contributions program depend on the outcome of this exercise and the particular cells in which the most obvious lack of fit occurs. Most Western businesses would probably concentrate on resolving gaps in the dimensions of missions, strategy, means, and structure. Scholars of Japanese management might argue, however, that Japanese firms might be most concerned with finding incompatibility in philosophy and values and style. Now that the Japanese are beginning to launch their own corporate philanthropy programs, it will be interesting to see how these programs exemplify the corporate cultures of their sponsoring companies.

For those individuals who complete this exercise and find their programs closely aligned with their corporate culture, the outcomes can indicate which characteristics are important to maintain and even strengthen in the years ahead. The exercise will help other managers reveal areas in which the mesh is weak or nonexistent. Ideally, the examples cited in this chapter will suggest ways to address particular issues. One word of caution, however. Corporate cultures are unique, as people are. A clear understanding of a spe-

Figure 8.1. Mesh Between Corporate Contributions and Corporate Culture.

Corporate Culture Element	Obvious in Company by:	Reflected in Community Involvement Function by:
Philosophy/values		
Mission		
Strategy		
Structure		
Means		
Style		

cific cultural environment is a prerequisite to adopting another firm's good ideas.

Edgar H. Schein, Sloan Fellows Professor of Management at the Massachusetts Institute of Technology, once wrote (1986), "An examination of cultural issues is essential to a basic understanding of what goes on in organizations, how to run them, and how to improve them." The same can be said for corporate community involvement programs.

References

Cross, D. W. "Corporate Culture." *Managers Magazine,* May 1988, pp. 3–4.

Hall, M. S. "What Do They Think of Us?" *Foundation News,* Sept.–Oct. 1988, pp. 55–57.

Macdougall, N. "How You Should Evaluate Company Culture." *CMA Magazine,* Sept.–Oct. 1987, p. 71.

Pascale, R. T., and Athos, A. G. *The Art of Japanese Management.* New York: Simon & Schuster, 1981.

Schein, E. H. "Are You Corporate Cultured?" *Personnel Journal,* Nov. 1986, pp. 83–96.

Smith, C. "Giving Green." *Corporate Philanthropy Report.* May 1989a, p. 1.

Smith, C. Oral remarks at INDEPENDENT SECTOR Annual Meeting, Pittsburgh, Penn., Oct. 1986b.

Svicarovich, J. *Commitment to Community.* Tacoma, Wash.: Weyerhaeuser Company Foundation, pp. 23–25.

PART THREE

Today's Key Issues
in Corporate Grantmaking

Chapter Nine

Why Give?
Notes to a New CEO

Jack A. MacAllister

Early in this century, John Lorenzo Hubbell, one of the first and most widely respected of all Indian traders, explained why he labored to improve the lot of the Navajos: "No intelligent Indian trader desires to live among a community of Indian paupers. . . . The first duty of an Indian trader . . . is to look after the material welfare of his neighbors. . . . This does not mean that the trader should forget that he is here to see that he makes a fair profit for himself" (Blue, 1986). It is not likely that Hubbell ever heard of expressions like *community relations* and *social responsibility*. They would not have meant much to him anyway. They are dull words, dry and dusty. But Hubbell did know that his business could prosper only if those around him fared well.

For more than half a century, during a time in the history of the American West when Indians suffered greatly with the coming of new settlers, Hubbell became known to the Navajos for his honesty and for, more than any other white man, the help he gave to his neighbors. He was friend, student, teacher, and merchant. And he became the foremost Navajo trader of his time. He died in 1930 at age seventy-seven, but the Hubbell Trading Post, now a National Historic Site, is still operated in the traditional manner on the Navajo reservation in Arizona.

Hubbell, in his way, was a classic chief executive. He managed for the long pull, knew his customers and served them well, set out to earn a fair return on his investment, recognized the importance of community, and saw that the success of his business depended on his responding to the needs of people. Over the decades, no one has improved much on that concept of good management.

Yet there are those people who say that a modern corporation's only job is to make as much money as possible for its shareowners. They believe that good schools for our children, shelter for the homeless, and opportunity for the disadvantaged are things for someone else to attend to. But corporations that do attend to these issues, they argue, just penalize their shareowners.

Do not believe it. The CEO's job is to make sure the business succeeds, but a business cannot succeed if society fails. We cannot market successfully if the marketplace does not prosper. We cannot compete if graduates of our schools cannot read, write, and reason. Every citizen, every business, and every organization has a responsibility to promote the common good. Time and money used to further economic and social progress do require the same accountability as other corporate resources, but to ignore the problems of society is to fail the test of leadership and to do a disservice not only to shareowners, but also to customers, employees, and communities where you do business.

So think of community involvement not as charity, but as an investment in a way of life and in the future of your business. Each company may get involved differently. We can help the young, the aged, or the homeless. We can help improve our schools, expand the arts, protect the environment, or provide health and human services. But, in grantmaking as in business, there are some basics: the need to focus our efforts to get results; the need for trained, competent management; and the need for involved leadership. We must set objectives and expect results. In all, I think there are six principles to successful grantmaking.

Involve Yourself

Chief executive officers need to know their communities for the same reason they need to know their customers. Get educated. Learn about the issues, and gain an understanding of what the community needs. Talk—and listen—to educators, health and human services workers, environmentalists, community leaders, and your own employees. This means giving time, which can be difficult. But a CEO's personal involvement is absolutely essential to successful grantmaking. Grantmaking needs the same attention you give to marketing, finance, and operations.

Involve Others

It is important to build community involvement into the culture of your company. Get the board of directors, senior staff, and your employees involved.

You won't find more good ideas, more enthusiasm, or more willingness to get involved anywhere than among your employees. I learned about the problems of the homeless—and that most homeless people are neither drug dependent nor unstable—when an employee invited me to join her on visits to homeless shelters in our area. She introduced me to men and women who lacked hope as well as homes. We have since joined with other businesses to provide jobs, training, and social support to homeless families.

Be Strategic and Innovative

Do not try to support every worthwhile cause. Throwing money at problems does not work and, moreover, there is never enough money to go around. Find ways to make a difference. Encourage agencies to work together on areas of common concern. Look for plans that have long-term value. In society, as in business, it costs more to fix things than to get them right in the first place. U S WEST focuses much of its help on early childhood education because a nation plans its future by how it nurtures its young. Dayton Hudson supports quality family child care. Allstate Insurance Company helps minority high school youngsters develop their business abilities.

General Electric and Atlantic Richfield Company help young people broaden their appreciation of the arts. Thousands of companies work with local school systems.

Set Objectives and Expect Results

Write down the areas of greatest interest to your company. The values of your business, your budget, and the needs of your communities will all determine the nature of your involvement. Thinking through your objectives and communicating them to employees and the community will give meaning and purpose to your program.

Be sure your grantmaking staff is professionally trained and understands both the needs of the community and the objectives of the business. Be sure they are as competent in their fields as your financial and marketing people are in theirs. They should have the respect of the community, know the needs of the community, and know how to relate community needs to company objectives.

You have a right—a responsibility—to expect organizations that seek resources from you to have their own objectives and strategies to achieve them. They probably will not be objectives that can be achieved in the next quarter or the next year, but nonprofits should achieve measurable results. Be prepared to stay involved for the long term: make an investment of yourself as well as funds, and know the disappointments as well as the successes. I like to ask managers at U S WEST what they tried that did not work and what they learned from their mistakes; their answers speak volumes about their willingness to take meaningful risks.

Do More than Write Checks

Ways in which a company can get involved in the community are limited only by the creativity of its management. For example, you can be a forceful advocate for change. Chances are, when you speak out, the community will listen. Just be sure you know what you are talking about. Remember the admonition of the poet Alexander Pope: "A little learning is a dangerous thing. Drink deep or taste not the Pierian spring" (Bartlett's, 1955, p. 310b). Drink deep.

You and your managers can be immensely helpful to school

districts, social services agencies, charitable organizations, and others on matters from setting budgets to personnel development, from planning to communicating. You will get many requests for loaned executives; consider them only when objectives and timetables are clear to all.

You can share equipment, space, facilities, and technology. Westinghouse Electric Corporation provides consulting services to potential new businesses. Amoco's National Center for Neighborhood Enterprise provides professional management training and technical assistance to residents of public housing. U S WEST invited school teachers to join its training programs on leadership development, risk taking, and management techniques, areas that teachers said they needed help with. The teachers are enthusiastic about attending these classes, and their participation makes the classes more valuable for our managers, too.

Recognize Good Work

Encourage and recognize employees for the good work they do. Many companies match contributions, up to specified limits, that their employees make to charitable organizations. Some contribute specified amounts to an organization for every hour an employee volunteers to it.

This, I am sure, is an incomplete list. Any CEO could add to it, quite probably improve upon it. Like our friend John Hubbell, we must recognize that the right to do business includes a responsibility to the community. I think you will find that fulfilling that responsibility through community participation is one of the easiest things to do—and one of the hardest things to do well. Good luck.

References

Bartlett, J. *Familiar Quotations.* (13th ed.) Boston: Little, Brown, 1955.

Blue, M. "A View from the Bullpen: A Navajo Ken of Traders and Trading Posts." *Plateau, 57* (3), 1986, pp. 9-17.

Chapter Ten

Determining the Scope
and Boundaries
of Corporate Grantmaking

Judith K. Healey

When Alice encountered the Cheshire Cat sitting high up in a tree in a fork in the road, she was lost. She asked politely for directions. The Cheshire Cat asked where she wanted to go. To tell the truth, she did not know. "Well, then, if you don't know where you are going, take any road. Any road will get you there," said the sassy cat. And so it is in corporate grantmaking. If you do not know where you are going, any road will get you there. But where will you be?

Mission Statements: The "Why" of Corporate Grantmaking

In most corporations, grantmaking has evolved for a variety of reasons: the personal charitable interests of the chief executive officer, the recognition by the corporation that it wants to be perceived as a "good corporate citizen" in its community, the desire to make the community an attractive place for employees to live and work, the desire to be associated with some tangible effort such as the arts, the decision of the company's executives that profits generated by the corporation should serve some general public good. Any one of these elements or a combination of them is a legitimate reason for corporations to make grants and contributions.

Many times the grantmaking of a corporation has evolved over time through some or all of these rationales. Rarely does a company develop a mission statement before the first grant is made. And while increasing numbers of corporations are publishing guidelines, often the guidelines are predicated on the current grants program rather than being a more reflective statement of purpose for the company's grantmaking. A grantmaking program that is unplanned may accomplish much good, but most corporate executives would agree that such drifting is generally not acceptable in other departments of the company. In fact, allowing the grantmaking program to function in an unplanned way frequently puts it at risk in the fast-changing scene of corporate America.

Dangers and Opportunities. Corporate grantmaking is coming of age. It is becoming increasingly more sophisticated in its approach, process, and administration. The money committed to grantmaking, despite dire predictions to the contrary, continues to rise annually. At the same time, competition for grants is increasing. Less money is available for several segments of the nonprofit sector, and critical needs for assistance in basic human requirements such as food and housing are apparent. Homeless people are affecting all of our major urban environments. Large numbers of people in this country are sleeping on our city streets. Hunger is a headline item and a constant topic in our churches, foundations, and United Ways. The government is providing less in the way of assistance for many in need. As the nation's institutional funders struggle to address these compelling issues, the arts, too, argue that they have increasing costs and, since "man does not live by bread alone," a valid claim to whatever grants and gifts are available.

In this time of turmoil and change, corporate grantmaking is deluged with competing requests from the community. In addition, because many corporations have not thought through a mission statement and have produced only the broadest of guidelines, discontent with the grantmaking program inside the corporation may grow. In the worst situation, the company, struggling with needs to compete in its industry and perhaps operating with the impending threat of a merger or acquisition, becomes increasingly disenchanted with its grantmaking program. Often, in times of stringent budget cutbacks within the corporation, the funds for contributions are among the first to be reduced since senior managers may not see in this department the important bottom-line contribution they so readily see in others.

The Chinese character for crisis embodies both the concept of danger and that of opportunity. The corporate grantmaking program today, sometimes under siege from within and without, should seize the opportunity inherent in the situation. Development of a clear mission statement and guidelines will provide the rationale to persuade the company to protect the program in volatile times; it will also explain the company's program to the multiple interests in the community seeking funds, thereby improving community relations for the company as a whole.

Reflection of Company. Every contributions and grantmaking program should have a well-thought-out mission statement. Such a document is the "why" of the program. It explains the necessity of the program to those inside the corporation as well as to the public. It can be used to explain to shareholders why the company gives away their hard-earned money as well as to instruct the public on the intent of the company's grantmaking program. The mission statement is the basis of the guidelines that will be published, and, more important, it is the internal standard against which requests should be measured as grant funds are allocated. Ultimately, it contributes to the value managers of the company will place on the grantmaking function.

Every corporation should have a mission statement that is unique for its grantmaking program because every corporation is different. The mission statement should be a reflection of the corporation's interest; it should include the philosophy of senior management or the board of directors on the purpose of a grantmaking program. And it should be useful for the staff of the program to design day-to-day guidelines that ultimately will determine the mix of projects funded by the grantmaking program.

Many years ago, I interviewed the corporate secretary of a medium-sized manufacturing company in the Midwest. I asked the executive, "How does this company make its grants? How does it decide which requests to honor and which to decline?" There was a long pause as he looked out the window thoughtfully. Then he swung his eyes back to me. "The chairman and I just sit down every year in December and go through them. If he likes a group, he'll give the O.K." Undoubtedly, there was no mission statement in that grantmaking program! The company is now out of business; if you do not know where you are going, any road will get you there.

A mission statement should be broad enough to encompass the company's interests and flexible enough to provide for a variety of contingencies. It should also reflect the company's rationale for making grants. A broad mission statement is necessary because any company's business interest may expand suddenly with an acquisition or a merger, an increasing likelihood these days for both strong and weak companies. A flexible mission statement is an enabling document that does not tie the hands of the grantmaking staff as changes occur in the company. The mission statement should indicate that senior managers have given the company's rationale for making grants serious thought and have made a considered decision that some of the company's resources will be directed to grantmaking to enhance the company's business purposes.

A mission statement may be as simple as the following, from the General Mills Foundation: "The ultimate goal of General Mills' corporate citizenship activities is to make a significant and lasting impact on our communities. Through the continuing commitment of both philanthropic and volunteer resources, and in its own policies, the company supports efforts that offer long-term benefits to individuals, families, and the community, and reduce future costs to society" (General Mills 1990 Corporate Citizenship Report).

It is never too late to develop a mission statement for a grantmaking program. Even if a company has been operating for some time without one, any moment is opportune for senior officers to examine the motivations for giving and create the statement that explains these motivations. Mission statements should be periodically revised, as well. Many corporations review both grantmaking guidelines and mission statements every five years, but any regular time period will do.

If the thought of developing a mission statement leaves you cold with fear as you gaze on your already overburdened desk, be of good heart. A mission statement need not be long. Sometimes three or four paragraphs say more than five pages. Also, you have models to review. A number of corporations have developed (and sometimes refined) mission statements for their grantmaking programs. Call a few colleagues; ask how they devised their statements and dealt with their boards or committees in adopting the statements. You may find your task (and your mind) considerably eased by these conversations.

Guidelines: The "How" of Corporate Grantmaking

Once the mission statement has been developed and agreed upon by your board of directors or management committee, the guidelines should be easier to develop or revise. The guidelines are the corporate grantmaking program's most important public document. They are the voice of your intent. The eager grantseeking public will peruse your guidelines statement as if it were the Holy Bible, seeking ways to represent their various cases to you for funding in your own terms. This interaction between corporation and hopeful grantee through the published guidelines is not a bad system; it is a realistic one. The greatest favor that you can do for nonprofit groups and potential grantseekers is to be clear about the interests of your company's program.

Whereas the mission statement represents the "why" of your company's interest in grantmaking, the guidelines represent the "how." Guidelines should be considered an announcement of current program interests. They should be reviewed annually or biennially to determine if the grantmaking program overall has been consistent with the guidelines. If the program and the guidelines are not consistent, the guidelines should be revised on the theory that they clearly do not represent the interests of the company, or the process of making grant allocation decisions should be examined, as it may need some fine tuning.

Guidelines should also be reviewed to allow for revision to include new and emerging interests for the company in the grantmaking area. This is a common sense practice: if a corporation provides funds to make a better community in which employees may live and work, the community's needs change. Likewise, if human service is a focus, those needs also may change; witness the rise of the visible homeless in the last ten years and the corresponding response from grantmaking organizations.

Guidelines should be clear, so that grantseekers understand the program's interests, thereby reducing the gamesmanship of this exchange and saving everybody time. To this end, be clear about the company's real interests in giving contributions. If the company has a special interest in a certain program area, for example, early childhood or literacy, it should be outlined so that prospective grantees may assess your interests against their plans to see if their application for funds would be sensible. Clear guidelines save everyone on both sides of the grantmaking table time and frustration.

Be thoughtful. Put yourself in the grantseekers' place; tell them what you are *not* interested in. The community needs to know what is definitely out of bounds; corporations do not usually fund capital campaigns, religious causes, and fund-raising or charity dinners. Some corporations do not like to contribute operating funds to nonprofit organizations, but many other corporations find this a very convenient way to support a variety of efforts, especially in the arts and human services, that enhance the community. The guidelines also should be clear about geographic boundaries. This is the easiest exclusion to define.

Be brief. Do not make grantseekers read through unnecessary pages of puffery to ferret out your real interests. Ultimately, this will save you and your staff time as well. A reasonable and useful set of guidelines may be easily set out in less than one page. The guidelines should also contribute to public knowledge of the company and its community and philantrophic commitments.

Risks and Pitfalls. Establishing a contributions program involves some risks, although these are minimal. Nevertheless, these should be considered as guidelines are developed. The overall purpose of the grantmaking program undoubtedly will be to enhance the

standing of the company in its community. One would hope that
grants programs would not generate a negative view of any corporation. Nevertheless, sometimes grants are made to causes that are
unpopular with certain groups. For example, in the past fifteen
years, a retail food company and a newspaper both made unpopular
grants to Planned Parenthood. A write-in campaign was organized
to deliver bags of mail to intimidate the corporate executive responsible for grantmaking in the retail food company. The newspaper
received a complaint about the grant through its "readers complaints" column. To the credit of both corporations, they were not
intimidated by the response of a few and continued to make grants
to this organization.

This story illustrates the importance of having clear guidelines. The guidelines provide the public rationale (as the mission
statement provides the internal rationale) for the grantmaking of
the company and can be invoked in instances where some people
might take issue with the company's individual grants.

Corporations also should be aware as they are setting up
guidelines that these guidelines should serve the needs of the corporation, not the needs of record keepers. Some years ago, a very useful
institution was founded. The Foundation Center in New York City
was established to provide information for grantseekers on various
sources of private-sector funds. However, in order to manage efficiently the large amount of data that was collected, it was decided that
grants should be divided into certain categories for purposes of collecting data. Since private foundations formed the core (at that time)
of this data base, the categories were established primarily on the areas
of interest of those grantmakers. The general categories of human or
social services, arts, and the environment were used for years as grantmakers, both corporate and private, began to develop guidelines for
their individual programs. Oddly, corporations kept inserting a category called "civic" in their guidelines and annual reports, one which
was not in the general grantmaking lexicon. Why? Many corporations, unlike private foundations, were developing grantmaking programs in order to contribute to their communities as good citizens.
Therefore, they provided funds for a range of efforts that defied easy
sorting to correspond with the approved categories. For example,
recently, economic development has become a major focus of corpo-

rate contributions, as have certain types of housing support and investment for low-income residents. These are highly sophisticated areas of grantmaking and in most cases are designed to promote grantee self-sufficiency rather than provide charity in the traditional sense. Yet they do not fit under the categories called human service or social service, the traditional categories for assistance to the underprivileged.

INDEPENDENT SECTOR has undertaken an effort to revise the national taxonomy of categories for grantmakers. This is a worthy effort. It is undoubtedly helpful when contributing data on your corporation's grantmaking program to use the approved categories. But you do not have to develop your guidelines, nor think of your grantmaking, in these terms. The cart of record keeping should not be placed before the horse of sensible and meaningful program design.

Where to Start. In designing or revising your company's guidelines, it is well to give some thought to the following questions:

1.   What is the nature of your business?
2.   Where do you operate?
3.   What do your executives and/or corporate directors see as important problems of our time?
4.   Do your employees have a contribution to make to the design of the grantmaking program?
5.   What do you want your grantmaking program to contribute overall to your corporation?

In developing a program, and subsequently the guidelines, it is important to take time to reflect. The questions offered above may be helpful to start this process.

What is the nature of our business? is the first question to ask. If the industry is a national oil company, the grantmaking program may be very broad. If, on the other hand, a small local manufacturing company wishes to make grants, the program will undoubtedly reflect more local interests and may also reflect the business. A retail company will be conscious of families in its community, a food company may think about hunger, and a media company may want to provide help for community vitality or the arts or literacy. Whatever the outcome, a good point of departure for program discussion is the nature of the business.

Where do we operate? is the next and perhaps the most important question a corporation may ask. Whom should these grants benefit? Are we a community-based corporation? Perhaps the grants should be local. Do we have plants or subsidiaries in several communities? Perhaps we want to be visible "good citizens" in those communities as well. Are we a broad national or international company? Then grants to national organizations may be in order.

What do our executives/corporate directors see as important problems of our time? is a significant question. Corporate grantmaking is always discretionary. It is initiated by executives within the company or on the board and should reflect their sense of important contemporary topics that require attention. In devising a mission statement, some of these ideas will be revealed; however, in developing the guidelines, they begin to take shape in a more concrete way. In fact, the grantmaking executive has an excellent opportunity to engage senior managers in dialogue about the program while developing guidelines. Based on these discussions, the grantmaking executive will begin to shape the program, be it broad or more well defined. And senior managers may develop a sense of program ownership through these discussions, a good thing to encourage in these times of internal corporate uncertainty.

Do our employees have anything to contribute to the design of the grantmaking program? is the next question. The inclusion of employees in the design of the grantmaking program depends solely on the culture of the company. In some instances, it is wise to give the employees a sense of pride and ownership in the company's grantmaking program. Even more important, however, employees may be the most underutilized resource in grantmaking today. They have ample knowledge of the corporation's community and, in some cases, of the problems in the community. Employees, after all, are the heartbeat of any community. Through their families, their children in schools, their struggles with chemical dependency or other personal experiences, or through their volunteer activities, they understand the community. They can be used as channels of information for the grantmaking executive and as evaluators of existing programs. Of course, it is neither feasible nor appropriate to involve employees in every company grantmaking program, but their potential should be kept in mind.

Finally, you must ask the big "R" question: what do we want our grantmaking program to contribute overall to our corporation? What are the *results* of this commitment of effort, time, and resources? What is the philanthropic return on investment? This is a most legitimate question. How do we measure and publicize the good our grants have accomplished? This is not to say that corporate grantmaking is crass, nor merely done for public relations purposes. But when a company commits resources that could be channeled to expansion, higher wages for employees, or more profit for shareholders, it has a right to ask if the results justify these decisions.

The question of return on investments is an appropriate one to raise as guidelines are being developed. The guidelines issued to the public will generate proposals from which the company will choose in giving its grants. The program should produce a planned result, whether relief of poverty in the community or a better appreciation of the company as a good neighbor to the community that it calls home.

Guidelines for a corporate foundation might easily be the following:

The XYZ corporation, and its foundation, offer the following guidelines:
1. Because the business of the XYZ corporation is furniture manufacturing, we have an ongoing interest in the conservation of the nation's timber resources. We welcome applications for projects that protect the environment or provide for environmental education.
2. The XYZ corporation has its major factory sites in three cities: Cleveland, Ohio; Raleigh-Durham, North Carolina; and Sacramento, California. In order to contribute to the development of these communities, the corporation will consider applications for projects that enhance the quality of living in these communities. Program interests are the arts, human services, and the education of young children.

3. With the exception of environmental projects, the XYZ corporation does not review applications for projects of national scope or from national organizations.
4. The corporation does not fund capital requests, requests for endowments, religious organizations, fund-raising dinners or events, or requests for scholarships or endowments. The corporation does not provide funds for travel in its grants, and does not make grants to individuals for any purpose.
5. Proposals should be no more than five pages in length and should address the background of the organization, the need for the project, the plan for implementation, the plan for evaluation, and a one-page budget summary. The budget should indicate the complete fund-raising plan, including source of income in addition to the request to XYZ company.
6. Proposals should use the accompanying cover sheet, which requests certain summary information. In addition, the most recent financial statements of your organization should be included, as well as a list of your current board members.
7. Applications are accepted at any time during the year. The period of consideration is usually less than two months.

Grantmaker as Executive

In all of this discussion about designing a philanthropic program's mission and guidelines, it should have become apparent to you that the process requires a manager, an initiator: one who begins, designs, convenes groups, writes and rewrites, and convenes the groups again. These tasks are part of the job description of the executive in charge of the grantmaking program. In some companies, the person in charge of grantmaking will be the director of public affairs; in others, the president of the company foundation or vice-president for external affairs. The executive as grantmaker or the grantmaker as executive is a topic deserving of an entire chapter. This person must have extraordinary talent, vision, courage, and persistence to shape the grantmaking program. The grantmaker should have personal skills to move the company and its senior executives to see the value of the grantmaking program, public skills to represent the company and its program to the community, imagination to envision the future and to believe in the prospects for so many programs presented for funding, and persistence to initiate and complete the process described in these pages. (For a more complete description of this remarkable person, see the brief essay "Who Is that Grantmaker in the Mirror" in the Council on Foundations' book, *Mapping Careers in Corporate Grantmaking*.)

It is up to the grantmaking executive to orchestrate the process I have described. The grantmaker must propose the idea to the chief executive officer that the grantmaking program needs a mission statement if none exists. This person will have to write the drafts, meet with the committee or other internal managers, revise, return to the drawing board, and meet again. The grantmaker will have to draft the guidelines and shepherd them through the same process.

The payoff for this hard work will be enormous. Once senior managers have been engaged in the development of missions and guidelines for the company's grantmaking program, they will be shareholders in the program. They will take an interest because they will have been a part of it.

The initiative, however, must come from the executive most closely aligned with the program, and most responsible.

Not Just Any Road . . .

The most important concept of those just discussed is that of intentionality. One veteran corporate grantmaker tells a story about a colleague who moaned about the stack of "paper" (applications) on his desk. He confessed, when questioned, that he let all of the requests for funding to his small company pile up until he could get to them. Then he worked his way down the stack until the money was gone. He rarely read the last two-thirds of the proposals.

This man did not know where he was going with his company's charitable contributions program. He probably did not even know where he had been! His giving was not intentional, not planned. No corporate giving program can afford to operate that way in the 1990s.

Companies must know why they are giving and what results they want, and they must be able to explain that to their various communities and stakeholders. In these times of increasing need and corresponding cutbacks in the corporate world, "just any road" will no longer do. To plan a course of action, to choose the road, is a necessity. The best corporations will move into the 1990s with mission statement and guidelines ready. And even Alice would understand that!

Chapter Eleven

Cause-Related Marketing: Potential Dangers and Benefits

Cynthia D. Giroud

The relationship between marketing and grantmaking has been the subject of great debate in recent years. Critics say that linking the two jeopardizes traditional corporate grantmaking, exploits non-profit organizations, and jeopardizes the survival of organizations that are less visible and trendy. They also believe these links could reduce the contributions made by individuals since they can say that they gave at the supermarket. I believe any of these concerns could be valid. However, companies can overcome these criticisms by developing programs that respect the needs and concerns of nonprofit groups and the community at large.

If you are considering linking marketing and philanthropic strategies, viewing programs that link the two from a variety of perspectives will help you. This chapter strives to present a broad view of the definition of cause-related marketing, the strategy's risks and benefits, the consumers' position on such marketing, the types of programs that are currently in use, and the process for developing your own program.

Cause-related marketing is a term that has been registered by American Express to describe the concept many say was pioneered by that company. Cause-related marketing is based on the premise that consumers will purchase products or services that offer an emotional bonus in the form of a contribution to charity. Usually, the contribution is triggered by a coupon redemption. In other cases, a portion of the purchase price of an item is designated to support a charity. The idea is driven by sales volume; greater sales translate into more funds for the charity.

Risks Involved with Cause-Related Marketing Programs

Since it is always better to enter into a situation with your eyes open, you should examine the risks associated with integrating marketing strategies into your grantmaking program. Some of the most commonly cited risks and ways they can be minimized through careful planning follow.

Charities May Be Selected Mainly on the Basis of Their Attraction to Consumers. Market-driven programs have, in the past, tended to select charities on the basis of their attractiveness to consumers rather than on the basis of effectiveness and need. This is not necessarily the case today. As cause-related marketing has matured, programs employing it have gradually shifted away from traditional charities. Newer programs have departed from the norm to benefit groups such as AIDS patients, battered women, and the homeless. Johnson & Johnson's campaign is a prime example of this trend.

Believing their target audience of families, women, and children would feel strongly about the critical problems facing battered women, Johnson & Johnson created a promotion called Shelter Aid. The promotion included nine brands of products and resulted in positive returns for the company and the cause. Over $1.5 million was raised for the National Coalition Against Domestic Violence (Freeman and Walley, 1988). A portion of the funds were used to staff and operate a national toll-free hot line. The company realized a significant improvement in market share when its feminine care products line experienced a dramatic sales increase as a result of the promotion.

Corporate grantmakers should not leave the selection of a charity to fate. As the in-house experts on charitable organizations and social issues, we must make the marketing group aware of the most pressing social concerns and the organizations in the best position to address them.

Charities May Be Exploited. In this country, 800,000 nonprofit organizations compete for a limited pool of funds (Levine, 1987). They are operating in an environment of decreasing federal and state funds, fewer tax incentives for individuals, and a general decline in corporate giving dollars. To survive, organizations must find new sources of revenue. Under these conditions, we cannot discount the power of cause-related marketing to raise much needed income for nonprofits.

Corporate grantmakers can work with marketing groups to develop clear and ethical principles for managing cause-related marketing programs. These principles should reflect the needs and concerns of both the benefiting charity and the company.

Prior to entering into our first cause-related marketing initiative, we at Scott Paper Company developed the following principles for a line of products called Helping Hand. With every purchase, Helping Hand products offered consumers the opportunity to contribute a nickel to six charities that helped children with special needs. The principles established for this program became a touchstone for subsequent cause-related programs that the company introduced. They may also be a useful framework for developing your own program.

- Money contributed to the participating organization truly helps children and society.
- All stakeholders realize how the program benefits them or meets their objectives.
- The brand builds a credible record of accomplishments.
- Scott develops a strong relationship with the benefiting charities so they are full partners in the program's success.

- Scott provides a credible and consistent explanation to the consumer of how the money is generated and allocated.

The Public Could Attack the Charity You Have Selected. You must select the right organization for the right reasons. If you simply select the trendiest organization, you risk losing your public credibility. Your company will be in a much better position to respond to criticism about the selection of a charity if you developed clear criteria for the selection.

At Scott, we developed some basic criteria for selecting the Helping Hand charities. Each charity needed to have:

- A primary focus on the Helping Hand priority of helping children with special needs
- IRC status
- A strong national presence and substantial size
- Strong public recognition and support of its efforts nationwide
- A professional operation that is above reproach with a long track record of success
- A good reputation with the pediatric community
- Strong local presence in communities across the country
- Demonstrated reliance upon volunteers rather than several administrators to operate the program
- Capability to be actively interested in supporting the brand's success to build a mutually beneficial partnership

The Public May Not Believe the Money Is Reaching the People Who Need It Most. To have a successful program, you must be frank about how the funds are being raised; what limitations, if any, exist; and the allocations process. Your corporate image is riding on this frankness. Equally important, you need to work with the benefiting charity to identify the best way to leverage the contributions. The results created through the program also become powerful marketing tools for future promotions.

Programs Are Generally Short Term and Can Leave Charities with a Major Shortfall When Discontinued. Cause-related marketing by its very nature has different objectives than traditional grantmaking. It is oriented toward building consumer awareness, trial, and repurchase of the company's products or services. If cause-related programs do not demonstrate improved consumer response over other types of promotional strategies, their continuation is not justified. Consequently, program discontinuation is an inherent risk charities take when involved with cause-related programs.

If an organization becomes totally dependent upon a company for support through a cause-related program or traditional grantmaking, the company has not truly leveraged its funds or helped to secure the organization's future. You must work with the beneficiaries to channel the funds in a way that strengthens their long-term viability. This could be accomplished by helping them to build their donor base, renovate facilities, or create an endowment. You could also extend your relationship with the organization beyond just cause-related marketing. Employees could become involved as volunteers. Public education materials could be developed to supplement the advertising campaign. And you could recruit employees from among the organization's clients.

My experience with the Helping Hand program demonstrates that it is possible to discontinue a program without jeopardizing an organization's future. After five years and nearly $3 million in contributions to the participating charities, Helping Hand was discontinued because of constraints in manufacturing capacity. The benefiting charities were very much our partners in the development and implementation of this program. Therefore, they were kept apprised of the results being achieved in the marketplace.

This open communication ensured that the charities received considerable advance notice of the end of the program. Additionally, the allocations process was organized so that grants were made to existing programs, research efforts, or new programs that would be carried on by other funding sources. In this way, we were able to track our results over time, but the organizations were never solely dependent upon Scott for their continued operation.

Cause-Related Marketing May Jeopardize Traditional Philanthropy. Any program that does not meet its objectives is in jeopardy. It is important to understand your company's objectives for the grantmaking program and develop a plan that illustrates how the program will meet the company's objectives and further the company's vision of success. Company leaders should approve the plan and receive regular updates on its results. If we take this more results-oriented approach with the grantmaking program, there is ample room for both grantmaking and cause-related marketing to coexist and together enhance the company's image and impact on critical needs.

Potential Benefits of Cause-Related Marketing

Rather than dwell on the risks, I would like to mention a few of the benefits that can be accrued through cause-related marketing.

The Visibility of Charities Can Be Increased Through Funds Normally Devoted Only to Product Marketing. Reebok International Ltd. created the Reebok Foundation to underwrite the Human Rights Now! world concert tour organized by Amnesty International. Top performers toured five continents and gave concerts before more than one million people. Reebok supported the tour with videotaped news releases, a Home Box Office special, and an elaborate publicity program aimed at teenagers and young adults. They also launched an annual Human Rights Award for young people who have significantly raised awareness of human rights.

According to Reebok's public relations agency, Reebok's management has a genuine concern for human rights, and it is willing to take risks as part of the marketing concept. Last year, Reebok's award winner was denied a visa on political grounds. The extensive news coverage brought notoriety to both Reebok and Amnesty International.

Charities Can Gain Access to the Talents of Marketing Professionals. Marketing professionals can provide technical assistance that could have a lasting impact on charitable organizations. This was one of the major benefits identified by the Helping Hand charities. Working with our advertising agency and marketing group gave them insight into the planning process, the analysis needed for program development, and ways to evaluate the results of their efforts.

Corporations Can Increase Their Sales. The godfather of cause-related marketing, American Express, has demonstrated that strong results can be gained through this approach. Its campaign to renovate the Statue of Liberty yielded $1.7 million for the statue (Webster, 1989). By giving $.10 to this cause each time one of its credit cards was used, the company increased card usage by 30 percent. Based on these results, American Express moved strongly into cause-related marketing by spending over $23.5 million to advertise sixty-seven charitable promotions. These promotions generated over $9.3 million in contributions to nonprofit organizations around the world.

Corporations Can Enhance Their Image. Ralston Purina sponsors a program called Pets for People that helps senior citizens adopt pets. For every coupon redeemed, the company donates $.20, or up to $1 million, to the Humane Society.

This program is not simply a sales-generating promotion. The company has gone to great lengths to develop a comprehensive program that not only places the pets but provides medical care for the pets and follow-up contacts with the senior citizens after the placement is made. As a result of the program, Ralston Purina has been able to fund up to 10,000 adoptions per year through ninety or more shelters and has achieved critical business as well as grant-making results ("Charities in the Marketplace," 1987). Through this program, the company was able to have an impact in an area with which its consumers strongly identified and, therefore, achieve solid business results.

Grantmakers Can Broaden Their Ability to Address Critical Needs. Nike has an unusual marketing dilemma. Nike's products are coveted by inner-city youth who are plagued with a multitude of problems that often prevent them from earning the income needed to purchase the products. Nike decided to focus its giving program on inner-city issues. It funds groups that deal with drug and gang problems and donates its products to inner-city groups. Nike's marketing department has been drawn into the focus through an ongoing national sports charity partnership with Boys Clubs of America. It donated $1,000 to the Boys Clubs for every point scored by Michael Jordan during an NBA All Star Game. It supported the program with an advertising campaign called "What Makes Michael Fly?"

The Direct Impact of Cause-Related Marketing Makes It the Most Strategic Form of Grantmaking. Ben and Jerry's Ice Cream has only been in business for ten years, yet it has firmly established itself in the minds of consumers as a company that cares about social issues. The company's strategy is based on a sincere commitment on the part of the owners to using their products as a vehicle for creating positive social change. This commitment is demonstrated throughout the manufacturing process. Rainforest Crunch candy and ice cream present excellent examples. Ben and Jerry's works with Cultural Survival Incorporated (CSI), an advocacy program for the world's indigenous peoples. CSI manufactures the candy that goes into Ben and Jerry's Rainforest Crunch Ice Cream. It also sells the candy directly to the public.

Ben and Jerry's creates a winning formula through this product from a number of perspectives: the income of the people in the Brazilian rain forest is increased by three to four times; rain forest preservation groups receive 40 percent of CSI's profits; Peace for Understanding receives a 20 percent share; the company gets 30 percent; and Ben and Jerry's employees gain 10 percent toward their profit sharing plan (Rob Marchalak of Ben and Jerry's). Packaging also plays an important role in achieving the company's goal of positive social change. Each pint of ice cream carries a message about the rain forest and its importance. Ben and Jerry's success indicates that a company can prosper by creating a synergy between marketing and grantmaking.

The Forgotten Stakeholder: The Consumer

Much of the debate about the risks and benefits of cause-related marketing has been dominated by fund-raising consultants, grant-makers, advocates for responsible philanthrophy, and marketing professionals. Little attention has been paid to the consumer's perspective. Of course, it can be said that consumers vote with their wallets. If that is the case, the votes would be overwhelmingly in favor of cause-related marketing since it has resulted in sales records for many of the sponsoring companies.

The Better Business Bureau conducted a nationwide survey of 850 consumers who either subscribe to its newsletter or wrote to the bureau in May or June 1987 requesting information. The responses provide an excellent perspective on issues to consider in the development of a cause-related marketing program ("Charities in the Marketplace," 1987). Respondents were asked to comment on the circumstances under which they would support such a marketing approach. Respondents were overwhelmingly in favor of cause-related marketing campaigns, with a few key reservations: they wanted quality products for a fair price, quality charities, and financial accountability. The following list shows the percentage of people surveyed who responded affirmatively to each item presented.*

1. I found out about joint promotions of a charity and a product from one or more of the following:
   (40%) newspapers
   (35%) cents off coupons received in the mail
   (32%) displays in stores
   (31%) television
   (18%) other
2. I might choose to buy a product that helps support a charity:
   (81%) only if I were familiar with the quality of the product.
   (14%) even if I were not familiar with the quality of the product.
   (5%) no answer
3. I might choose to buy a product that helps support a charity:
   (40%) as long as the product cost the same or less than my favorite brand.
   (35%) only if the product were my favorite brand.
   (17%) even though the product cost more than my favorite brand.
   (8%) no answer

Note: For a full copy of this article, contact the Philanthropic Advisory Service, Council of Better Business Bureaus, 4200 Wilson Boulevard, Arlington, Va., 22203.

4. I might choose to buy a product that helps support a charity.
    (89%) only if I were familiar with the work of the charity.
    (8%) even if I were not familiar with the work of the charity.
    (3%) no answer
5. Would you like to see more (joint-venture) marketing?
    (47%) yes
    (43%) no
    (9%) unsure
    (1%) no answer

Types of Cause-Related Marketing Programs

According to the Promotion Marketing Association (Freeman and Walley, 1988, p. 34), cause-related marketing is growing at about 10-15 percent per year. The programs are providing over $1.8 billion in contributions to nonprofits. The approaches to cause-related marketing are limited only by the imagination. The programs can be broken down into three major categories: corporate image, annual product promotion, and permanent products.

Corporate Image. Corporate sponsorship of a special event helps the nonprofit organization defray costs while at the same time giving the corporation significant visibility. For example, corporations are recruited to become everything from the official fast food restaurant to the official credit card of the Olympic Games. Many companies also develop auxiliary short-term promotions to stimulate sales. Other corporate-sponsored events include Hands Across America, Live Aid, and sporting events.

Corporations also sponsor radio and television programs that attract the company's target audience and reinforce the company's position on issues or areas of focus. Ashland Oil's sponsorship of "Car Talk," the popular public radio program, is an example of this strategy. Similarly, Cargill Industries, an agricultural products company, was one of the first sponsors of "A Prairie Home Companion."

A company may also link its name to a particular charity or cause. Allstate Insurance has successfully linked its name on a national level to its Issue Forums. At the regional level, Bell of Pennsylvania has achieved positive results with the Bell Institute, a two-and-a-half day planning seminar for nonprofit groups.

Annual Product Promotions. Annual promotions are normally tied to product sales or coupon redemptions. Repeating the promotion each year enables the company to build a credible record of accomplishments, save on promotion development costs, and create strong customer and consumer awareness and support. Procter & Gamble's Special Olympics coupon redemption program raised over $12 million in 1987. Oscar Mayer Foods Corporation's sales-related promotion donates up to $1 million each year to youth baseball ("Charities in the Marketplace," 1987). Oscar Mayer's program has two parts. The company donates a nickel to the cause per each purchase of hot dogs and cold cuts, and customers can also redeem proof of purchase seals for baseballs, bats, mitts, and other gear to aid the teams. Donations are made to the United States Baseball Federation to be distributed to teams that need additional funds to survive.

Permanent Products. Some companies sell products throughout the year with the commitment that funds from their purchase will be directed toward specific causes. This type of promotion is used less often than annual product promotions because of the costs associated with manufacturing and marketing a permanent brand. The products range from Ben and Jerry's Peace Pops and Paul Newman's products to Celestial Seasonings teas. Financial service companies have also entered this category. MasterCard International's Choose to Make a Difference campaign exemplifies this trend. Based on a national survey that found which health and social issues consumers considered most important, the company selected six causes to which it would donate $.07 each time a card was used or MasterCard Travelers Cheques were purchased between Thanksgiving and Christmas. Cardholders determined how much of the donation was allocated to each organization. The program raised $3.1 million for the charities in 1988. A $15 million advertising budget was used to promote the campaign with excellent results. Following the campaign, MasterCard's image was better than Visa's image for the first time in years, and use of MasterCards increased 19 percent.

Developing a Cause-Related Marketing Program

The appropriateness of linking grantmaking and marketing in your company is strongly related to the company's philosophy about grantmaking and the mission of your corporate giving program. Companies generally hold one of three philosophies about philanthropic contributions. For some, contributions are purely altruistic and must be totally independent of corporate interests. At the other extreme, some companies require giving programs that return a tangible benefit to the corporation in the form of increased sales. Of course, there is also a middle ground, which could be defined as enlightened self-interest. Giving programs that fall into the middle area earn a less tangible return through an enhanced company image, improved employee morale, better communities in which to live and work, and access to a skilled work force. If your company's corporate giving philosophy is something broader than altruism, you should probably begin looking at your program's mission and priorities to determine how you can integrate marketing strategies into your operation.

If you decide to add a marketing dimension to your program, you need to determine which type of program best fits your corporate philosophy about grantmaking. For example, companies that favor the middle ground would probably confine their strategies to an internal assessment of their current philanthropic initiatives for their applicability to a corporate image campaign. If you work for a company with a broader agenda, you must reach out to the marketing department, understand their objectives and challenges, and identify the areas of mutual interests. For example, the Scott Paper Company Foundation has a focus on children in need. Our marketing group targets young mothers with children. We have collaborated on three cause-related marketing initiatives that are targeted toward children in need. Besides Helping Hand, we also have introduced a promotion to raise funds for Ronald McDonald Houses around the country and a second initiative called Learning Tools for Schools, which provides educational materials and equipment to elementary schools.

The first step in the process of developing a cause-related marketing program is to explore with the marketing department objectives, target audience, current initiatives, and future directions.

1. What are you trying to accomplish through your corporate grantmaking program? What are your areas of focus and priority? How do you go about achieving your objectives? What is the marketing department trying to achieve? What is its focus and priority? How does it achieve its objectives?
2. Who is the target audience for your company's products and services? How does this audience view the world around them? Which issues do they perceive to be most critical? Do the priorities of marketing's target audience in any way complement the priorities of the corporate grantmaking program?
3. What strategies are currently being used to reach your company's target audience? What programs are you supporting or initiating that might relate to the target audience or benefit by marketing's involvement?
4. What voids do you currently see in your grantmaking effort that could be filled by a partnership with marketing? Is marketing planning any programs that could benefit from a charitable dimension?

If this meeting turns up opportunities for collaboration, the next steps are dictated by the type of promotion that is selected. However, it is clear that a few safeguards need to be incorporated into almost any initiative. I believe you need to ensure that the following questions can be answered to your satisfaction:

1. Are you thoroughly familiar with the reputation, credibility, and financial management of the charity being considered?
2. Do you have a formal agreement with the charity that gives you permission for the use of its name and specifies how the money will be allocated, the duration of the campaign, and the steps that will be taken if problems arise?
3. Does the promotion clearly specify how the funds will be raised

and allocated and any limitations such as a maximum amount to be contributed?
4. Does the promotion meet all applicable state regulations?
5. Have you established a separate account to manage the funds?
6. Have you planned a financial report that describes the results of the program to the public?

I believe corporations and nonprofit groups can gain a great deal through cause-related marketing. As corporate grantmakers, we are all too aware of the infinite needs that exist in our communities and the all too finite and in many cases declining size of our contributions budgets. To truly address the needs in our communities, we must access the larger budgets available through our marketing departments. We must work in partnership with marketing to help that department navigate the strange waters of community involvement and ensure that any initiative achieves its full potential to make a difference in the community. We must lead in the selection of a charity and the development of an allocations process that can create a real impact on the target issue. We must work as partners with marketing on the development of program goals that demonstrate a clear regard for the interests of all stakeholders in the program's success. By taking the lead, we can make cause-related marketing a valued part of our arsenal for addressing the ever-growing needs in our communities.

References

"Charities in the Marketplace: A Look at Joint-Venture Marketing—Part 1." *Insight* (a publication of the Council of Better Business Bureaus Philanthropic Advisory Service), Issue 2, 1987, p. 3.
Freeman, L., and Walley, W. "Marketing with a Cause Takes Hold." *Advertising Age,* May 16, 1988, p. 34.
Levine, "Selling a Cause." *Incentive Marketing, 161* (12), p. 39.
Webster, P. J. "The Case for Cause-Related Marketing." *Foundation News,* Jan.-Feb. 1989, pp. 30–33.

Chapter Twelve

Choices in Giving: United Ways and Alternative Funds

Mary E. Pickard

America's corporations and United Ways across the country have a strong tradition of working together. This partnership has served both well over the past 100 years, raising more money for human service organizations than any single private effort. But changes in the United Way, in the communities it serves, and in corporations that support it have created changes in the partnership itself that present challenges and opportunities to contributions professionals.

The United Way is an important part of most corporate giving programs. About 48 percent of corporate contributions to human services nationally and about 15 percent of all corporate and small business contributions are given through the United Way, totaling $726 million (Conference Board, 1988). Of even more significance is the money contributed by employees: $1.426 billion. While this is only a small fraction of the total $86.7 billion contributed to nonprofits by individuals (most of it to religion), it is more than 50 percent of all money collected by the United Way. Together, businesses and their employees accounted for 77 percent of the $2.78 billion in cash raised by the United Way in 1988.

Changes in the Alliance of Business and the United Way

The alliance between corporate America and the United Way started around the turn of the century, when communities were looking for an efficient way to both give and raise money to meet the human service needs of people. They formed local community chests: "one-stop shopping" for both contributors and beneficiary agencies. The nonprofit sector was much smaller at that time than it is now, community chests included most charitable activity in a community, and government funding of human service endeavors was practically nonexistent.

Circumstances have changed over the years. Government has entered the picture since the United Way began its work and has helped to produce the human services industry we have today. The number and types of human service agencies have expanded significantly, and these agencies provide 42 percent of federally funded human services ("Giving, Volunteering, and the Nonprofit Sector"). United Way funded agencies are only a fraction of the total number of nonprofit groups in most communities today. There are 400,000 nonprofit charitable organizations in areas such as the arts, environment, legal rights, health care, education, and public policy.

United Ways nationwide raised $2.78 billion dollars in 1988. They are second to the federal government in human service funding. The United Way provides only partial funding to the 37,000 programs it supports. The combined annual budgets of these funded groups in 1988 was $10 billion ("Giving, Volunteering, and the Nonprofit Sector"). Recognizing that nonprofit organizations require funding beyond what United Way can provide, many corporations have lifted their traditional ban on funding individual United Way agencies. When corporate managers find their businesses giving money to both the federated campaign and the individual agencies, they begin to question the value of a federated appeal.

Federal spending for social welfare was cut 39 percent from 1980 to 1985, putting more pressure on United Ways and the agencies they fund (Abramson and Salamon, 1986). This trend intensifies the competition for both individual and corporate dollars.

Over the past fifteen years, corporations have hired their own professional staffs to administer grants programs, review grant requests, and make recommendations to senior management. Given this decision-making capability, some managers question the need for contributing to a federated drive, which, in turn, regrants corporate money. Some corporations are not satisfied with simply contributing to good causes. They want to focus on specific issues—sometimes those that are related to business interests—making the federated approach potentially less appealing. Some nonprofit organizations have come together to gain access to the employee solicitation and payroll deduction privileges previously offered almost exclusively to the United Way, another erosion of the notion that one campaign is sufficient.

Advantages of Federated Campaigns

All of these changes raise some questions: Why should a corporation give to federated campaigns? Have they outlived their usefulness? If federated campaigns are desirable from a corporate viewpoint, how does management determine the nature and level of its involvement? If a corporation supports a federated approach, should it expand access to employee solicitation and payroll deduction privileges to other federated fund drives in addition to United Way?

The traditional nature of the United Way and the large amounts of money it raises sometimes lead us to take it for granted. But the proliferation of new federated fund drives is a testimonial to the benefits of consolidated efforts. Access to payroll deduction significantly increases contributions from individuals that would not be available without collective efforts.

If we did not have the United Way, we probably would invent it. That is not to say it works equally well in each community. Often there is room for improvement. But on whole, federated appeals provide many important benefits in addition to fund raising.

1. They bring people together within the community to raise funds for what they believe in.
2. They can be efficient for both donors and nonprofit agencies.
3. They provide annual program and operating funds to non-profit organizations—money these groups can count on from one year to the next—promoting organizational stability.
4. They encourage individuals to contribute to their communities and, in the case of employee campaigns, provide a means for employees to learn about the many organizations that serve the communities where they live.
5. They allow nonprofits, through consolidating their resources, to work together to advocate for their own interests and those of their clients.
6. They allow nonprofit organizations to work together to provide administrative and fund-raising services at lower prices, for example, telemarketing, group health plans, accounting services, and management assistance.
7. They provide a way for small, relatively unknown agencies to be part of a large and publicly visible fund-raising effort. In some cases, they provide an umbrella under which organizations can grow from small and fledgling to large and mature.
8. They provide a vehicle for volunteers to connect with organizations in the community. The allocations process encourages research, discussion, and consensus building within a community or among a group of agencies.
9. They constitute a "critical mass" of private nonprofit organizations that can work collaboratively with government and business.
10. They provide an efficient way for corporations to target money. For example, some United Ways are creating initiatives around issues such as AIDS, literacy, child care, or homelessness.

Rise of New Federated Campaigns

Given these benefits, the corporate giving professional faces some hard choices. The United Way has had 100 years of experience and has a tradition of deep corporate commitment. The results achieved by the United Way have generally been positive. The United Way has tremendous stewardship responsibility, both to preserve the benefits it now gives and to change to meet new challenges within our communities. The rise of other federated fund drives puts this stewardship challenge squarely in the forefront and presents ethical dilemmas for all concerned.

Since 1960, more than 100 alternative federated fund drives have gained access to payroll deduction campaigns in government workplaces, nonprofit organizations, and businesses. These alternative fund drives are expected to raise about $105 million in 1989 for about 2,000 groups, according to the National Committee for Responsive Philanthropy (NCRP) (*Workplace Giving: The New Era,* 1989). The NCRP acts as a clearinghouse of information on alternative fund drives—part of its role as watchdog of private philanthropy and advocate for increased access for all charities to philanthropic giving by corporations, foundations, and employer payroll deduction systems.

The NCRP gives special attention to the payroll deduction system, rather than corporate gifts. Corporate giving is important, but individual giving provides significantly more potential for growth in contributions to the nonprofit sector. Of the $104.37 billion given to charity in 1988, 4.6 percent was contributed by corporations and 83.1 percent by individuals (AAFRC Trust for Philanthropy, 1989). For the United Way itself, employees contribute twice what their employers give. When individuals have the chance to have small amounts taken from a paycheck regularly, they are more likely to contribute larger gifts.

The NCRP puts fund drives into two categories, traditional and nontraditional. It calls funds that provide money to social action organizations (also known as progressive advocacy organizations) and groups serving women and minorities nontraditional. Such funds include the Black United Funds, Women's Funds, Environmental Funds, and other social action funds. Funds distributing money to the arts and various health organizations are labeled traditional by the NCRP. They include the United Arts Funds, the Combined Health Appeal Drives, and Sharing International.

The distinction between traditional and nontraditional funds can be important. Corporate giving programs generally have preferred to contribute to direct service organizations that could be called traditional rather than to advocacy or social change organizations. However, these labels are usually loaded with political overtones and are not always relevant. Many "traditional" organizations serve minority groups and women and advocate for social change. Many "social change" and "advocacy" organizations provide direct service. Nevertheless, the labels remain, and they influence the ways in which corporate executives respond to each fund.

Further complicating the discussion and increasing the polarizing influences is the notion that if a new federated fund is trying to gain access to payroll deductions, it is "against" the United Way. This creates a win-lose proposition. Corporate executives can be forced to "take sides."

The corporate contributions professional sits in the middle. (Although it is not always the contributions or community affairs people who run these campaigns. In some corporations, it is the human resources people.) A corporate grant officer must be a facilitator, dispassionate as to the end result but passionate for open discussion within the corporation and, potentially, within the wider community.

Issues to Consider in Supporting Federated Campaigns

When faced with the question of whether or not to support other federated campaigns, corporate professionals often focus on the operational issues—how to manage the payroll deduction and computer systems. While not small questions, these should be the last questions. The operational issues will probably work themselves out if and when grants officers and management develop a clear corporate consensus and the vision to implement it.

A corporation's managers need to answer some fundamental questions to ascertain whether or not they are willing to consider support for federated campaigns other than the United Way. First, how does the annual employee solicitation campaign fit into the corporate culture? Is there a tradition of employee participation and ownership of the campaign? Does company management encourage individual choices among employees with programs such as flexible compensation or quality circles?

Second, what is the purpose of the company's annual solicitation of employees? Does management view the payroll deduction system as a method to encourage employee giving generally, regardless of the purpose of the nonprofit organizations? Or does management view payroll deduction and employee solicitation privileges as implying corporate endorsement of each agency that is funded? If the latter, management may feel a responsibility to employees to ensure that the organizations participating are philosophically congruent with corporate viewpoints.

Third, how do key constituents view this issue? Preliminary discussions could be conducted with United Way executives, others in the nonprofit community, management in other local corporations, community leaders, and employees.

Competing federated fund drives depend largely on government employees for significant growth potential. By introducing enabling legislation, new organizations have gained access to workplace giving in local, state, and federal governments, where the large number of employees at one work site creates efficient solicitation. Nonprofit employers and small businesses have also been relatively open to alternative funds. The United Way, on the other hand, looks to large corporations as a key to growth for the same reasons of efficiency and because corporations provide access to other important resources: in-kind giving, corporate leadership, and volunteers.

For some corporate managements, consideration of expanded payroll deduction will be out of the question for one basic reason: concern that it will reduce the amount of money collected for the United Way. Not much research is available on this subject. A survey by NCRP in 1988 showed that giving to United Ways increased 75 percent of the time in multiple-choice charity campaigns. Total giving by employees increased 93 percent of the time (*Report on the Effects,* 1988). The survey included fifty employers who had conducted 227 annual campaigns over several years. NCRP admits the sample is small, since nearly 4,000 employers now conduct multiple-choice workplace charity drives. Until the research is more conclusive, the fear of harming the United Way may supersede other values, such as increased employee giving overall and increased choices within the workplace.

Changes in the United Way

Many proponents of expanding payroll deduction to charitable funds assert that the increased competition has improved local United Ways by encouraging them to be more inclusive and more responsive to emerging community needs. Whether as a result of competition or not, United Ways are changing.

The mission of the United Way used to be focused on fund raising. Now, it is "to increase the organized capacity of people to care for one another" ("Second Century Initiative," 1986). Funding used to be directed toward specific agencies. Now, most United Ways focus on program funding with specific program goals. In some communities and on the federal level, the United Way is taking an advocacy role, lobbying on behalf of specific legislative issues such as income tax deductibility for charitable contributions and welfare reform. Increasingly, local United Ways are taking on a convening role, bringing nonprofit groups, business, government, and individuals together to wrestle with community-wide problems such as homelessness.

In communities where alternative fund drives have taken hold, United Way has taken steps to cooperate in order to advance two of its key strategies: (1) to encourage a single community-wide campaign for health and human care services and (2) to become as inclusive as possible of people, programs, agencies, and natural geographic market areas. In Hartford, Connecticut, for example, the United Way and the Combined Health Appeal conduct one campaign instead of the previous two. In Philadelphia, the United Way conducts a donor option campaign so that employees can use payroll deduction to contribute to any charitable human service agency, whether or not the agency is part of the United Way campaign.

Options for Giving

The competition between federated funds has also changed the ways in which some corporations approach employee giving. Some options have included:

- Expand the matching-gifts programs beyond education to include a wider range of nonprofit groups.
- Promote the matching-gifts program and advocate contributions to specific organizations or local community issues.
- Provide solicitation privileges only to the United Way, but allow employees to use payroll deduction to contribute to other agencies. This approach can vary from providing unlimited donor options to allowing employees to give to a preapproved list of nonprofits.
- Conduct one generic campaign with an employee committee deciding which organizations receive the funds.
- Allow several solicitations at different times of the year.
- Provide employee solicitation and payroll deduction for several funds, with each fund providing its own solicitation materials.
- Provide employee solicitation and payroll deduction for several funds, but have a generic employee campaign with its own theme and campaign materials.

Regardless of the options they consider, contributions professionals should know that even entering the debate can be risky. The key to successfully resolving this issue within a corporation depends on senior management's willingness to listen to and consider the pros and cons of multiple charity campaigns. A contributions manager must clearly articulate the advantages and disadvantages of different funding options, understand constituent points of view, anticipate and accept consequences, and have a strong resolve for whichever values ultimately are chosen.

Some federated funds seek access to payroll deduction, but some such as statewide private college and independent school funds do not. Their primary focus is on corporate gifts and senior management leadership for fund-raising campaigns. Other organizations, such as coalitions working to stock emergency food shelves, are looking for in-kind contributions. Whatever the resource to be distributed, it is often easier for a corporation to contribute through a federated group of nonprofit organizations than to receive and act on each request individually. The efficiency is appealing. The effectiveness of such a strategy ultimately depends on a corporation's giving goals.

By contributing to a federated fund drive, business gives up its decision-making role. There are several reasons a corporation might want to give up this role.

- To support employee and retiree giving, perhaps through matching gifts.
- To support a communitywide effort and to be a "team player."
- To support the benefits outside of fund raising that accrue in a federated fund drive such as organizational cooperation and management services.
- To provide the much needed ongoing operating grants to a large number of organizations efficiently and without having to differentiate between organizations. Some corporations support a diversity of groups because of commitment to the nonprofit sector and corporate goals.

Often, corporate management is also looking for ways to express its special corporate giving interests. In an effort to capture the funding for some of these interests, federations have developed special initiatives. For example, the Minnesota Independent School Fund has a minority scholarship program. The United Way in Pittsburgh developed a literacy project.

As several nonprofit executives regularly point out, special programs are important, but nonprofits have to pay their utilities, too. A corporate program can balance its general support for the nonprofit sector and special targeted giving, in part by determining the size of gifts to federated campaigns. In one of its workbooks, produced for its National Corporate Leadership Program, the United Way of America lists six different ways to compute a corporate contribution: match employee gifts, give a percentage increase equivalent to the community goal increase, make a contribution equivalent to others in your industry, determine a gift on corporate profits per employee, provide a base gift to each community and reward with bonuses those that demonstrate outstanding service, and use an evaluation of overall campaign success and community support to determine the gift. It seems to me that there are two issues for corporations to be concerned about: not giving enough and giving too much, compared with the corporation's total contributions budget. Again, such a judgment depends on the company's goals.

One of the biggest fears of contributions professionals is that "formula giving" (programs such as matching gifts, federated fund drives, and annual gifts that are keyed to percentage increases) will consume budgets, leaving little discretionary money for new and emerging issues or focused giving, especially when budgets are flat or decreasing. It pays to monitor the relative size of formula giving to the entire budget and discuss its size with senior management as a strategic issue.

Perhaps more typical is giving too little. Remember, a federated fund drive represents several organizations. An exercise that I have found enlightening is to compute the relative gift the company is making to each organization and think about whether it is commensurate with what management might contribute were the organizations to approach the company individually. I am not suggesting it should be. Although the gifts may seem small in many instances, the company might not give anything to some of the organizations if it were not for the federated fund drive. This technique is just another way to analyze corporate giving and think about the company's position.

In addition to employee solicitation and corporate gift contributions, companies can provide in-kind contributions, corporate leadership, and volunteers. Gifts in Kind, an organization of the United Way of America, reports that from 1984 through 1988 it distributed $175 million worth of products to 50,000 nonprofit agencies nationwide (Wargo, 1989). The capacity to distribute large quantities of materials through a national network is a significant attraction to and service for corporations with products to donate.

Whether through direct grants, employee solicitation privileges, products, or even volunteers, federated drives are able to organize groups together for a common cause and to celebrate a common set of beliefs. The purpose of an organization delivering services or a corporation distributing resources is the same: to affirm our capacity for working effectively as a community.

References

AAFRC Trust for Philanthropy. *Giving USA, 1989*. New York: AAFRC Trust for Philanthropy, 1989.

Abramson, A., and Salamon, L. *The Nonprofit Sector and the New Federal Budget*. Washington, D.C.: Urban Institute Press, 1986.

Conference Board. *Survey of Corporate Contributions*. New York: Conference Board, 1988.

"Giving, Volunteering, and the Nonprofit Sector in the United States." Fact sheet published by the United Way of America.

Report on the Effects of Different Types of Workplace Campaigns on Employees' Total Giving and Giving to United Ways. Washington, D.C.: National Committee on Responsive Philanthropy, 1988.

"Second Century Initiative: 1987-1991." Pamphlet published by the United Way of America, 1986.

Wargo, M. Memo to Mary Pickard, Sept. 29, 1989. Wargo is with United Way of America.

Workplace Giving: The New Era. Washington, D.C.: National Committee for Responsive Philanthropy, 1989.

Chapter Thirteen

The Whirlwind of Corporate Restructuring: New Realities for Corporate Philanthropy

Lizabeth G. Sode

Depending on your point of view, the wave of mergers in the United States is either the market's way of correcting its course to improve the efficiency of management or an assault by greedy corporate raiders to accumulate wealth at the expense of other corporate stakeholders. Whatever your conclusion, the 1980s long will be remembered as a period of restructuring, punctuated by some of the largest-ever mergers, acquisitions, and leveraged buyouts in U.S. business history. Despite predictions of imminent legislation to curtail such activities, as well as the October 1987 stock market crash, 1988 proved to be a banner year for corporate reorganizations, an upsurge that took many Wall Streeters by surprise. These events also caused considerable anxiety to nonprofit managers who worried about their possible impact on corporate philanthropy.

Business Week reported that for 1988, "by December 31, take-over specialists had closed 42 transactions, each worth $1 billion or more—a record by far." Although the number of transactions dropped for the second consecutive year, the aggregate value of these deals grew by 25 percent to $222.6 billion. "And that doesn't include the precedent-breaking $25 billion buyout of RJR Nabisco, the $5.8 billion takeover of Pillsbury, or nine other billion-dollar deals started in 1988 but uncompleted by year end," according to *Business Week* ("The Merger Game Went into Hyperdrive," 1989, p. 35). The average price of the deals increased, and buyers paid big premiums for their acquisitions. Information about the charitable activities of the companies involved was not included.

Business restructuring can include a wide array of techniques such as employee stock ownership plans, asset sales, liquidations, initial public offerings, stock buybacks, recapitalizations, or privatization. Most frequently discussed are mergers and acquisitions (M & A) or leveraged buyouts (LBOs). For the purposes of this chapter, references to M & A include the entire gamut of restructuring methods.

Mergers, acquisitions, and leveraged buyouts, in the simplest terms, can be distinguished as follows:

> A *merger* is a procedure whereby one or more corporations merge into and become a part of another corporation. The corporation that merges into the other corporation ceases to exist after the merger. For example, the computer companies Sperry Corporation and Burroughs Corporation merged to create Unisys Corporation, and R. J. Reynolds Company merged with Nabisco to form RJR Nabisco.

> An *acquisition* occurs when one company buys another and the former becomes the new owner. The identity of the company that is acquired may or may not be maintained intact. Unilever acquired Chesebrough-Pond's; PepsiCo acquired Kentucky Fried Chicken; The British Petroleum Company acquired The Standard Oil Company of Ohio; Philip Morris Companies acquired Kraft; Campeau acquired Federated Department Stores; and Eastman Kodak Company acquired Sterling Drug.

> A *leveraged buyout* occurs when an individual or small group of investors, often company management in con-

junction with an investment banking firm, uses the company's assets as collateral to borrow funds to acquire the company by purchasing all of its outstanding stock at a premium. Commonly, high-yield, high-risk securities (junk bonds) are sold to accumulate the cash necessary for an LBO. The resulting company is highly leveraged, with a significant debt burden. This debt forces much of the cost savings and increased efficiency associated with the LBO. In addition, the debt results in tax savings to the new owners based on the tax deductibility of interest paid on borrowed funds (*The Chicago Fed Letter,* 1989). Companies that have been purchased through a leveraged buyout include Borg Warner, Burlington Industries, Fort Howard, Montgomery Ward, Stop & Shop, and Beatrice Company.

Each transaction has it own origin, purpose, pace, and style. M & A activity, by its very nature, is complex and multifaceted. Generalizations are easy to make but are often hard to apply to such diverse situations. The key to surviving through a restructuring (and perhaps even enjoying it) lies in understanding the dynamics of the transaction as well as the corporate culture and values that result.

Pros and Cons of M & A

The huge size of recent M & A deals has captured the attention of economists, the press, legislators, academicians, and corporate executives, who continue to debate the long-term economic impact of these deals. Despite various efforts to quantify and accurately predict the economic effects of mergers, acquisitions, and leveraged buyouts, the data remain largely inconclusive. Convincing case studies exist to support both advocates and critics of M & A activity.

Dozens of bills to restrict takeovers have been introduced in Washington in the last few years. The Business Roundtable, a collection of CEOs of the 200 largest corporations in the United States, has pushed hard for restrictions. Andrew C. Sigler, president of the Business Roundtable, charges: "It is nothing but a grubby asset play. They are acquiring the greatest accumulation of wealth of all time—greater than the Rockefellers or the Rothschilds—they are doing it by snapping it out of companies, thus damaging the capabilities of the economic system to perform" (Linowes, 1987, p. 7). Critics argue that M & A distract corporate management, disrupt the lives of corporate employees and their communities, induce corporations through tax breaks to take on excessive debt, and prevent corporations from investing adequately in their products and services to remain viable competitors in the international marketplace.

On the other hand, Kohlberg Kravis Roberts & Company (KKR), which has sponsored a number of LBOs over the past twelve years—including those of Beatrice Company, RJR Nabisco, Safeway Stores, Owens-Illinois, and Motel 6—analyzed data from the seventeen companies acquired through LBOs in which KKR still has an ownership position. "The data demonstrate that, contrary to statements and generalizations which are frequently made, leveraged buyouts are an effective technique for acquiring a company and result in more efficient and more profitable operations which increase employment, increase research and development, yield higher taxes to the federal government, keep capital spending strong, are able adequately to handle negative events such as economic downturns, and not run with a view to quarter-to-quarter earnings, and yield high returns to investors" (Kohlberg Kravis Roberts & Company, 1989, p. 64).

Regardless of your point of view or the clarity that only future events will yield, corporate restructurings are a fact of business life and must be managed as prudently as any other type of change. Corporate restructuring happens all the time and always has (in one form or another) throughout American business history. "In fact, there have been other waves of mergers and acquisitions— if not leveraged buyouts—in times past, and there is simply no evidence that they had a negative impact on the growth of total corporate contributions," says Hayden Smith of the Council for Aid to Education (Smith, 1989, p. 23). Restructuring, in its broadest sense, includes an array of management methods for increasing shareholder value, the often-stated primary purpose of business. Change is inevitable, and managing change is what business is all about.

Impact of M & A on Corporate Contributions

Leaving the debate on the merits and perils of M & A to the financial experts, I will focus in the remainder of this chapter on the effects of these activities on corporate grantmaking. To date, very little research has been done on this subject.

In the Conference Board's *Corporate Contributions Outlook, 1987,* Anne Klepper concludes, "Mergers and acquisitions are clearly changing the corporate landscape. While their impact on corporate contributions and memberships is yet to be measured, it is evident that some contributions programs have disappeared. Although new programs have been born from corporate spin-offs and divestitures, it is not possible to predict whether they will equal in size and scope the programs that have fallen" (Klepper, 1987, p. 3). Although M & A have continued at the same pace since 1987, research on their effects on corporate grantmaking has not progressed much since that time.

Research has been hindered by several factors, including the variety of definitions for *restructuring,* the difficulty in framing questions to elicit comparable responses, the inaccessibility or unavailability of respondents with the appropriate data, and the complexities of the deals themselves. As a result, we are left with anecdotal, not statistical, information. Figures that are available do not bear out the real stories and too often are selectively chosen to support either critics' claims or public relations strategies.

According to Klepper, "A thorough research job would be quite difficult" (personal conversation with author). In 1989, for example, the Conference Board included only one segment dealing with corporate restructuring in its annual survey of corporate contributions. The questions asked were: Have you restructured? Will your corporate contributions budget increase, decrease, or remain the same? Restructuring in this context is meant to include mergers, acquisitions, leveraged buyouts, and stock buybacks.

Responses to these questions, however, may not provide reliable data. Profitability may have a greater effect on the level of corporate contributions than does restructuring. Statistics can confuse the two. For example, in 1986 Standard Oil of Ohio reduced its budget for corporate contributions from approximately $17 million to $13 million. Since the company anticipated continuing declines in profitability, a further reduction of $10.3 million was planned for 1987 (Lance C. Buhl, personal communication with author). Both of these reductions were a direct result of the dramatic drop in oil prices and had no relationship to the 1987 takeover of Standard Oil by British Petroleum, resulting in the reorganization of Standard Oil as BP America. Yet a cursory review of the company's charitable contributions statistics may have led some people to conclude that a change in corporate ownership was the cause of the subsequent reduction in contributions. "We have been most gratified not only by the acute interest of British Petroleum in our contributions program, but also by the active endorsement of our programs' emphases by senior management," said Lance C. Buhl, manager of corporate contributions, for the company (personal communication with author).

In an article entitled "Don't Blame Mergers and Buyouts for the Slowdown in Corporate Giving," Hayden Smith (1989, pp. 23–24) wrote, "It is doubtful that there has been more than a marginal impact on total corporate contributions—if indeed it has had any impact at all. To infer that total charitable giving by corporations has decreased just because the giving by companies involved in restructuring has decreased is akin to what logicians call the 'fallacy of composition.' It also totally ignores the very dynamic nature of the corporate community. The corporate population itself changes daily, with births, deaths, mergers, spinoffs, and other events. This is a constant process, and the current wave of restructuring is one example of such dynamics."

We do not really know what measurable impact M & A have had on corporate grantmaking. But several programs have been virtually eliminated or severely curtailed following a corporate reorganization. In 1989, George Kennedy, chairman and CEO of IMCERA Group, estimated that since 1984 at least fifty-five major companies with headquarters in the Chicago area had been bought or restructured. However, in a recent article published by the Donors Forum of Chicago, entitled "Merger Mania Beclouds Corporate Philanthropy's Future," authors Cleopatra and James Alexander conclude: "While all too many Chicago corporate names and faces have changed due to mergers and restructuring, it appears that in the aggregate the philanthropic effects, while wrenching, have not been fiscally disastrous" (Alexander and Alexander, 1989, p. 3).

The grantmaking function is not a major consideration in M & A transactions because contributions are financially immaterial within the context of the overall deal. Budgets for corporate contributions are relatively small when compared to the purchase price of current deals. In 1988, the average price of an M & A deal climbed 39 percent to $130 million ("The Merger Game Went into Hyperdrive," 1989). By contrast, the average total expenditures (cash and noncash) of 550 corporate giving programs in 1988 reported in the 1989 Taft Corporate Giving Directory was slightly less than $4 million. The yearly contributions average represents only 3 percent of the average purchase price of a deal and is an inflated figure because only 550 of the largest contributions programs are included in the calculation.

Corporate contributions will take a backseat to other more immediate and financially significant issues in M & A deals. Contributions managers are likely to face a long period of uncertainty, during which the resolution of major issues in finance, marketing, law, and human resources takes precedence.

Dynamics of M & A

In the early stages of a potential merger or acquisition, an acquirer and a target may decide to make a deal. Or an acquiring company may be interested in making an unfriendly offer for a target company. In either case, "the main problem is competition" according to Leo Herzel, senior partner, Mayer Brown & Platt. "Secrecy is therefore very important," he says (Herzel, 1986, p. 5). Often, the companies involved desire "to delay publicity for as long as possible, as long as they can legally and practically do it, because of the problem of competition." At this time, rumors may abound. Word of mouth is a pervasive, although often unreliable, form of communication. The prudent manager will remain calm.

"For companies that are vulnerable, the mere threat of outside action of this nature may lead to bizarre forms of recapitalization that result in downward pressures on contributions budgets," says Hayden Smith. He points out that "even potential takeovers are believed to have negative effects on contributions," according to some observers (Smith, 1989, p. 23).

Once a deal has been finalized, new strategies are often implemented immediately. Michael Jensen, a professor at the Harvard Business School says, "Restructurings usually involve transfers of ownership and major organizational changes (such as shifts in corporate strategy) to meet new competition or market conditions, increased use of debt, and a flurry of recontracting with managers, employees, suppliers and customers. This activity sometimes results in expansion of resources devoted to certain areas and at other times in contractions involving plant closings, layoff of top-level and middle managers, staff and production workers, and reduced compensation" (Jensen, 1987, p. 1).

Proponents of M & A argue that takeovers occur because new technology or market conditions require a major restructuring of corporate assets. In some cases, incumbent management is slow to respond to these changes or tends to build empires at shareholders' expense. According to Jensen, "When the internal processes for change in large corporations are too slow, costly and clumsy to efficiently accomplish the required restructuring or change in managers, the capital market, through the market for corporate control, is bringing about substantial changes in corporate strategy" (Jensen, 1987, p. 2).

A change in control results in a new set of priorities aimed at improving the efficiency of the organization's financial structure, manufacturing, distribution, sales, marketing, or advertising. Particularly with mergers and acquisitions, the objective is to develop synergy between two companies, to find ways in which the combined companies can benefit from their association, reduce overhead, and become more efficient. The corporate culture desired by the new company following a merger or acquisition is one in which business units work together and seek new opportunities that could not have been realized before the merger or acquisition.

This emerging culture places a premium on problem solving, creativity, and teamwork. For an alert, ambitious contributions manager, this environment can provide new opportunities to bring the contributions function into the mainstream of the company's new operating goals and objectives. Becoming part of a problem-solving team is an asset for all managers and is more proactive and constructive than bemoaning one's fate and waiting for decisions about the contributions program to be made by others in the company.

In an environment in which virtually everything is being reexamined from a new perspective, the goals and objectives of the contributions program will also be scrutinized—eventually. Sometimes, this examination is overdue. A company that has plodded along giving grants to the same organizations year after year, without asking what the return is or how the system might be improved, is ripe for a critical review. After a merger or acquisition, practices that have been unquestioned for years are evaluated against modern standards for corporate responsibility, in the context of today's social issues and tomorrow's business needs. Restructured companies that are measuring the impact of all money spent eventually will pose several questions to the contributions program: What is being accomplished? What is the return on these social investments? How can grantmaking programs be shaped to better benefit the corporation in the long run? How can the programs be organized to improve efficiency and reduce administrative expense? How should the programs be positioned and marketed to communicate the company's new values?

After the 1987 LBO of Burlington Industries, combined foundation and corporate giving of approximately $3 million was scheduled to be reduced by 50 percent over a two-year period. Executive Director Park Davidson said, "This was a wonderful opportunity to get a lot of 'politically initiated' contributions off our list. We had contributed to a number of the same groups every year and our revised strategies helped us clean out a lot of things with a logical explanation." Nonprofit recipients, Davidson argues, also benefit from this housecleaning approach. "It's healthy for donees who took our annual contributions for granted to confront change. It forces them to reexamine their own perspective as well" (personal communication with the author).

The self-examination by the contributions department takes place at a time when senior managers must focus their undivided attention on several critical issues. For example, the reduction of debt and the sale of assets are important factors in the post-LBO phase. Tax questions must be resolved and appropriate provisions made to take advantage of new tax opportunities. Preservation and growth of market share and adequate investment of capital in profitable operations require the immediate attention of corporate and division management. These are the areas in which the restructuring must succeed if it is to be successful and if the company is to continue to support its philanthropic activity.

To the extent that the contributions program is tied to the goals and strategies of the company, it will require time to take shape. To become an integral part of the restructured business, the grantmaking staff must fully understand what that business is and how it will be managed. The contributions program cannot be refocused overnight. For a while, the company's contributions program may fall between two worlds—not what it used to be, but not yet what it is destined to become. Patience is a necessary virtue in such an environment.

Critics of M & A are particularly concerned about ownership of American companies by foreign-based corporations. However, it is still unclear what effect such acquisitions have on corporate grantmaking. "Foreign owners seem to understand that at the very heart of their business is the need to learn the rules of the host country," said Lance C. Buhl. "BP management, for example, recognizes that their vulnerability to charges of insensitive foreign ownership entails a risk. They have been supportive of our contributions program from the beginning of our relationship. Quite pragmatically, they recognize that their license to operate requires careful adaptation to the values and customs of the host country" (personal communication with the author). Making the counterargument, Charles Mannatt, former chairman of the Democratic National Committee, wrote, "Japanese firms doing business in America have brought their attitudes with them. Although some Japanese corporations have recently improved their charitable activities, most still lag far behind American firms in corporate giving" (Mannatt, 1989).

Management of Contributions During Restructuring

A change in corporate ownership may affect corporate foundations differently than other corporate giving programs. A corporate foundation is a separate, independent legal entity sponsored by a corporation but not necessarily owned by it. The company receives its charitable tax deduction when it contributes funds to the foundation. Once these contributed funds are transferred to the corporate foundation, the company no longer includes these assets on its balance sheet. Therefore, if the company's assets are sold, it does not necessarily follow that its corporate foundation is acquired by the buyer. If the foundation's bylaws provide for governance by a self-elected, independent board of directors, not appointed by the corporate sponsor, this board of directors in effect controls the foundation. In contrast to a "pass-through" foundation in which transferred funds equal current obligations, an endowed corporate foundation or one with accumulated assets could operate independently from an acquiring company. Such a foundation may even go on to operate under a new identity, depending on the provisions in its charter or bylaws.

The history of the Beatrice Foundation is a case in point. The foundation was incorporated in 1953 as the Swift & Company Foundation. In 1973, when Esmark was created as a holding company for the businesses that had constituted Swift, the foundation became the Esmark Foundation, with continuity in its board of directors. In 1984, Beatrice Companies acquired Esmark and the foundation became the Beatrice Foundation. The directors of the Esmark Foundation (who had been officers of Esmark) elected executives from Beatrice as the new directors of the Beatrice Foundation, triggering this voluntary change of control.

In 1987, E-II Holdings was spun off by Beatrice to become a publicly traded holding company and, subsequently, the foundation was renamed the E-II Foundation. The old Beatrice Foundation directors elected several new board members from the senior management ranks of E-II Holdings and approved the name change. However, when E-II Holdings was acquired by American Brands in 1988, the foundation, as an independent entity, was not likewise acquired by the buyer. The directors of the E-II Foundation elected to change the name back to Beatrice Foundation and today continue to govern the Beatrice Foundation's activities.

A corporate contributions program is more vulnerable than a foundation in a corporate restructuring. Corporate contributions appear as a line item on the company's expense budget. The period after the restructuring—particularly in an LBO, through which the company incurs significant debt to finance the transactions—is characterized by an all-out effort to reduce expenses in order to meet interest payments on that debt and provide the ongoing businesses with sufficient capital to generate future income. Every corporate "cost-center" is examined by management. Management often concludes that one feasible place to pare expenses is the contributions budget, in which reductions are not likely to immediately affect the company's ability to generate enough cash to service the debt or support its business operations. Indeed, many people might argue that reducing contributions is an efficient use of a highly leveraged company's financial resources.

Furthermore, it may be inappropriate to maintain the same level of corporate contributions at a time when employees may be terminated because of redundancies in the work force. An acquaintance of mine whose company had recently been restructured informed me that she had been asked to remain in her position as manager of corporate contributions. She was quick to say, however, that the most painful part of the process was justifying her position, while dozens of her fellow employees packed their desks and left the company. "They asked me how it was possible that the company would continue its contributions program even while laying off employees in other departments," she said in a personal conversation with me. She was already the only person in the department, and the elimination of her position would have brought the contributions function to a complete standstill, a situation her CEO personally found unacceptable.

Today, the size of corporate contributions staffs often reflects the "lean and mean" cost consciousness many corporations adopted in the 1980s. In 1987, Brian O'Connell, president of INDEPENDENT SECTOR, conducted an informal survey of the staff sizes of approximately seventy-five private foundations and seventy-five corporate contributions programs. He found, "In these 150 programs of equal grantmaking size, the private foundations have, on average, one professional staff person for each $1.2 million of grants, and the corporations have one staff person for each $2.3

million of grants, a ratio of approximately 2 to 1" (O'Connell, 1987).

For an already small contributions staff, the additional pressures and responsibilities following a restructuring can be staggering. In addition to the normal work load, contributions managers must prepare program assessments and alternatives, brief new management or new owners, address staffing issues, and field a barrage of calls from anxious donees. Keeping the lines of communication open with constituents (nonprofit groups, community and civic leaders, corporate management, and so on) before long-term strategies are approved can be time consuming, to say the least. But by taking the time to communicate, contributions managers can present their program as thoughtful and strategic in responding to organizational change.

It may be useful for the contributions manager to develop a short-term agenda for managing the program in the early stages of restructuring. By resisting the temptation to remain silent until decisions are final, proactive contributions managers can allay much of the community's concern by explaining the purposes of the restructuring and giving a broad time frame for decision making. Contributions managers are in contact with a constituency that may not be reached directly by the company's traditional communications to investors and the financial media. Yet this nonprofit constituency will also be affected by the company's restructuring and needs to be kept informed. Remaining calm, professional, and accessible from the beginning of the restructuring reflects positively on both the contributions executive and the company.

Burlington Industries asked their plant managers to meet with local community leaders to explain the company's LBO and the effects it would have on Burlington's contributions. In a videotaped presentation, Chairman Frank Greenberg outlined the purposes and consequences of the LBO. Plant managers explained that the company did not plan to make drastic reductions in its support of nonprofit groups located in plant communities but that it would make necessary cutbacks by reducing the amount of support provided to national organizations such as the Red Cross, the Boy Scouts, the Girl Scouts, and others. Local support of these organizations would continue, they said. "The response from our community leaders was quite positive," Burlington's director, Park Davidson, said in a conversation with me.

Nonprofit executives who have had a positive and helpful relationship with the company may want to convey their support of the contributions program to senior management or new owners. This is a way for the newcomers to learn of the reputation the company has earned by virtue of its past giving history. At this stage, contributions managers may guide the nonprofit executives to be constructive in their comments and to encourage the company to maintain its standard of excellence in grantmaking, if, indeed, the grantmaking program has met high standards. Many of the other stakeholders of the company are likely to be voicing their views at the same time. The nonprofit sector should not go unheard at these early and critical moments.

"It is in the best interest of the community to speak out for itself when a merger is first announced. If the nonprofits sit on their hands, decisions will be made without their input. It's especially important for small organizations that depend on those grants to have their voices heard," according to Ron Coman, in a conversation with me. He was the director of community affairs for Kraft, which was acquired by Philip Morris in 1988.

By the time a takeover occurs, the contributions program must stand on the reputation for accountability and impact it has already earned. James Alexander, a Chicago-based consultant in corporate philanthropy, says, "It's tough to look like Sophia Loren at 50 if you didn't look like her at 20" (personal communication with author). On the other hand, contributions programs that have earned the respect and appreciation of the communities in which they operate, may experience a ground swell of support from civic and nonprofit leaders in the event their programs appear to be threatened.

The *Chronicle of Philanthropy* documented this point in its coverage of one recent takeover:

The Pillsbury Company has become one of the first corporations ever to negotiate preservation of its charitable-giving program into the terms of a takeover agreement. The provision was written into the company's merger accord with

Grand Metropolitan, P.L.C., which last month succeeded in a hostile bid to acquire the company for $5.7 billion.

This fall, in a show of concern for the giving program, representives of more than 300 nonprofit groups packed the lobby of the company's Minneapolis headquarters and brought letters testifying to the importance of Pillsbury philanthropy. Carol B. Truesdell, Pillsbury's former vice president for community relations, said that the company's lawyers were unaware of any similar stipulations in other merger agreements ["Pillsbury Preserves Giving in Takeover Accord," 1989].

The role of the contributions manager has been described as to serve as an interpreter between the corporation and the nonprofit sector, communicating the values and realities of each to the other. An interpreter must be fluent in two languages, an expert in each. Becoming an authority on both the corporation and its nonprofit constituents gives the contributions manager credibility with both internal and external audiences. This capability is especially important during restructuring, when reliable information is sought by all parties. Being an authority increases the likelihood of participation in decision making and impels others in the company to seek and consider this unique point of view.

Two studies conducted by the Council on Foundations (in 1982 and 1988) concluded that the corporate chief executive officer "plays a pivotal role in both shaping and implementing corporate giving policies. Two in three CEO's across the board describe themselves as the major influence on their companies' corporate giving policy" (Daniel Yankelovich Group, 1988, p. 13). Clearly, this is a key relationship for the contributions manager, who must have discipline in order to present information and recommendations to the CEO that are as strategic and responsible as any provided by others in the company. When a new CEO takes over, the contributions manager must take into account that CEO's background, preferences, and overriding corporate objectives. This is another area in which the contributions manager must become expert and must clearly articulate the specific benefits of the contributions function to the chairman. To do so effectively will require a comprehensive understanding of the company's future opportunities, management challenges, marketing objectives, and vulnerabilities.

Problem solvers routinely question things and do not readily accept the status quo. That is why they are in such demand in restructuring corporations. They have the capacity to replace programs they have helped to create with revised agendas that reflect new conditions. They are adaptable and persistent. They understand and manage with the big picture in mind. In these uncertain times, such characteristics will serve the contributions manager well in producing results with the resources at hand. Bemoaning fate or resisting change is futile. Integrating creativity, responsiveness, and good communication into a contributions program is what strategic philanthropy and professionalism are all about in any event. No matter what the future rate of new mergers and acquisitions, corporate grantmakers will be well served and well advised to refine these essential skills.

References

Alexander, C. B., and Alexander, J. N. "Merger Mania Beclouds Corporate Philanthropy's Future." *The Forum* (published by the Donors Forum of Chicago), *6*, 1989, pp. 2-3.

The Chicago Fed Letter. Jan. 1989, p. 1.

Herzel, L. "How Mergers and Acquisitions Work." Paper presented at seminar of the Public Relations Society of America, Bloomingdale, Ill., May 29, 1986.

Jensen, M. C. "The Takeover Controversy: The Restructuring of Corporate America." *From the Podium,* Sept. 1987, pp. 1-5.

Klepper, A., and others. *Corporate Contributions Outlook, 1987.* New York: Conference Board, 1987.

Kohlberg Kravis Roberts & Company (with Deloitte Haskins & Sells). "Leveraged Buy-Outs." *Journal of Applied Corporate Finance, 2* (1), 1989, 64-70.

Linowes, D. F. "Is the Merger Mania Good for the Nation: Should There Be Regulatory Restraint?" *From the Podium,* Sept. 1987, pp. 5-8.

Mannatt, C. "Japanese Firms, Corporate Citizens." *Chicago Tribune,* Aug. 8, 1989.

"The Merger Game Went into Hyperdrive." *Business Week,* special issue, Spring 1989, p. 35.

O'Connell, B. "Corporate Philanthropy: Getting Bigger, Broader, and Tougher to Manage." Paper presented at the National Conference on Corporate Community Involvement, Atlanta, Ga., May 13, 1987.

"Pillsbury Preserves Giving in Takeover Accord." *Chronicle of Philanthropy,* Jan. 10, 1989. p. 5.

Smith, H. "Don't Blame Mergers and Buyouts for the Slowdown in Corporate Giving." *Chronicle of Philanthropy,* Mar. 7, 1989, pp. 23-24.

Daniel Yankelovich Group. *The Climate for Giving: The Outlook of Current and Future CEO's.* New York: Council on Foundations, 1988.

PART FOUR

Administering Corporate
Grantmaking Effectively

Chapter Fourteen

The Keys to a Well-Run
Grants Program:
A Checklist

George M. Collins

When the senior managers call you in and tell you that they want you to create and operate a grants program or to take over a program already in operation, you may see this as the end of your career in the corporation—instead of one of the best opportunities you have ever been offered!

Your first impression may be based on your lack of knowledge of what a corporate foundation or grantmaking program is all about. Like any new assignment, you know that it is a change—and someone said we all shy away from change—but hopefully, we will begin to demystify the operation in this chapter.

In 1982, I knew absolutely nothing about professional grantmaking. But I did know the members of the newly created Boston Globe Foundation's board of directors. In fact, I had known three of the six directors for forty-two years and the other three for up to thirty years. So, may I suggest that the most important item on your agenda is to know your teammates.

Know Your Teammates

If you are assigned as a staff member to a foundation, start by getting to know your fellow staffers and your staff leader. If you are assigned as a foundation's staff leader, get to know your staff, your directors, and your CEO—who, if you are lucky, will also be the corporation's CEO. Begin by asking these questions:

- Who are your teammates?
- How do they think?
- Are they altruistic to a fault?
- Does their compassion make for poor grantmaking?
- Are they only interested in the bottom line in the corporation's earnings report and so look at the grantmaking program as "spending" the firm's monies and not as "investing" the firm's funds in the community?
- Are any of the directors or staff narrowly focused in their grant-making priorities, or are they serving on boards of directors of nonprofit institutions seeking grants?
- Is your staff—if you have one—geared to a nine-to-five life-style over a five-day week?

If your staff is geared to a conventional work week, and you are hopeful that your local grantmaking is going to be important to the community, then you need to have a serious talk with the staff. This is not a nine-to-five kind of job, but it can be a great one.

After you have quietly assessed the people around you, I advise you to recognize that your role is to serve them—the staff, the directors, and the grantseekers. Keep in mind that the better you know their personal wants and needs, the better you can garner their support of the grantmaking program.

And depending on the system in place in your company, you will also want to include the line executives in at least your in-house reports about grantmaking. Executives who see themselves as the money earners of the firm will only see the foundation as a money spender unless they know what the foundation is doing locally, nationally and internationally. In a majority of corporate grantmaking efforts, you will be able to influence almost all the grant decisions—except when the "old-boy/old-girl" network holds sway.

But in many companies—if not most—the old-boy/old-girl network or the historic back-pocket grantmaking of privately held firms has been a dominant factor in the creation of a corporate program with a professional delivery system. The corporate foundation is an "arms-length" instrument that permits the chief executive officer and other top executives to refer all requests for grants out of their offices if they so desire. They never have to say no to anyone. The foundation can do that for them if the grant is not approved. If the grant is approved, they can be the bearers of good news to the applicant or to their fellows in the old-boy/old-girl network. Thus they still can have input in all major "bricks and mortar" grants.

Learn by Doing

Different people have different ways of doing things. And there are many ways to do things in grantmaking. If you do not know much about corporate grantmaking, you do not know what does or does not work. You should be eager to learn, mostly by doing.

You may make a bad grant but probably only once. You will find that nonprofit agencies need your support so desperately that they will not let you be easily victimized by badly operated agencies. And the network of grantmakers, in your company and outside of it, will usually delight in telling you their experiences.

But let us suppose that you have accepted the position of corporate grantmaker—executive director of the program, regardless of title. You will probably find a file of requests awaiting your attention.

My files were not in a cabinet. They were in piles on two captain's chairs in a conference room—one emblazoned with the crest of Harvard College and the other, with the crest of Dartmouth. I thought, how appropriate. These two schools really know how to raise money for their "nonprofit" lives, and the proposals on the chairs were from real nonprofits, asking for grants that usually amounted to less than half of one year's room, board, and tuition at these Ivy League citadels.

Back files indicated gifts made to agencies and institutions over the previous fifteen years. They gave me a first inkling as to how at least three of the foundation directors thought, to whom they gave support, and to whom they may have made commitments for the future.

My next step was to call attorney John Edie of the Council on Foundations to find out what was required of our foundation before it could be accepted into the Council. If your foundation already is a Council member, you only need to check your membership charter so you will not inadvertently place your membership in jeopardy. If you are not a Council member, you should take a serious look at what they can offer you in service and savvy—and check with nearby foundations, not just corporate foundations, to get their opinions of its value. Then your first selling job to the directors and the CEO may be for a Council membership fee.

Working with the CEO, you will want to set up the dates and times of meetings with the board of directors for presentations of staff recommendations for grants. This will allow you to begin planning your operation.

Time commitments are naturally followed by funding commitments. Some corporate grantmakers have secured funding from company trusts. Others must receive annual grants from pretax earnings ranging from less than 1 percent up to the legal limit of 10 percent. The best of all worlds may be to have no "chiselled in stone" dollar amount but a percentage figure approved by the corporate board of directors annually and a "guesstimate" as to how much that will mean over the foundation's fiscal years. Meeting dates and times and money in hand, you now can look at the proposals already in house.

Develop Communications Systems

If you are going to use a computer from the beginning—perhaps not advisable even though there are good software programs available—you will need some help, or you will never find the time for site visits to your grantseekers. Perhaps a better idea is to begin to create a file of proposals through which you can become a business-like organization.

You will want to have postcards printed acknowledging the receipt of each proposal and stating that you will follow up at a later date. This will cut down to some degree the flood of telephone calls from grantseekers. Later, when you are more experienced, you will develop a set of guidelines for people seeking grants. These guidelines must be approved by the foundation's directors. Without such approval, you will have constant strife over what your foundation really does or does not fund. With unanimous approval by your directors, you are armed—and so are they—with a document that is the "constitution" of your grantmaking effort.

Directors find it very comfortable to refer requests to the foundation's staff leader, particularly if money is tight or the support requested is questionable in light of the foundation's guidelines. If you are creating a foundation, you will want to develop a form for reporting the grant requests that can be supplied to the directors. This form, which I will detail later in the chapter (Exhibit 13.1), should probably have the following information.

1. Name of organization
2. Address of organization
3. Executive director's name
4. Single paragraph description of what organization does
5. Amount of funds requested
6. Single paragraph description of what organization proposes to do with the grant
7. Percent of the organization's annual budget that this request would fill
8. Staff assessment of agency
9. Staff recommendation of whether grant should be made and in what amount

In a new organization, this form may be the most that you can provide the directors, along with a copy of all the agency documentation, but be open to constant review and ready to change your reports to your board members. Several grantmakers have told me that after six or eight grantmaking meetings, their directors usually ask not to receive all the agency materials. At that point, approval of grant proposal guidelines and the attendant request form becomes a priority.

If your area has a regional association of grantmakers with a research library, this should be your first stop in seeking to develop guidelines and forms or brochures. You might also ask—off the record—several grantmakers which grantmaker has the best system of operation: Who acknowledges requests and how? Who does the promised follow up and how? Whose criteria are fair and not excessive? Then scan the guidelines and visit your colleagues and if you agree with the guidelines, do not hesitate to ask permission to use whatever fits your needs.

Over the years, many grantmakers in specific areas of the country have seen the value to the grantseekers of coordinating their guidelines. And your board of directors will quickly realize the value of the use of a single form that makes financial comparisons all oranges or apples—not a mixed bag.

Prepare your guidelines for proposals and have them printed as quickly as possible. When agencies see such forms and other criteria for grantseeking, they will generally comply with all your requests.

A standardized proposal form will give you the opportunity to ask grantseekers questions that generally are not answered in a cover letter such as: What is the makeup of the agency staff and directors? What is the total budget of the agency and how is it spent? The first set of answers (about agency staff and directors) tells you quickly whether they really represent the people "served" by the agency.

The proposal form also allows you to tailor your postcards to groups acknowledging receipt of a proposal by listing any deficiencies in the proposal and including any additional forms the grantseeker may need. It is difficult in this era for an organization serving persons with varied disabilities and handicaps to have no persons with disabilities or handicaps on its staff or board. It should also be expected that agencies serving battered women and their children may not have any men on either their staff or board. In fact they may not allow men to make site visits to their shelter because it is too traumatic to their clients. You must respect such restrictions; certainly all efforts to urge staff and directorships to reflect the agencies' programs and aims should be of a persuasive nature, not an "either/or" message tied to a grant.

There may come a time, though, when the need for accurate financial data will result in specifying that unless a competent fiscal operation is put into place there will be no more funding. To handle such an event fairly you must make the effort to provide help in securing such financial talent.

On occasion this can provoke an amusing and often a frustrating result. The Globe Foundation once made a $4,500 grant specifically for the hiring of an accountant for an agency which had not provided up-to-date fiscal data for three years. We informed them that we would expect to see the audit before we would be able to continue any further support. One year later we received a request for several thousand dollars for operating use and we reminded them that we needed the audit report.

"Oh my," the agency director replied, "the week after your check arrived last winter our furnace blew apart and it cost us $4,500 to get a new one installed." We gave him an "A" for creative answers, but we still haven't seen an audit—and he has stopped asking for money.

In another instance, after being assured for several years that an agency board would expand their minority representation on staff and board—with no results—we ceased all funding to them and explained clearly the reason. The director thanked us for our past support, agreed that what we sought to achieve was his desire and that our requests had given him strength in asking the board members for compliance . . . but candidly admitted that there would have to be several retirements or deaths on his board before he would be able to bring his agency hierarchy into this century. This also is the time when you can send a polite letter to the petitioner specifying that the request does not fall within the foundation's guidelines so that the petitioner will be able to get on with the financial search.

You may wish at this time only to receive a basic outline of the project and its proposed budget from the grantseeker, with detail to follow should you wish to proceed toward a grant. Our process moved rapidly, at the suggestion of other grantmakers, toward a series of questions that endeavor to place every grantseeker on the same level playing field.

The information we seek may seem to be extensive and involved. The Boston Globe Foundation's directors have found over the years that every time they have asked for an executive summary of this material, they more often than not also wanted an answer to one or more of the proposal guideline questions. Exhibit 14.1 presents a proposal form that should be of assistance in evaluating an agency and its staff.

One concern of the Boston Globe Foundation from its early days has been to know whether physcially challenged persons have access to all of the nonprofit agencies or institutions we might consider for grants. Exhibit 14.2 presents a questionnaire that is incorporated into our grant proposal form and has been of great benefit to us in gaining this information.

If you commit to seeking this data, you need the backing of your directors before you begin because you are going to receive many requests for funding to upgrade nonprofit offices and facilities. You may also want to have a person skilled in the field of architectural barriers visit your own building and make recommendations that will bring your own offices and plant up to code.

You will hear complaints from some grantseekers that your proposal forms are too restrictive or too tiring to fill out or to comply with. But what you may really be guilty of is allowing forms to take the place of human contacts. Too many grantmakers get a reputation of being unavailable to grantseekers. Simple rules of courtesy—returning your telephone calls, writing quick notes telling of receipt of a proposal or rejection of a proposal because of guidelines or by the directors—coupled with a high visibility in making site visits—will go a long way in reducing this criticism to the minimum.

If you have a staff of associates or program officers, you will want to assign them the incoming proposals as quickly as possible. It is unfair to assign a proposal to a staff member who serves on the applicant-institution's board or participates in the group as an active member. This potential for conflict of interest is a major impediment to objective, unbaised grantmaking. You must be aware

Exhibit 14.1. Proposal Form.

PROGRAM INFORMATION (Please type)

Name:
Address:

Telephone:
Executive director:
Contact person:

FUNDING REQUEST

Amount requested:
Purpose of request:

Total to be raised for project:
                for agency:
Total received to date for project:
                for agency:
Previous BGF grants:
    1982 $; 1983 $; 1984 $; 1985 $
    1986 $; 1987 $; 1988 $; 1989 $
Other potential funding sources and amounts:

SOURCE	AMOUNT PROPOSED	RECEIVED

PROGRAM

Description of program:

Specific objectives:

Evidence of need and that program would not duplicate existing services:

History of agency's experience operating similar services:

Exhibit 14.1. Proposal Form, Cont'd.

Public relations efforts:

Coordination/collaboration with other agencies:

Hours of operation:
Duration of program:

POPULATION SERVED

Target population:

Number served: (by individual program if available)

Ages:

Income level(s):
Ethnic group(s):
Geographic distribution:
Handicapped/disabled involvement: (Are building/facilities accessible
according to code for disabled/handicapped?)
*Please fill out attached Accessibility Questionnaire and return with this
grant proposal.*
Enrollment versus capacity:

PROGRAM INFORMATION

Site:

Location:

Occupancy: Own/rent:
If rent, annual cost:
      In-kind?:
Accessibility to target population: (including handicapped accessibility)

Feasibility of space for program:

MANAGEMENT

Number of staff: (administrative, program, clinical, custodial, etc.)

      F-T: P-T: Others:

Composition: (m/f, racial/ethnic background)

Experience of F-T staffers:

Exhibit 14.1. Proposal Form, Cont'd.

Training and orientation of staff:

Supervision of staff:

Ratio of staff to clients:
Use of volunteers:

Staff turnover in past two years:

BOARD OF DIRECTORS
Board functions:

Composition of board: (professions, etc.)

Number of board members:
Sex: Male/   Female/
Race: W/   B/   H/   O/
Average attendance at board meetings:

EVALUATION MECHANISM used by the agency to evaluate its program(s):

FINANCIAL MANAGEMENT
Board-approved agency budget this fiscal year: (Attach line-item budget.)

Board-approved program budget: (Attach line-item budget.)

Fiscal year dated:
Description of in-kind goods and services:

Evidence of long-term funding or efforts at making agency self-sufficient:

What do you see as the greatest challenges facing your organization in the next two or three years?

Evaluate briefly your organization's strengths and weaknesses:

Are you a United Way Funds recipient: Yes: No:
If yes, this year/:   Total U.W. funds received:
What percentage of current F.Y. budget are U.W. finds?:

Copy of IRS Form 990
Copy of IRS 501(c)(3) letter of determination

Exhibit 14.2. Accessibility Questionnaire.

Organization's Name: _____

In order to determine how best to address the problem of barriers to people with disabilities, The Boston Globe Foundation is gathering information from all grant applicants on accessibility to programs and program spaces. It is an effort to gather data and assess where our grant applicants are in terms of access. All applicants must complete the following questionnaire.

In answering questions about accessibility please consider the entire building your office is located in including hallways, elevators, parking areas, and door widths (at least 32″).

1. Is your office space physically accessible for people using wheelchairs?   Yes ☐   No ☐

2. Do you have a TDD (telecommunications device for the deaf)?   Yes ☐   No ☐

3. Is the TDD's number listed on your letterhead and promotional materials?   Yes ☐   No ☐

4. Has your staff received training on how to use the TDD?   Yes ☐   No ☐

5. Do you hold your public and in-house meetings and events in physically accessible locations?   Yes ☐   No ☐

    a. Briefly list the accessible spaces you use to hold meetings and events.

6. Do you make your printed programs, brochures, annual reports, etc. available in large print or on tape for people with visual impairments?   Yes ☐   No ☐

7. Do you publicize your accessibility in your promotional materials, announcements, etc.?   Yes ☐   No ☐

8. Do you use a sign language interpreter for meetings or events?   Yes ☐   No ☐

9. Have you ever requested information from ticket buyers or event attendees regarding their access needs?   Yes ☐   No ☐

10. Do you do any special outreach to notify people with disabilities about your programs, events, or services?   Yes ☐   No ☐

11. Do you have any employees with disabilities?   Yes ☐   No ☐
    people with:
    Mobility Limitations   Yes ☐   No ☐   Visual Limitations   Yes ☐   No ☐
    Hearing Limitations   Yes ☐   No ☐   Learning Disabilities   Yes ☐   No ☐

12. Do you have any board or committee members with disabilities?   Yes ☐   No ☐
    people with:
    Mobility Limitations   Yes ☐   No ☐   Visual Limitations   Yes ☐   No ☐
    Hearing Limitations   Yes ☐   No ☐   Learning Disabilities   Yes ☐   No ☐

13. Do you have a designated staff member responsible for access and dealing with Chapter 504 regulations?   Yes ☐   No ☐

14. Could you use technical assistance to become more accessible in your programs, services, or facilities?   Yes ☐   No ☐

15. Is accessibility a part of your organization's long-range plan?   Yes ☐   No ☐

of connections by you or your staff or directors with grantseeking institutions to retain your image as an objective grantmaker.

If you become the leader of a corporate program with support staff, you will be able to avail yourself of a computer system and tailored software to develop a record-keeping system. Some of the areas you will want this system to cover include:

1. Guidelines material that you deem necessary for storage and reference
2. Date proposal received
3. Response sent to grantseekers
4. Staff associate assigned to follow up
5. Director's meeting date at which proposal will be presented
6. All funding data on the organization, such as past grants for at least five years
7. Assurance that the organization has an IRS 501(c)(3) designation and that the latest copy of such status is included in the file

You will also want to have a systems structure that allows you to call up a list of all proposals assigned for a given meeting and a way to indicate whether they are complete and if a recommendation to fund the proposal has been made or if not, why not.

Grantmaking software systems have been available for purchase as a package, with individual tailoring possible, for almost a decade. Funders using them rarely return to their old paper filing systems.

Of major importance in the communications system of your grantmaking program is knowledge and creativity in keeping your directors and other corporate officials and employees posted on what you are doing. You can involve these people in the grantmaking process in many ways. For example, you might develop employee teams to determine the national corporate programs where they would like to see their "plant grants" be invested locally. The local executives in such a program certainly want to be included in the decision making—even if they only receive a list of grants and amounts before hearing what great people they are at the weekly local Kiwanis Club luncheon. Remember also that the next CEO

and other top officers of the company will not know how important
it is to invest in the community through the corporate grantmaking
operation if they are always excluded from your actions. In all prob-
ability—depending on company policy—you will find that middle
managers are very active personally in many of the agencies seeking
grants and that they can provide accurate information on what the
applicant agency is really accomplishing.

It is impossible to overstate the importance of letting a broad
spectrum of corporate employees know what the foundation is doing and impressing upon them the importance of such community
investment. Many employees are volunteering service to the agencies you support, and knowing that their corporation also believes
in the institution they are helping is a tremendous boost to their
morale.

I would like to conclude this effort by restating the basic
importance of communication at all levels.

1. Know who your in-house grantmakers really are.
2. Get to know your staff and rely on their experience and
   expertise.
3. Get to know your grantseekers.
4. Keep your grantseekers posted, by mail if you have a staff. Let
   them know they are not forgotten.
5. Remember that your grantseekers are not the enemy. This is
   not an adversarial relationship unless you make it one.
6. Establish an applications system that puts applicants all on
   the same level playing field in their proposals.
7. Remember that your "investment program" in the community may be more important than anything else the corporation
   does to seek good public relations.
8. Develop a filing or computer system that not only allows you
   to respond quickly and compassionately to grantseekers but
   also allows you to have fingertip knowledge of how, where,
   and in what areas you have invested your time, energy, and
   funds during the life of the program.
9. Exhibit a posture that you represent the will of all the people
   in your company and its corporate philosophy as responsible

philanthropists—not an image that you are giving charity to those less fortunate than yourself.

10. Remember that "good grants" make a grantmaker look good, and many of the best grants are those with the word *risk* attached.

Operations Checklist

Let me list again a possible, but by no means the only, scenario for foundation operation.

1. The proposal arrives.
2. If it is on and in the proper form (*in* is more important than *on*), a file (color-coded by year and area) is opened.
3. If the proposal is not in the format requested in your guidelines, the material should either be returned in its entirety—with reasons for such action—or a file should be created and a card sent to the grantseeker should specify what additional information is needed before the staff can move the proposal forward.
4. A card acknowledging receipt of the proposal should be sent to every grantseeker. The card may specify when the staff plans to seek action from the board of directors or trustees.
5. Be sure the file indicates the date on which the receipt card was mailed and the dates of any other correspondence. This information will be very helpful if documents are lost at the applying agency.
6. The new files should be assigned to a staff member and placed in a pending proposals file. Arranging this file by date of proposed board presentation can be helpful.
7. Establish dates for site visits to all grantseekers. You should be able to learn more in a thirty-minute visit to an agency than you will ever garner from the slickest proposal.
8. Answer all telephone calls as quickly as possible, and your reputation as an accessible grantmaker will be your best public relations tool when you have to reject a proposal.
9. Prepare a brief personal letter for use in telling a grantseeker that the foundation's directors have not awarded them a grant.

Get this response out as quickly as possible so that grantseekers are able to pursue other funding sources.

Checklists supposedly let you know how to perform at top level in whatever field of endeavor they apply to. But they also indicate all of the levels at which something can or may go awry.

Earlier I suggested that the best part of this job of grantmaking was the ability to learn by doing and particularly by taking risks. I cannot reinforce these appeals too strongly. You have just "lucked into" the best job the company can offer you—enjoy it!

Chapter Fifteen

Legal Standards
for Corporate Foundations
and Contributions Programs

John A. Edie

The ability of a private American citizen to obtain an income tax deduction for a charitable contribution dates back to 1917. Similar corporate income tax deductions were first permitted in 1935. This long tradition of encouraging private, nongovernmental charitable initiative is not unique to the United States, but the incentives here are the most generous in the world.

To prevent misuse of this tax deduction system, Congress has set forth certain limitations and requirements that must be followed. The Internal Revenue Service (IRS) and the local attorney general in most states oversee these rules and prevent abuses. Perhaps the most basic limitation in the law is that charitable deductions can only be obtained for gifts or contributions for charitable purposes. The question then arises, What is a charitable purpose?

Definition of Charitable Activities

The variety of activities that fall under the term *charitable* is constantly evolving. However, the term has been liberally interpreted and is not limited simply to assisting the poor. Generally, activities that promote health, education, science, culture, art, the enhancement of knowledge, the environment, religion, human values, social welfare, and human rights all fall under the broad definition of charitable activities.

As one mechanism for ensuring that deductible contributions are used for charitable purposes, the law requires that each contribution be given to organizations that the IRS has verified as charitable. Contributions to individuals, no matter how charitable the purpose, cannot be claimed as charitable tax deductions.

The tax code lists many types of organizations that are exempt from income tax (Section 501), but the vast majority of these organizations do not have charity as their primary purpose (labor unions, trade associations, and chambers of commerce, for example). Section 501(c)(3) is the primary section of the tax code that classifies charitable organizations. Every nonprofit organization wishing to raise funds will want to tell prospective donors that their gifts can be claimed as charitable deductions. With a few minor exceptions, an organization cannot make this claim unless it has a letter from the IRS stating that it satisfies the requirements of Section 501(c)(3). To qualify as charitable this section states that an organization must be "organized and operated exclusively for religious, charitable, scientific, testing for public safety, literary, or educational purposes." Examples of Section 501(c)(3) organizations are: churches, schools, nonprofit hospitals, private foundations, community foundations, corporate foundations, museums, symphonies, operas, United Ways, environmental organizations, and many more.

This same section of the code specifically restricts the charitable organization from performing certain types of activity. First, it strictly forbids the organization from privately enriching any person or shareholder. Although reasonable compensation and expenses can be paid for services necessary to accomplish charitable goals, such payments cannot be excessive. (Jim and Tammy Bakker's PTL Club lost its Section 501(c)(3) status because of excessive enrichment.) Second, none of the assets or funds of a charitable organization can be used in election campaigns to support candidates. And third, no substantial part of the budget of a charity can be used for attempts to influence legislation (lobbying).

So long as an organization applies for 501(c)(3) within fifteen months of the date of its creation, the status as charitable will be retroactive. Thereafter, depending on its size, the organization will be required to file an annual tax return with the IRS and, from time to time, the IRS will audit the activities of the charity to ensure compliance.

An often-repeated truism is that corporations or their foundations can give only to Section 501(c)(3) organizations. An important exception to this rule is a gift or grant given to a governmental entity. Units of government (city councils, school boards, high schools, county fire departments) are not required to obtain Section 501(c)(3) status, yet corporations and company foundations may make grants to such units and obtain a charitable deduction so long as the funds will be used for a charitable purpose. Not all activities of government would fall under the broad umbrella of the term *charitable*. Manufacturing machine guns and B-1 bombers, for example, would hardly qualify; nor would most governmental activities to promote business. For example, a for-profit company that owned a major theme park could not obtain a charitable deduction for a grant to the city for a tourism campaign that prominently advertised the park. Therefore, in making grants to governmental units, corporations need to specify clearly the charitable uses to which the funds are to be put. Grants for charitable purposes to certain veterans organizations and nonprofit cemetery companies are also deductible, even though these organizations are not exempt under Section 501(c)(3).

Limits on Contributions

What limitations are there on how much a corporation may deduct as a charitable contribution? In general, a corporation may deduct as charitable contributions in any given tax year up to 10 percent of its taxable income. For the vast majority of American corporations, this limit is not a realistic limit since it is extremely rare for any company to reach the 10 percent level. Generally speaking, the national average for corporate giving is around 1 percent annually. If, however, under unusual circumstances, gifts adding up to more than 10 percent are contemplated, the corporation may carry over the excess and deduct it in future years, for up to five years (*Corporate Contributions 1989 Data*, 1990).

Assuming the corporation stays within this 10 percent limit, is all of a contribution deductible? The amount deductible depends on the type of gift and to whom it is given. Gifts of cash are simple; they are always 100 percent deductible within the 10 percent limit. Gifts of appreciated property (stocks, bonds, land) can be more complicated, however. Gifts of appreciated property to public charities are generally deductible at their full market value. Except for gifts of publicly traded stock, however, such gifts (such as land or privately held stock) must meet specific and detailed reporting requirements as to their true valuation. An approved appraisal is required by the IRS for each such gift.

As will be explained in the next section, private foundations must follow a stricter set of rules than other Section 501(c)(3) charities. One difference in their treatment is the deductibility of gifts of appreciated property. Therefore, when a corporation is considering a gift of appreciated property to its private company foundation (or to another private foundation), it must proceed with caution.

Within the 10 percent limit, gifts of appreciated property from the corporation to the company foundation are fully deductible so long as the property is publicly traded stock. Other types of property gifts are limited in deductibility to their cost (or basis). For example, a gift of publicly traded stock originally purchased for $10,000 and now worth $110,000 may be deducted at the full fair market value. However, if the property were land, the deduction would be limited to the cost, or only $10,000. Gifts of products made by the corporation (known as gifts of inventory) are sometimes deductible depending on the product and who will use it. Rules for these deductions are complicated and technical and will require careful examination by corporate legal counsel before a company proceeds.

Direct Corporate Giving Program
Versus a Company Foundation

Hundreds of companies have established private foundations through which they channel the bulk of their charitable giving. The establishment of a company foundation often signifies to the public at large a company's serious intent to become a helpful contributor to the community. Unlike most private foundations created by wealthy persons or families, company foundations usually have very small or negligible endowments. Instead, they act as "pass-through" foundations, wherein corporate profits are annually channeled through the foundation. However, approximately ninety companies have endowed their foundations with amounts in excess of $10 million (a few are endowned with over $100 million) (*The Foundation Directory*, 1989).

Just what is a company foundation? Technically, it is a separate legal entity organized under state law either as a nonprofit corporation or as a charitable trust. It has its own separate board of directors or board of trustees, although members of the board are usually directors or employees of the company. Once formed at the state level, the company foundation makes formal application to the Internal Revenue Service (Form 1023) for recognition as a Section 501(c)(3) charitable entity that is also a private foundation. Once this status is approved, the foundation will be exempt from federal income taxes and contributions to it will be deductible as charitable contributions within the limits noted earlier.

Corporations without company foundations normally give their contributions directly to the charitable grantees. Under such a direct giving arrangement, the corporation usually establishes the giving program as a staff function located in an appropriate office such as public affairs or community relations. Occasionally, the company will appoint senior officers or other key employees to a committee that will choose the grantees for a given year.

As noted earlier, all private foundations must follow a stricter set of rules than those set for public charities. These tougher restrictions are the price of being private, of having all of a foundation's resources coming from one source (one person, one family, or one corporation). Faced with abuses uncovered by congressional investigations in the 1960s, Congress determined that private foundations should be more closely regulated. The Tax Reform Act of 1969 set out a number of new restrictions under which all private foundations must operate. Attached to many of these rules are penalties that can be imposed on the foundation and occasionally on the foundation manager personally.

Briefly, six new limitations are now in place. First, each private foundation must pay a 2 percent excise tax on net investment income (dividends and interest from any endowment). The tax can be reduced to 1 percent if certain tests are met. Second, there can be no self-dealing; the assets of the foundation may not be used to benefit any disqualified persons (members of the board, employees, and substantial contributors to the foundation, naturally including the company providing all the funding to its foundation). Third, the foundation must distribute the equivalent of 5 percent of its net assets each year as a charitable payout. Fourth, the foundation may not hold a controlling interest (usually 20 percent) in any business. Fifth, the foundation may not make any risky investments that jeopardize its ability to carry out its exempt purpose. And sixth, certain types of expenditures, such as for lobbying, electioneering or political campaigns, and noncharitable purposes are subject to penalty. Other expenditures (grants to individuals such as scholarships, voter registration, and grants to organizations that are not charities), while not prohibited, will incur a tax unless specific guidelines and regulations are followed.

Advantages of Foundations. Given all these additional restrictions, what advantages does a corporation receive from establishing a company foundation? To begin with, several of these rules just come into play for company foundations. Since the majority have very small endowments, the amount of investment income is minimal, and the 2 percent (or 1 percent) tax is insignificant. Also, the minimum 5 percent payout requirement is essentially irrelevant since 5 percent of endowment assets is a figure much smaller than the total amount of pretax profits flowing into the company foundation each year and then flowing out as grants.

A company gains several advantages by establishing a foundation. The process of forming a company foundation can serve as a valuable aid in clarifying and defining the goals and objectives of the company's charitable giving program. Once established, the foundation can serve as a buffer between the chief executive officer and grantseekers; the foundation officer can explain that the company has a foundation and that all contributions must go through the established procedures. Perhaps the most attractive feature of a company foundation is its ability to serve as a holding tank (or reserve) for funds to assist the company in evening out its annual grant levels. Most companies make annual contributions to many of the same charities. When the company makes less profit than usual, it would prefer not to cut back on its normal level of charitable support. Annual giving levels can be maintained by building up the reserve in profitable years and dipping into the endowment in low-profit years.

Direct corporate giving programs are not permitted a charitable deduction when making contributions to non-U.S. charities. However, grants from company foundations to foreign charities are permissible as long as specific rules are followed closely. Thus, the company can obtain a deduction for funds contributed to its foundation, and the foundation can make gifts overseas.

Corporations without foundations cannot make contributions to noncharities and obtain a charitable deduction. However, so long as specific procedures are followed, a company foundation can make such a grant. The procedure is called *exercising expenditure responsibility*, and it has four parts: (1) conduct a pre-grant inquiry of the grantee, (2) enter into a written agreement specifying how the funds are to be used and limiting them to charitable purposes, (3) obtain regular written reports on the status of the grants from the grantee, and (4) indicate on the foundation tax return that an expenditure responsibility grant has been made and describe its current status. Two examples of grants to noncharities in which expenditure responsibility might come into play are: a grant to the local chamber of commerce to assist in their program to train hard-core unemployed and a grant to a for-profit opinion survey company to assess the public's perception of the availability of health care services.

In this day of mergers and acquisitions, the existence of a company foundation may provide permanence in the company's giving program, especially if the foundation has built up an endowment. As a separate legal entity with a defined governance structure, a foundation may survive various corporate restructurings, particularly if its assets are not included as part of the parent company's assets.

A company foundation also has the potential to provide significant tax savings to the parent company, especially when the company wishes to sell appreciated property. By treating the company foundation as a conduit or pass-through foundation for a particular tax year, the company can avoid capital gains taxes and obtain a full charitable deduction even though the property involved is not publicly traded stock. For example, if a company wished to sell a piece of land worth $1.1 million that it purchased for $100,000, it would be facing a capital gains tax of up to 34 percent on the $1 million gain. By not selling the land, it could save $340,000 in capital gains tax. Instead, by giving it to the company foundation, it could obtain a $1.1 million deduction from its taxable income, thereby saving another possible $374,000 in income tax. As noted earlier, however, a corporation making a gift of appreciated property (other than publicly traded stock) may only deduct the cost (or basis) of the property ($100,000 in the example). But, by treating the company foundation as a pass-through foundation, the full $1.1 million may be deducted. To satisfy the rules for a pass-through foundation, all gifts and income of the foundation must pass through the foundation and out as "qualifying distributions" within two-and-one-half months after the tax year in which the gift was received. In the example given, the normal procedure would be for the company foundation to sell the land shortly after receiving it then to use the proceeds to make grants to eligible donees within the time limit required.

Disadvantages of Foundations. What disadvantages are there to establishing a company foundation? Without question, a foundation requires additional administrative time and paperwork. Depending on the complexity of the grantmaking program, this additional administrative work may be minimal and may be easily provided by other corporate departments (corporate counsel, accounting). Yet a complicated tax return must be filed each year and sufficient staff must become well educated on the legal requirements of private foundations to avoid pitfalls and potential penalties to the foundation and to corporate officials.

Violations of the self-dealing rules are often the most difficult to avoid for a company foundation. Once funds are given by the parent company to the company foundation, the money may not be used to provide any private benefit to the corporation or to its key employees. For example, in thanks for a grant, the local symphony might provide the foundation with free tickets. If these tickets were made available to top officials of the company, the foundation may have violated the self-dealing rules. Each company foundation manager needs to be keenly aware of grants that might result in tangible benefits (for example, tickets for events, free dinner and entertainment at a fund-raising gala) to the corporation. Generally, if the benefit received has an intangible value (name of company or foundation in the program or the company name on a building or plaque), then self-dealing does not occur. However, if the benefit received is tangible and has a distinct economic value, self-dealing is likely.

Some of the most experienced corporate grantmakers maintain both a company foundation and a direct corporate giving program. Most grants flow through the foundation, but potentially troublesome grants for the foundation are made directly. For example, purchasing a table at a major fund-raising gala would be done through the direct giving program to avoid any possible self-dealing problems.

Other Legal Issues

In addition to the basic legal issues noted above, corporate grantmakers should keep in mind a number of more specific concerns. The rules for each of these issues can become complex, and no attempt is made here to be comprehensive. But the reader should be familiar with the basic issues and seek expert guidance when needed.

When making grants through a corporate grantmaking program, what kind of documentation is required, and how long must it be kept? As noted earlier, a company can only claim a charitable deduction for gifts to certain organizations, and those organizations must have 501(c)(3) status or be a governmental unit. During an IRS audit, the burden will be on the company to demonstrate that all claimed deductions qualify.

The Internal Revenue Service publishes the *Cumulative List of Organizations* described in Section 107(c) of the Internal Revenue Code of 1986. This document, also known as *Publication 78,* is reissued annually by the IRS and is supplemented quarterly. It contains a list of all organizations that the IRS has ruled to be eligible for charitable contributions, but it does not contain local affiliates of large national organizations (like the Red Cross) that obtain their tax status under a national "umbrella" ruling. The list also is prone to errors and does not include the names of organizations that have recently lost their eligibility for deductible contributions. These names are published from time to time in the *Internal Revenue Bulletin.* In light of the inherent problems with *Publication 78,* it should only be used as a convenient starting point or reference guide. Obtaining a copy of the IRS tax determination letter of each grantee and keeping it on file is clearly the better solution.

The tax return of a company foundation must include specific information for each grant made: name and address of grantee, amount of grant, and purpose of grant. Obviously, more complicated grants such as those made to overseas charities or in which expenditure responsibility is required will demand more documentation. Obtaining the tax determination letter from the grantees of company foundations is also sound practice. The IRS normally examines documents only from the previous three years in its audits, so retaining documentation for that time period is essential. However, to be safe, most foundations save documents for six or seven years.

The use of fiscal agents should be avoided. Many people in the world of charities believe that when gifts by donors or grants by foundations cannot be made directly, they can simply be laundered through a fiscal agent. For example, when a charitable organization does not yet have its tax determination letter, the company foundation might wish to give the grant to a local united fund or church and direct it to make the grant. Similary, grants from direct corporate giving programs to non-U.S. charities are not eligible for deductions so might be funneled through an intermediary charity. Unfortunately, IRS rules clearly state that these types of grants from donor to intermediary grantee to secondary grantee are, in fact, grants directly to the secondary grantee if they are earmarked. *Earmarking* is defined to mean subject to any written or oral agreement whereby the intermediary grantee lacks control and discretion over where the funds are to go.

Under a direct giving program, when gifts or grants result in economic benefits coming back to the corporation, care must be taken not to claim too great a deduction. The general rule is that the corporation may only deduct that part of a contribution that exceeds the fair market value of any tangible benefit received in return. In effect, only the "gift" part of the contribution is deductible. For example, the purchase of a $500 plate for a gala fund raiser is worth only a $400 deduction if the value of the food, drink, free parking, and entertainment is $100.

Company foundations need to exercise particular care in attempts to set up a company scholarship program through the foundation. The Internal Revenue Service may question whether or not the scholarship program (for which the company is obtaining a charitable deduction by funding it through the foundation) is not really a disguised additional fringe benefit for employees. The rules and limitations here are complex, but several companies have established such programs through their foundations. Scholarship grants in any one year may not exceed 10 percent of the number of eligible children of employees who actually applied or 25 percent of the number of employee's children who were eligible to apply. Technical assistance in managing corporate scholarship programs is essential.

As noted earlier, making grants to overseas charities cannot result in a charitable deduction unless the company arranges for the grant through its company foundation. Foreign charities are rarely registered with the Internal Revenue Service, and the company foundation must take extra precautions to see that the funds are used for charitable purposes. If the potential foreign grantee is not willing to obtain charitable tax status with the IRS, the company foundation has two possible approaches. It may exercise expenditure responsibility, as explained previously, or it may obtain a written opinion from the grantee's lawyer or its own lawyer that advises the foundation that the grantee would be the equivalent of a U.S.

charity if it had been established here. Obviously, the specifics of such a procedure call for careful review.

In summary, when first becoming involved in a corporate charitable giving program, it is essential for any corporate grant-maker to be well grounded in the basic legal requirements for corporate grantmaking. This basic knowledge is important whether the corporation has a direct giving program, a company foundation, or both. Yet, despite the complexities one can encounter, flexibility and varied options are available for creative grantmaking.

References

Corporate Contributions 1989 Data. New York: Conference Board, 1990.
The Foundation Directory. (12 ed.) New York: Foundation Center, 1989.

Chapter Sixteen

What Grantmakers Should Know About Today's Grantseekers

Jon Pratt

This chapter is intended to offer some insights into the role and mission of nonprofits in the United States and to suggest ideas for developing good working relationships between corporate grantmakers and nonprofit grantseekers. Because the nonprofit sector differs in several important respects from the business world, corporate grantmakers need background information to be able to fairly evaluate and to understand specific organizations.

Distinguishing Characteristics of Nonprofits

Nonprofit organizations are well accepted as a factor in the economic, social, and political life of the United States, based on their number, budgets, employees, participants, and history. The 970,000 nonprofit organizations in the United States now represent 5 percent of the U.S. gross national product, and their 7.4 million employees represent 7 percent of the work force. Between 1972 and

1982, nonprofits accounted for 13 percent of new job growth (Rudney and Weitzman, 1984).

Three important points are central to understanding nonprofits. First, when nonprofits provide services, they often act in ways that are qualitatively different from for-profit or government service providers active in the same area. Second, nonprofit groups play an important societal role in strengthening democracy. Third, the autonomy and flexibility of the nonprofit model are essential to the achievements of the nonprofit sector.

Given the size and history of the nonprofit sector, one would assume that the differences in service effectiveness between nonprofits, for-profits, and government would be well documented, but they are not. However, studies have shown the following:

- Nonprofit child-care centers tend to be of higher quality than for-profit child-care centers (Wittbrook, 1989, p. 18)
- Nonprofit nursing homes use fewer sedatives than for-profit nursing homes (Weisbrod, 1988)
- Nonprofit vocational training has lower loan default rates than for-profit vocational training (U.S. Department of Education, 1983).
- Nonprofit housing suffers fewer tenant-caused damages than private or government rental housing (Morse, 1990).
- Clients of nonprofit service agencies often report that they feel better treated than clients of governmental agencies.

In each of these cases the relationship between the nonprofit service provider and the individuals served showed high levels of trust, service quality, and responsibility. This flexibility, effectiveness, and high level of public confidence in nonprofits has inclined units of local government to increase their use of nonprofits as the vendor of choice when contracting out service provision.

Although nonprofit groups provide many valuable services and are generally efficient and effective service providers, the essence of the nonprofit sector is not simply service provision. Every service delivered by a nonprofit could be delivered by a private enterprise. A key explanation of the existence of nonprofits is their role as independent centers of initiative and criticism.

Robert Johnson makes this point in *The First Charity* (1988), in which he focuses on community organizations as important tools in making democracy work and describes in detail nonprofit organizations in Baltimore, Denver, and Chicago.

The First Charity sets out five reasons why people favor democratic governance: (1) protection from tyranny, (2) reconciliation of private individual concerns with public community concerns, (3) invigoration of the individual citizen, (4) inclusion of everyone in public life, and (5) maintenance of a satisfying representative government. Based on these assumptions, an effective nonprofit is not simply one that has a positive cash flow but rather one that has an inclusive, diverse community board; collaborates with others in the community; is involved in public policy issues that affect its clientele; and brings people together and invigorates the community.

It is worth noting that in the Soviet and East European reform movements of 1989, one of the first outcomes of democratic reform was the creation of new nongovernmental organizations. These organizations may well be in the best position to lessen the public conflict and casualties between the retreating state authority and the emerging market economy. The worldwide development and democratic role of voluntary associations were predicted by Alexis de Tocqueville (1988 [1830]) in *Democracy in America*: "Associations must multiply as quickly as conditions become equal."

This democratic role of nonprofits is underscored by some of the most important contributions nonprofit groups make to this country: influencing policy (abolition, environmental laws), increasing participation (universal suffrage, voter registration drives), representing minority interests (National Association for the Advancement of Colored People, National Federation of the Blind), furthering social innovation (child-care centers, battered women's shelters), and promoting public debate (Common Cause, League of Women Voters). This public role is encouraged under the IRS code, in which charitable organizations are given considerable latitude to communicate with government and influence legislation. Up to 20 percent of the first $500,000 of an organizations' expenditures can be used for lobbying, 15 percent of the next $500,000 can be used, and declining percentages of the remaining portion of expenditures. Although private foundations (including corporate foundations) cannot earmark a grant for lobbying purposes, they are free to make grants to organizations that use other funds for legislative activity.

The Nonprofit Economy

A common misconception among the general public is that most of nonprofit groups' income is donated. This mistaken impression is reinforced by the frequently quoted statistic that 90 percent of charitable contributions come from individuals (AAFRC Trust for Philanthropy, 1989). While technically correct, this figure does not help a grantmaker understand the organizations that seek grants. Most individual contributions go to religious organizations, not to arts, human services, or educational organizations. Turning the issue around presents a fuller picture of the nonprofit economy: Where do nonprofit grantseekers get their funds?

Table 16.1 shows the income sources for the overall nonprofit sector, excluding colleges, nursing homes, and hospitals. (These institutions are important but disproportionately large and fee based, skewing the results for an examination of typical grantseekers.) Even excluding these large fee-based institutions, most nonprofit income is from governmental sources and fees. Charitable donations supply only a quarter of nonprofit income, with individual contributions accounting for only 6.4 percent—a far cry from 90 percent.

The mixture of income types within this economy varies based on organizational size, activity area, and geographic location. The highest degree of reliance on corporate contributions is among organizations with budgets between $50,000 and $500,000, arts organizations, and organizations in large urban areas (Leherman and Salamon, 1982).

Grantmakers naturally want to know what impact a grant will have and what the other sources of funding will be for a project. Put another way, the question is, Without this grant, what would happen? Within the nonprofit economy, it is possible to identify areas where a given grant is a more significant portion of a nonprofit agency's budget, and arguably makes a bigger difference.

Exhibit 16.1. Funding Sources of U.S. Nonprofit Organizations.

Funding Source		Percentage of Total Funding Base
Government		38.4
Fees, Dues, and Charges		29.6
Private Giving		21.3
Individual Contributions	6.4	
United Way	5.4	
Other Federated Drives	1.5	
Corporate Contributions	3.2	
Foundation Grants	3.5	
Religious Organizations	1.3	
Endowment and Investment		4.6
Other (includes sources of income such as sale of products, special fundraising events, rental of facilities, etc.)		5.7
Unspecified		0.4
Total		100.0

Source: Leherman and Salamon, 1982.

Employment in the Nonprofit Workplace

The commitment of nonprofit employees is a major strength and distinguishing characteristic of the nonprofit sector. Management consultant Peter Drucker lauds nonprofit staffs for their loyalty, imagination, ethical behavior, and ability to be driven passionately by the dictates of their heart (Peterson, 1987). Nonprofit employees' relationship to their work differs from that of for-profit employees in several respects: Self-selection has attracted a group of people who tend to relate personally to the mission of their organizations. They have increased expectations of flexibility and participation in decision making, and they work in smaller workplaces.

Nonprofit employees generally report greater overall job satisfaction than business employees, except with regard to compensation. Many nonprofit employees are motivated to find intrinsic rewards and seek a flexible work environment where the content of the work is important. A survey of Minnesota nonprofit employees found high levels of satisfaction in most areas, with particularly high responses to three items: the chance to do different things from time to time, the chance to do things for other people, and being able to do things that do not go against the employee's conscience (Pratt and Davies, 1990).

Compensation for nonprofit employees overall is approximately 20 percent less than for government employees and 25 percent less than business employees, though the gap is gradually narrowing. One factor in low compensation is gender—as in the teaching profession and now corporate contributions positions, two-thirds of nonprofit employees are female. To varying degrees, women work in the nonprofit sector because of exclusion from other professions and attraction to the public service nature and supportive work environment of nonprofits. In a sense there is a trade-off for the nonprofit employee—the potential for greater job satisfaction and autonomy, but less pay.

The nonprofit employer also experiences a trade-off: reduced management prerogatives because of employee participation in decision making, balanced by a highly motivated and committed work force. Although relationships between nonprofit management and employees may appear convoluted to someone from business, they are supported by the lesson of industrial psychology: Satisfied employees are more productive than dissatisfied employees.

Nonprofit compensation patterns also differ in that they tend to exhibit less steep gradations than is true in business so that the range between top and bottom salaries is less pronounced. Nonprofits are much less likely than government to offer comprehensive employee benefits, which may explain why employees often work in the nonprofit sector for five to fifteen years and then move to government jobs.

The appeal of the nonprofit workplace and employees' commitment to it are partly the result of less burdensome work rules and fewer external constraints. Reducing nonprofit autonomy would hurt nonprofit service quality, a point made by Mirvis and Hackett (1983):

The increased monitoring of nonprofits by funding sources and agencies, and the wholesale importation of motivational, training, incentive, and performance appraisal systems are all seen as ways to improve efficiency in . . . nonprofit organizations. But will they truly improve productivity and the quality of worklife? Standards designed to increase accountability and efficiency could also centralize authority, limit flexibility, stifle innovation, and create pressures toward achieving measured goals of work quantity at the expense of quality. Tighter controls could limit professionals' freedom and rigid measurement systems could lead administrators to demand too much from already time-pressured subordinates. Or worse, these people, dedicated as they are to their jobs, might assume a greater load but at the expense of their health and satisfaction and under a threat of loss of their livelihood.

The irony in all this is that just as the for-profit sector seems to be "loosening up," the [nonprofit sector is] "tightening up." In our view, the move to run . . . nonprofits "more like a business" needs to be carefully considered. If not, they may lose their identities and employees' motivation and satisfaction may actually suffer.

Although the largest and most visible nonprofits (colleges, hospitals, major arts institutions) may appear more similar to major corporate employers, 85 percent of nonprofit employers have less than $1 million in annual expenditures. For nonprofits with staff, the Minnesota study showed, on average, a paid full-time equivalency (FTE) staff of 11.9 persons per organization (Pratt and Davies, 1990). Part of the creativity, flexibility, and low pay of the nonprofit sector reflects this modest average staff size.

Self-Determination in Nonprofit Organizations

Since the nonprofit sector's steady growth from the 1960s, it has promoted an identity as the "independent sector" and has even inspired a national organization by the same name. Nonprofits see themselves as the initiators of change, as the challengers of the public and private sectors, and as the sector that has been willing to take risks by addressing controversial issues and providing innovative types of services. Nonprofits consider their autonomous nature one of their distinct qualities.

A major source of the independence of nonprofits is structural; by law nonprofits do not have private ownership and cannot return profits to equity partners. Instead, governance is in the hands of a board formed to uphold the organization's charitable mission. The volunteer board, made up of community members without a financial stake in the organization, is free to act in the community's best interest. Ideally this board represents the economic and cultural diversity of the community and can serve as overseer, policymaker, quality controller, and, at times, fund raiser for the organization.

Arguments for the integrity and democratic role of nonprofits are based on the assumption that these organizations are not subject to external control by government or private donors. The initiative, autonomy, and community orientation valued in the nonprofit sector are compromised when nonprofit organizations become agents acting on behalf of, and under the control of, funding sources.

Effective social movements owe some of their success to their financial self-sufficiency—being organizations that are strongly supported by their constituents, that retain their autonomy, and that can focus on their mission. One of the basic tenets of Alcoholics Anonymous, whose premise is that people need to take responsibility for their own life, is that the organization must be self-supported—and so it does not seek or accept outside contributions.

The simple solution of total financial self-sufficiency, based on many small donors or on service fees, is out of the question for most organizations.* Balancing the financial needs of an organization with the interests of government and private donors presents constant challenges to a nonprofit's concept of autonomy. The notion of nonprofits as an independent sector presupposes that all elements of society view nonprofits in the same way that nonprofits view themselves. The vulnerability of nonprofit autonomy is especially evident in funding relationships.

The Grantmaker-Grantseeker Relationship

Most nonprofits regularly spend 8–20 percent of their budgets on fund raising, more if they are dependent on direct mail fund raising.

---

*This treatment of nonprofit autonomy grew out of discussions between the author and two members of Minnesota Council on Nonprofits' research committee, Frederick W. Smith and R. Aburto.

Like marketing costs for business, nonprofit fund raising requires substantial expenditures to take a charitable case to the public and potential donors, including corporate grantmakers. These costs include direct mail postage, salaries, office equipment, office space, and so on. Standards for charitable organizations adopted by the National Charities Information Bureau include the requirement that no more than 30 percent of an organization's expenditures be used for fund raising and administration.

Fund raising is an important element of public accountability, but it has the potential to give major donors undue influence over an organization's priorities. A nonprofit group's main purpose is to fulfill its charitable mission. The cold reality of nonprofit existence is that nonprofits have a second imperative: the responsibility to obtain resources needed to carry out the charitable mission. What happens when there is a conflict between the two? What does a nonprofit do when money may be available for the organization but not exactly for its mission? This dilemma is one that most businesses do not face.

The nonprofit's need for funding presents a strong temptation to make pragmatic deviations from its mission. Funding pressures act as incentives for an organization to adjust its original mission to more closely match current funder preferences. At times, nonprofits are advised to recruit elite members of the community to assist in making fund-raising contacts, resulting in governing boards unrepresentative of the entire community.

The question How do we further our mission? is sometimes less compelling than What can we do to get funding? Nonprofits may trade away their autonomy for survival. Corporate giving officers actually have greater power over decisions in the organizations they fund than they do over many decisions made in their own companies. Based on the resource-driven willingness to adapt on the part of nonprofits, corporate grants undoubtedly influence nonprofit planning and service strategies.

The potential for contributions to unduly influence the actions of a grantee makes the role of a philanthropist particularly sensitive. Since the relationship between grantmaker and grantseeker tends to be unequal, honest communication between the two is difficult. Special effort is required on both sides to disregard the fact that one side has the cash. The funders of nonprofits can ask legitimate questions to determine that their funds are well spent and used for the purpose intended. Funders also have the right to decide what to support and what not to support. However, at a certain point, the funding process can shift the locus of control for key organizational decisions from the nonprofit board to the funding source.

Since nonprofits have a qualitatively different structure and social role from business corporations, they have a different responsibility when it comes to responding to market forces. The availability of a donor with money who has a project in mind does not mean that an organization should automatically accept the contribution. If the project is outside or tangential to the mission of the organization, the group should gracefully but firmly decline the contribution.

In an ideal world, every nonprofit group would have adequate funding for its authentic mission, but, realistically, every organization faces funding complications at one time or another. The difficult, ongoing challenge is for nonprofit boards and managers to successfully assert and maintain a strong focused mission and, simultaneously, get the resources necessary to carry it out. Nonprofits and their funders need to seriously discuss the trade-offs between achieving donor expectations and supporting nonprofit initiatives. It is inevitable that the grantmaking interaction brings out conflicts and different viewpoints—even opposite conclusions on the same aspect of the relationship.

Since identifying differences can be the first step in opening communication toward resolving differences, the following two lists are offered to identify conflicts between grantmakers and nonprofit grantseekers. Obviously not all of these perceptions apply to everyone, but they represent the strongest feelings on each side.

Ten Things Grantseekers Dislike

1. Corporations that are not sufficiently open to new organizations that seek corporate support.
2. Corporate giving officers who fail to take the time for meetings, site visits, or the careful review of proposals necessary to understand an organization's needs.

3. Grantmaking guidelines that lack clarity or use buzzwords whose meaning is clear only within the company so that reasonable people reading the guidelines can reach completely different conclusions about a corporation's funding interests.

4. Grantmaking staff members who are inaccessible, hard to meet with or reach by telephone, and do not return telephone calls.

5. Grantmakers who mislead organizations about the likelihood for funding, encouraging them to submit proposals or feel positive about funding requests when the actual prospect for support is slim or nonexistent.

6. Grantmakers who have quick-fix expectations. "Yes Minister," one of the wittiest British television comedies, portrayed the plight of an appointed cabinet officer manipulated by career civil servants. In one episode, the minister's chief aide described the four words to use in a memo to guarantee approval: *quick, simple, cheap,* and *popular.* The four words to use to guarantee rejection were *lengthy, complex, costly,* and *controversial.* To totally squelch a proposal, it would be described as *courageous.* Nonprofits feel buffeted by changing funding interests, with increasing emphasis on what a grant will accomplish this year.

7. Corporations that reject proposals by form letter, without giving specific reasons or an explanation of why the proposal was not funded.

8. Corporations that try to change what a nonprofit does or seek to achieve marketing or public relations goals through support of an organization. This self-serving pressure on a nonprofit presents a strong temptation for the organization to deviate from its mission. (By contrast, the number one nonprofit frustration with private foundations is their failure to provide general operating support. Corporate grantmakers have been much more willing to provide general support and tend to give many more but smaller grants than private foundations. Unfortunately, some corporations are increasing their preference for special project grantmaking.)

9. Corporations that violate their own grantmaking guidelines

or procedures, stating that they do not fund in a particular area but then making a grant in that area.

10. Grantmakers that communicate an arrogant attitude.

Ten Things Corporate Grantmakers Dislike

1. Organizations that fail to read the corporation's funding guidelines or that submit boilerplate proposals that do not address the corporation's focus areas.

2. Organizations that fail to submit agreed-upon progress and financial reports after a grant is received.

3. Grantseekers that fail to disclose major facts or changes that bear on an organization's proposal, ranging from key staff changes to funding and legal issues.

4. Grantseekers that read the grantmaker's guidelines but ask to be an exception to these rules or present a contorted argument about why their organization really should fall within the corporation's interest area. The argument presented is basically: "While our main purpose is x, here is an explanation of why what we do is actually something different, namely the thing that you want to fund," followed by a quote from the guidelines.

5. The failure of nonprofits to appreciate limitations on the corporate contributions program, including limited time, money, and staff authority.

6. Organizations that only call when they need money, that do not send thank-you letters, or that fail to take advantage of other resources available in the company (volunteers, in-kind contributions, or potential board members).

7. Grantseekers that do not accept rejection well, taking it personally and out of context.

8. Poorly organized nonprofits—lack of time-management skills, fiscal discipline, or self-sufficiency.

9. Duplication of effort—too many nonprofits.

10. Grantseekers who have a smug, self-righteous certainty that their own cause is the most important and that they act out of ideals while others act out of self-interest.

Since grantmakers and grantseekers need to work together, these differences are rarely expressed openly. The difference in the financial position of the grantseekers and the grantmakers presents an inherent inequality but does not preclude good working relationships or even partnerships.

Meetings between nonprofit groups and corporate staffs outside of the bottleneck of the grantseeking-grantmaking process can help both sides learn from the strengths of the other. Grantmakers can increase accessibility by making site visits, attending community meetings, making multiyear grants, and maintaining an adequate size staff. Reducing grantmaking staff to save administrative costs is a fool's bargain indeed.

The nonprofit sector is entering an era of change, in large part because of its growth. Nonprofits are no longer seen as well-meaning but amateurish efforts, but now appear to the public more like professional service providers, to business more like market threats, and to government both an avenue to privatize service delivery and a potential source of tax revenue.

Nonprofit organizations are vulnerable to shifts in the regulatory and donor environment and need the support and involvement of corporate grantmakers to discover their full potential. Grantseekers need to assert, and corporate supporters to respect, nonprofit autonomy as an essential ingredient of the nonprofit sector. As in other walks of life, the most effective relationships are based on respect, trust, and candor.

References

AAFRC Trust for Philanthropy. *Giving USA, 1989.* New York: AAFRC Trust for Philanthropy, 1989.

de Tocqueville, A. *Democracy in America.* J. P. Mayer, ed. (G. Lawrence, trans.) New York: Harper & Row, 1988. (Orig. published 1830.)

Johnson, R. M. *The First Charity.* Cabin Johns, Md.: Seven Looks Press, 1988.

Leherman, B., and Salamon, L. *The Twin Cities Nonprofit Sector in a Time of Government Retrenchment.* Washington, D.C.: Urban Institute, 1982.

Mirvis, P. H., and Hackett, E. J. "Work and Work Force Characteristics in the Nonprofit Sector." *Monthly Labor Review,* Apr. 1983, p. 11.

Morse, A. Conversation with author on Oct. 23, 1990. Morse works in the Consumer Insurance Cooperative Agency in Minneapolis, Minn.

Peterson, J. "The Gospel According to Drucker." Los Angeles *Times,* Nov. 9, 1987, sect. 4, p. 1.

Pratt, J., and Davies, N. *Minnesota's Nonprofit Economy.* St. Paul, Minn.: Minnesota Council of Nonprofits, 1990.

Rudney, G., and Weitzman, M. "Trends in Employment and Earnings in the Philanthropic Sector." *Monthly Labor Review,* Sept. 1984, p. 17.

U.S. Department of Education. *Status of National Direct Student Loan Defaults as of June 30, 1982.* Washington, D.C.: U.S. Department of Education, Office of Student Financial Assistance, 1983.

Weisbrod, B. A. *The Nonprofit Economy.* Cambridge, Mass.: Harvard University Press, 1988.

Wittbrook, M. *National Child Care Staffing Study.* Oakland, Calif.: Child Care Employee Project, 1989.

Chapter Seventeen

Guidelines for Selecting Organizations and Programs to Support

Robin Reiter-Faragalli

Grantmakers, whether corporate, family, or individual, want to feel that they are making a difference in the community with the organizations they fund. They want to believe that their contribution will assist in the evolution of the organization, provide services to a constituency, and meet the challenging needs of the future. Grantmakers want to believe that the organization selected to receive the contribution is on the cutting edge of greatness and that the grant will add to the success of the institution and provide a long-term benefit to the community.

So much for what grantmakers want to believe! The hard reality is that with limited, modest resources available, the most difficult part of grantmaking is selecting the organization. With so many requests to choose from, with so many opportunities available, what goes into the selection process?

Corporate giving programs used to have the luxury of individual site visits, long lunches or meetings to get to know the or-

ganization, and a passing knowledge of all of the nonprofit organizations operating in their community. Not anymore. With the restructuring of corporate America, the proliferation of mergers and
acquisitions, and the emphasis on cost-containment programs in
most corporations, corporate giving staffs have decreased in size
while nonprofit organizations have multiplied, and the number of
requests for grants has tripled. Fewer dollars are available for a
greater number of funding opportunities. The selection of those
opportunities becomes even more important when one assesses how
best to meet the changing needs of a community and how best to
face the challenges of the 1990s.

Evaluation of Funding Requests

Evaluating funding requests does not have to be a time-consuming
or costly process. It does have to be an organized one. For example,
most corporations do not respond to direct mail, or "Dear Sir/
Madam," requests. If an organization has not done its homework
nor bothered to find out to whom it is writing, its future practices
may also be slipshod. Donors want to know with whom they are
dealing and applicants want donors to know who they are. Rule
number one in fund raising ought to be, know the person you are
seeking; do not shoot in the dark.

However, every absolute rule has exceptions. On occasion, a
company may respond to Dear Sir/Madam letters. When they do,
it is because the request comes from a small grass-roots, all-
volunteer organization that is run without the benefit of paid staff.
Just because the organization is small or all-volunteer, does not
mean that it is not providing a service or serving a constituency.
Corporations have funded several of these small organizations that
have grown over the years and continue to provide a needed service
to the community.

Many giving programs have geographic constraints. As a
Florida-based corporation, the Southeast Banking Corporation
generally does not support programs outside of Florida. As a part
of the first review process, a draft rejection letter is attached to each
of the out-of-state requests prior to its reaching the director's desk
to minimize the response time. However, this letter is only a draft

and not a final decision. We read and review all requests that come in. On occasion we will support a national organization if its program has an impact on our areas of interest or if it is in support of an effort that will benefit Florida-based organizations. For example, we have funded the Council for Community-Based Development, with headquarters in Washington, D.C., because the organization is available as a resource to those interested in supporting community development programs. Southeast Bank and its foundation have a long history of involvement with community development corporations. As an institution, the bank is concerned with maintaining the integrity of its philanthropic program and keeping in step with changing trends. This type of nationally oriented organization serves not only the needs of our corporate foundation but also the needs of community development corporations in our home state as well. However, because of the modest philanthropic resources available within Florida, it is rare that we fund out-of-state requests, and we do not encourage out-of-state groups to apply to our program.

The selection process for a small business or professional association is remarkably similar to that of a large corporation. Steel Hector & Davis, a Miami-based Florida law firm, is one of the most civic-minded firms in the state. It refutes the notion that lawyers generally do not donate to public charities and nonprofit organizations. Their contributions are made through a process equal in style to most major giving programs.

According to the director of communications for Steel Hector & Davis, in 1989 the law firm donated over $750,000 worth of pro-bono legal assistance to nonprofit organizations in Florida. Their cash contributions, in addition to the legal services provided, made them a leader among professional associations involved with community efforts.

At Steel Hector & Davis, a request for funds will generally only be reviewed if one of the lawyers in the firm is personally and significantly involved with the grantseeking institution. The firm is also concerned with the track record of the organization, the group's overall budget, and who else in the community may be funding the group. The firm does not consider marketing when making a decision and tends to be conservative in regard to the types of exposure it may receive from the grantseeker. The firm is less concerned with public awareness of its involvement in the community than in being involved in public concerns.

In determining what groups to fund, your primary concern should always be twofold: Is this decision good for the community and for the company? These two issues cannot be separated without doing a disservice to both the company and the community. Companies are always asked why they contribute to community projects, but rarely are they asked why they chose to fund a specific program or project.

Before considering what organization to fund or request to support, be certain that you know what your company is concerned with and what the priorities are for community participation. Without a clear understanding of the mission of your funding program, as broad or as narrow as it may be, you will be unable to respond to questions concerning your participation or lack of participation with specific organizations.

If you want your grants program to be on the cutting edge of creativity, if your company is interested in acting as an agent for change in the community, then do not be afraid of using some of your contributions dollars as venture capital—take a risk. The risk usually pays off if you have done your homework in reviewing the request, and very few contributions are wasted. Early contributions in the fight against AIDS, either for informational brochures or research requests, were considered quite risky back in 1985. Thankfully, many funding sources ignored the risks and responded to the needs of the community and organizations that were on the cutting edge of this disease.

Usually, when corporations have made risky contributions, the rewards have far outweighed the risks for both the corporation and the community organization. If you have a selection process in place for choosing groups to fund, then you minimize your risk by following your selection process.

Involvement of Employees in Evaluation of Requests

How do you determine whether to fund an organization if your office is in one city and the requesting organization is in another?

Corporations, both large and small, are made up of individuals who are interested in the well-being of their community. Consequently, they generally have a good working knowledge of their community and what makes it work. Use their input and advice. Use their eyes and ears.

A small corporate giving staff can add dozens of employees to the part-time staff by having them do site visits and evaluations. When we receive a request from an organization with which we are unfamiliar, we immediately send a copy of the request to one of our officers in that geographic area for review. We suggest that this person visit the organization or drive by the building before visiting in order to get a sense of the surroundings. We discourage the officer from providing information, either positive or negative, based solely on "community conversation" or hearsay.

To ensure that we are successfully providing contributions to worthy organizations, especially those outside of the immediate area, we rely heavily on the advice and counsel of our officers and managers in branch locations throughout the state. Although the foundation staff is able to travel the state and spends much time visiting locations and organizations, no one can provide more accurate and insightful information during the grant review process than the individual who lives and works in a community. Consulting these individuals enhances our ability to evaluate opportunities and gives our officers a sense of ownership in the program. If you ask for staff members' advice, they will be more supportive of the expenditure of dollars from an otherwise tight corporate budget and generally more inclined to volunteer and involve themselves with nonprofit organizations. Furthermore, they will be sensitized to the important role that the corporation can play in helping to develop a community. The phrase *quality of life* begins to take on a whole new meaning for employees who may otherwise not have been involved in their community issues.

Questions to Ask Grantseekers

In examining potential grant recipients, it is important for staff and trustees to ask several questions that will enable you to learn as much as possible about an agency's operation, its delivery system, and the scope of its commitment to serving the needs of the community and its constituency. When you make a general support contribution to an organization, you are supporting the institution; you are saying in essence that the institution is worthy of the grant, and that they will know how to spend the funds judiciously.

First, you should ask an organization the scope of its operation; is it national, statewide, or local? How long has it been in business, and does it work with a network of other similar organizations or alone in the field? Does it have a multiyear planning process or does it plan year to year? If it is affiliated with a national organization, how much of the contribution will stay in your city or state and how much, if any, will be allocated to the national headquarters?

Second, what is the organization's standing in the community? Is it an important service provider, or does it duplicate an existing or better effort? What is the caliber of the agency's staff, both administrators and service providers? (The issues are the same whether you are considering a social service organization or a cultural organization. In a cultural organization, the service provider is the artistic product. Is it top quality or merely adequate? In a social service organization, the service provider is often the social worker or counselor.)

Is the staff well qualified? Is it large enough to handle the type of program under consideration? Conversely, is the staff too large for the budget of the organization? Generally when administrative expenses exceed 16 to 18 percent of the overall budget, questions should be raised as to why. If more money is going into the operation of the organization than into meeting the needs of its constituency, the organization is out of balance and your funds may be better spent elsewhere.

It is important to distinguish between the administrators, managers, and service providers of the institution in order to fully evaluate the caliber of the organization. It takes all three to make an institution great. Is there an institutional balance between management and service providers? If the organization is top heavy in administrative staff and thin in the area of service providers, who will accomplish the goals as stated in the proposal?

Third, what is the composition of the board of trustees? Does the board reflect the ethnic, geographic, and corporate diversity of the community? If it does not, the best intentions of the staff may be in vain. Are there too many lawyers, doctors, bankers, or entrepreneurs on the board? If the board is not a healthy mix of representatives, the organization will find it difficult to carry out its mission, and the program or project could be in jeopardy.

You should always ask if all of the board members make a financial or in-kind contribution to the organization. It does not matter how little or how much each individual contributes, but they must all participate. After all, if the board does not support the organization, why should the corporation?

Do board and staff members communicate well with each other? It is always telling when you are invited to a meeting that includes a member of the staff and a member of the board, and the board member responds to a statement by saying, "Oh, I didn't know we were involved in that!" If internal communications are not in place, external communications will be faulty. Conversely, if the board member and the staff member are both speaking in tandem, you are generally assured that the organization is sensitive to the need to communicate and that what has been submitted to you in writing is in fact reliable. When reviewing a request you must also ask: Who will be in charge of the project? Who will take the lead in meeting the needs of the budget? Who will evaluate the effectiveness of the effort on an ongoing basis?

Questions to Ask Yourself

The corporate perspective, in addition to the community perspective, cannot be ignored. Corporations have many masters: shareholders, employees, customers, and community perception. Community perception often creates the greatest controversy for corporations establishing grants programs and making contributions to worthy institutions. Many communities believe that corporations do not actively support worthy organizations, and that when they do, it is only for publicity. In reality, many companies who do give, give quietly.

For example, many corporate giving programs participate with the United Way in local communities. Yet the United Way generally does not single out any one corporation or business for recognition. A company that supports the United Way does so to address the social service delivery system in the community, not to be congratulated for its effort. When selecting the United Way as a potential recipient of corporate contributions, a company makes a conscious effort to participate in a joint venture for the benefit of the community and not for the sole benefit of the corporation. This effort reflects the question raised earlier: Is this contribution good for the community and for the corporation?

Since the Southeast Banking Corporation Foundation made its first contribution in 1981, we have maintained the position that our contributions are an investment in the community. They are not giveaways. Just as the bank seeks investments that will pay dividends to our investors, so too does the foundation seek to make contributions that will reap dividends for the communities in which we do business.

Questions that most corporations must ask themselves include: How does our involvement with this group position us within the community? Have we been creative with our contribution, maximizing its effectiveness? Have we examined alternative avenues of support for the organization that may be more effective than a cash contribution? Does this grant have an impact on our employees or customers? Does it make a difference in the communities in which we do business?

The Steel Hector & Davis model, one that many smaller businesses and professional associations adhere to, is effective in recruiting new employees for the firm. The most valuable thing that a professional association has to offer is the service its professionals provide. If the lawyer, accountant, or architect is actively involved in a group, the nature of the involvement tends to bring others from the firm along for the experience. The group is then more likely to provide a cash contribution when the request is brought up for discussion.

Equally important is the question, Are others involved with this program or will we be the first? Many corporations are nervous about being number one when it comes to making a contribution to a nonprofit organization. They tend to wonder why others have not participated before. The Southeast Banking Foundation has never been shy about providing either the first dollars to an effort or committing, as a challenge, the last dollars to an effort. As a bank, we are used to starting with the number one, and the contributions program has been no different. The foundation looks at some of its grants funds as venture capital that can be risked.

The Ryder System Charitable Foundation, an extension of the Miami-based Ryder System trucking and transportation firm, has a similar philosophy. The Ryder System Foundation has a reputation for being involved in innovative leadership grants in the five cities nationwide where they support organizations. Ryder System is less concerned with following the crowd than with addressing new issues and facing challenges. The Ryder System Foundation has four primary focus areas in which it participates and rarely funds programs or projects outside of those areas. However, Ryder has established areas that provide a wide range of possibilities and do not limit the corporation's participation in community initiatives.

When your company agrees to provide seed money to a new effort, it is important to ask the organization how it is going to raise the rest of the funds and how it is going to carry on the project after the funding has expired. No one wants to commit funds to a program that has no hope for the future, unless of course it is a one-time-only effort. Remember my admonition about absolutes!

A small corporation is less likely to provide seed money because they do not feel that their limited resources will be enough to initiate a project. However, professional associations such as Steel Hector & Davis are in a good position to provide important start-up services as an in-kind contribution. Substituting services for cash at a crucial juncture can save an institution from many extraneous expenses in the long run. If you provide in-kind contributions, the selection process and the questions asked for nonprofit groups given earlier are still relevant. Steel Hector & Davis asks these questions prior to the grant request stage because they already have a partner or associate involved with the organization. There are generally no surprises when you target organizations that have a member of the firm on the committee or the board. However, with a large corporation, one that responds to requests to organizations whether there is employee involvement or not, the answers to these questions may mean the difference between a successful grant and failure. If the answers to your questions are unsatisfactory, then think twice about supporting the effort. The answer to these questions should have been explored by the organization long before it approached your company for a contribution.

Remember, it is not your money being used for grants, unless, of course, it is your own company and you use the company as a means of making all contributions, personal or professional. In most cases, however, the funds set aside for contributions belong to the company, the shareholders, the employees, and, in some cases, the public. This makes the selection process an important task.

If the public believes that the person in charge of the contributions program is using the position or the funds for self-aggrandizement or if there is even an appearance of conflict of interest in how the funds are used, the selection process and, indeed, the program itself are at risk. The selection process ensures the integrity of the program. And the integrity of the program ensures the long-term commitment of corporate involvement in the community.

If the selection process is open and accessible to community organizations, most will understand when they are denied contributions. Most will also understand that when they receive contributions, they will not necessarily receive funds in the future. It was simply the right combination of ingredients at the right time, meeting the available resources.

Once the selection has been made, the natural question, especially in a large corporation, is, Who gives the check? Small giving programs that draw on the expertise of officers and employees out in the field during the selection process, can have that individual or another more appropriate person in the region make the actual contribution. It is important for a statewide, centralized corporation to maintain a local geographic identity with the community in which its branch offices are located. By having employees in the area make the contribution to the local organization, the selection process has come full circle, the institution is identified as a part of the local community.

It will be the selection process that sets the standard for the rest of your program. With a process firmly in place, with the built-in flexibility to maneuver with changing times and trends, you will have provided a healthy guide to both community-based organizations and your corporate employees as well.

Chapter Eighteen

How to Manage
Gift-Matching Programs

Earl L. Gadbery
Helen L. Adamasko

Gift-matching programs provide an incentive for employees and retirees of a company to make donations to programs and organizations of their choosing. Some corporate foundations find it appropriate to match donations in several, or even all, of their categories of support. These could include a wide range of activities such as those devoted to health and welfare improvement; cultural enhancement; civic and community development; and support of youth programs, public radio and television work, and even volunteering efforts. Foundations contemplating broad gift-matching programs should consider quite carefully which activities will most effectively promote the use of their funds in conjunction with their grantmaking goals.

Alcoa's Gift-Matching Program

Alcoa Foundation elected, many years ago, to award matching grants solely in support of education. Since it was founded in 1952, the foundation has been committed first and foremost to supporting educational activities and programs. Educational gift matching has grown to be a highly successful component of that commitment.

Through the Alcoa Foundation Educational Gift Matching Program, Alcoa employees and retirees can help to meet the educational needs of particular communities. Many of them are communities in which Alcoa has plants or offices. The program represents a commitment between the corporation and these communities to improve educational opportunities and also heightens corporate visibility in a positive and useful way.

The foundation's educational gift matching also enables the participants to take ownership, or become direct decision makers, on how corporate funds should be spent. For this reason, foundations in general must be extremely sensitive to how far they wish to extend the gift-matching option. When a foundation broadens gift matching to include many areas of interest, it risks losing some of its discretionary control over where and how its dollars will be spent. In some cases, foundations have found that over 40 percent of their total budget is being directed to gift-matching obligations, which in turn means that a major part of their decision-making responsibility is removed from their direct control (*Matching Gift Notes*, 1989).

Employees could possibly make donations to institutions or programs that embarrass or cause concern to a foundation obligated to match such gifts. The effectiveness and integrity of the many noneducational organizations that become recipients of foundation funds is often quite difficult to determine, particularly if, unlike in the educational area, there are no accrediting agencies or other resources providing meaningful background information on the groups.

At Alcoa Foundation, we feel that matching gifts to accredited educational institutions is a very effective use of foundation funds. In fact, we double-match donations for education.

In 1988, the total number of donors who participated in Alcoa Foundation's gift-matching program was 1,870. Their contributions, made to 519 educational institutions, totaled $646,704; we contributed an additional $1,204,338. So the dollar amounts involved are substantial. We have had an average of 200 new donors annually. The largest number of gifts fall in the $25 to $50 range. However, the average gift is $228. During 1988, matching gifts were 11.2 percent of total grants paid.

A special mention should be made about Alcoa retirees. They have been a constant, very supportive group of participants in our gift-matching program over the years. They made up 41 percent of the total number of donors in 1988.

Procedure. The procedure for donors is not complicated. The donor makes a personal gift to an eligible college or university, and the foundation double-matches it, so long as the amount ranges from a minimum of $25 to a maximum total per donor of $5,000 in a calendar year. Thus, if a donor gives $100 to an eligible school, the foundation gives an additional $200. And the donor need not be an alumnus or have even attended the school.

However, the gift must be paid—not merely pledged—to an eligible school. It must be in the form of a check or marketable securities. Outright gifts of securities are valued at the closing market price on the date of the gift. Other types of gifts that are eligible for matching include real estate, bequests, and life income plans—such as a pooled income fund, charitable remainder annuity trust, and charitable remainder unitrust.

All institutions receiving donations intended for double-matching by us must be degree-granting colleges, unversities, or, two-year institutions that are fully accredited by a recognized regional or professional accrediting agency. And they must be recognized as tax exempt by the Internal Revenue Service. Alumni funds or foundations that exist for charitable purposes may also qualify for matching gifts if they are an integral part of an eligible school.

On the other hand, separately incorporated fund-raising entities such as athletic funds, booster clubs, sororities, and fraternities do not qualify. Other types of gifts that are ineligible for matching include:

• Tuition payments or gifts that reduce tuition
• Gifts such as scholarship or financial aid that benefit specific individuals
• Payments for books, student fees, alumni dues, magazine sub-

scription fees, insurance premiums, or other payments that are not direct gifts to an eligible school

- Gifts made with funds provided to the donor for donation purposes by other persons
- The value of personal services

A matching gift from Alcoa Foundation cannot lead to the donor's receiving any benefits with a monetary value, such as tickets to athletic or social events. Further, a matching gift cannot be used to reduce a church-related financial commitment, such as a tithe or an assessment.

To make a donation, an eligible donor sends a gift to an eligible institution and, with it, a signed form for the school's use. The chief financial officer of the school completes and signs the form and sends it to us. We issue checks to schools on a quarterly basis. The money can be used in any way the institution feels is appropriate.

When a check is sent to an institution, we address a letter to the chief financial officer that lists the names of the donors who made gifts during that quarter, the amounts of their contributions, and our matching amounts. If only a portion of a gift is eligible, we explain why so that the institution can maintain its own accurate records.

Day-to-day administration of the foundation's gift-matching program is the responsibility of a program assistant. The gift-matching process begins on a quarterly basis with receipt of the first completed application form sent to us by a college or university. Each application is carefully reviewed by the program assistant using a four-part test: Is this an eligible gift? Is the donor eligible? Is the institution eligible? Is the purpose of the gift eligible?

The application form must have been completed in its entirety by the donor and the gift certified by the chief financial officer of the institution. Forms that are incomplete or need clarification before processing are returned for correction to either the donor or the institution. Eligible applications are then ready for further review.

If the donor is a past participant, the information on the form is compared to our computer data base. Any changes in em-

ployee status or address are made to the record in the file. If the
donor is new to the program, all relevant information regarding
eligibility is verified with the corporate or local plant personnel
office. A new file is then added to the computer so that we can
quickly identify a donor when subsequent gifts are made.

Next, we check each institution's eligibility through our files,
and necessary information changes are entered. If the school is a new
entry, eligibility is confirmed through several sources so that we can
document eligibility of the school in accordance with our policies.
The *HEP Higher Education Directory* is one sourcebook that helps
us to determine whether a school meets our criteria. The directory lists
the nationally recognized accrediting agencies and associations, along
with professional and specialized accrediting bodies who may be contacted to verify an institution's qualifications.

Finally, we ask if the gift falls within the limitations of our
gift-matching guidelines. If not, we request additional information
to satisfy eligibility requirements. Both the donor and school are
notified if a gift cannot be matched.

Computer Systems. Once the application passes the four-point test,
it is processed in our computer system. It may be helpful to include
some background on how our automated system began. Prior to
November 1978, Alcoa Foundation's gift-matching commitment ratio was one to one. With the decision to increase the ratio to two
to one, the number of gifts increased by 50 percent, the number of
donors increased by 63 percent, and the number of schools receiving
gifts increased by 48 percent. Administration of the program became
more time consuming, and we decided to automate the process to
increase its efficiency.

Complete Computer Systems in Huntingdon Valley, Pennsylvania, was asked to help us design and develop a computer software system to administer the gift-matching program. The system
was brought on-line in 1981, and since then, it has provided efficient, accurate results and helpful graphics. The capabilities of the
system enable us to create a variety of reports and functions from
information contained in the data base.

For example, the computer provides quick verification of
specific information, compiles statistical reports, handles calcula-

tions, and processes check requests and related correspondence with institutions receiving funds. It also produces notifications to donors so that they know their gifts have been matched. New gift-matching applications are included with these notifications to encourage donors to become regular participants in the program.

One advantage of the computer system is that it enables us to easily track patterns of giving, allowing us to view a five-year history of a donor on a single screen. If unusual or erratic patterns of giving are apparent, we can identify trends that are occurring either at the plant locations, at the institutions, or with the individual donors.

Confidentiality. A word about confidentiality: confidentiality is one of the most important policies. Each donor and recipient organization must be assured that donation histories are kept in strictest confidence. Frequently, Alcoa Foundation receives requests from educational organizations asking us to supply them with names of employees in their locale or lists of alumni working for Alcoa. Although we understand this can be an effective fund-raising tool for some schools, it is nonetheless strictly against our policy to release such information.

We are also careful to distribute blank gift-matching forms to eligible donors only; they can be obtained from the foundation's office or plant personnel offices. Requests for large quantities of forms are questioned to ensure that employees are not being pressured by others or solicited aggressively by colleges and universities to make donations to these schools.

When checks are issued to recipient schools, copies of the letters that accompany them as well as check stubs are kept on file. Correspondence or acknowledgments that we receive from the schools are also kept. A copy of each quarter's statistics is included in the file for quick reference.

Communication. Communication between the foundation, donors, and institutions is crucial to the success of our program and must be ongoing. An open-door policy encourages our donors to call us at any time to question or discuss the appropriateness of their gift before it is submitted for processing. Institutions, too, are encouraged to call us to report any changes in their organization or in personnel who are authorized to handle and certify the gift-matching forms. In this way, questions concerning the eligibility of a gift can be discussed, and any special requests that do occur can be reviewed, approved, and handled expeditiously. For example, several company employees wanted to create a memorial fund in lieu of sending flowers for a fellow Alcoan when she died. She was actively involved in a particular university's activities, and the employees wanted to give money to that school in her memory. The foundation's board of directors approved the memorial and double-matched the total contribution.

Open discussions are the most effective way to talk through misunderstandings or misinterpretations that occur in implementing the program. For instance, an agricultural university called us to announce that it had received a prize-winning heifer as a gift. The administrator at the school wanted to know if they could place a dollar amount on the heifer and if it would qualify under the gift category we designate as "stock." Unfortunately, we could not find a rationale to support classifying livestock as marketable securities.

In another instance, an employee wanted to begin donating a portion of his personal art collection to a college and requested that we match the appraised value of the art as a gift to the school. We concluded that the art could be subject to inconsistent appraisal values, and, therefore, we decided not to include gifts of personal items in our program.

These are the broad requirements and restrictions of our gift-matching program. They have been established and fine tuned over the years to create a program that can be administered and controlled effectively. Control is particularly vulnerable when money is being sent to institutions for unrestricted use. Also, the institutions receiving money under this program are selected not by the foundation but by the donors associated with Alcoa.

Pitfalls in Establishing a Gift-Matching Program

Without question, there are pitfalls to avoid in establishing and maintaining a gift-matching option for education, as well as for other areas. We found it essential to limit our matching to accredited colleges and universities. To expand the program into other areas would be to run the risk of supporting programs that we already assist through other grants or that we do not wish to assist at all.

In any gift-matching program, the administrator must be constantly aware that problems can arise from time to time, and that warning signs of fraud or abuse can be very subtle or quite apparent. A policy must be in place to help identify potential problems and a system must be in place to deal with them. Some situations we have discovered that should "wave a red flag" within any foundation with an educational gift-matching program include the following:

- Levels of donations become erratic. A donor with a history of giving $50 gifts over the years suddenly donates $3,000 to $5,000.
- The percentage of annual gifts is too high in relationship to the donor's salary. For instance, a supply order clerk with two years of company service makes a $5,000 gift to a college. A retiree whose giving record was $25 suddenly transfers $4,000 in stock to a university.
- Gifts are made in odd amounts, for example, $853.11. This could perhaps be payment for a goup of tickets to an athletic event, tuition, books, room and board for a student, or alumni dues, none of which would be eligible for matching. One must be careful, though, in analyzing these figures, for a $83.33 gift could be the monthly amount necessary to enable a donor to make a $1,000 annual donation.
- Acknowledgments and thank-you notes are received from an organization's athletic department or from a public television or radio station, when gifts to such groups are restricted under the program's guidelines.
- Independent auditors for a school request verification of donor amounts for a specific period of time. Sometimes, the totals or names of employees do not match our records. Such inconsistencies must be investigated and resolved.

Each of these situations must be handled delicately, as the integrity of the donor, institution, and foundation are being challenged. All parties involved must understand that inquiries about the intention of a gift or a request to provide us with supporting documents to verify a gift are made only to clarify that our gift-matching policies are being followed and that our guidelines have not been misinterpreted and to remind everyone involved of our purpose, mission, and intentions for the present and future success of the program.

In one instance, a church-related college was the recipient of matching gifts that were made by employees in lieu of tithes to the church. Several gift-matching corporations nationally found that the local churches were allowing employees to submit their monthly tithe as gifts for matching to a group of church-affiliated colleges. Money was also being pooled by the church and given to employees who submitted the funds for matching as their own.

When the church was approached with these concerns, it was very cooperative and took steps to end the inappropriate use of these gifts. The church issued a "code of ethics" ensuring us that the churches affiliated with these colleges would no longer violate our policies. Future funds to these colleges could have been suspended or restricted if their representatives had not discussed the situation openly with us and invoked the code of ethics.

One of the policy changes that we made to our original gift-matching program took place in 1983 when the board of directors decided to discontinue matching gifts to secondary schools. At that time, over 50 percent of all grants we made went to education. Cutbacks in federal, state, and local allocations to many other charitable causes and organizations resulted in increased requests for funding. We decided to decrease support to secondary education in order to offer support to other appropriate areas. We had been encountering some problems in working with the secondary schools as it was. So we felt our decision was more than justified. It might be helpful to highlight some of the problems we had experienced.

- On occasion, employees were pooling their money. In one instance, an employee collected $4,500 from band parents and submitted the gift as his own for double-matching.
- Independent fund raisers sometimes gave money to employees to submit as their personal gifts for matching.

- Applications were submitted for double-matching amounts paid on premiums for insurance policies in which the beneficiary was a Christian secondary school.
- A high school principal set up an athletic fund to which donors made contributions. Corporate matching dollars were applied to this fund and the money was subsequently used to purchase a tractor for the high school. Both actions were ineligible for matching. Furthermore, the tractor was bought from his own hardware store, and he made a profit of $3,000 to $4,000!

If a foundation decides to include secondary schools in its gift-matching program, it must be alert to how requests are "packaged" and how the funds are subsequently used.

Networking and Resources

One of the most effective and enjoyable parts of handling a gift-matching program is networking. Networking, or keeping in contact with other administrators of gift-matching programs both locally and nationally, provides you with a wealth of resources available on the subject and increases your own visibility as well. Many times we have found that another company has researched or experienced a situation similar to one that is new to us. By consulting with people in other companies, we have been able to avoid "reinventing the wheel."

Recently, a major corporation was considering changes in its existing program and came to us for some ideas on how to effectively handle the communication of the changes to their employees, retirees, and recipient organizations. We were able to offer several suggestions, from the actual wording of correspondence and newsletter articles and the timing of the releases to changes in collateral materials regarding the program. The latter included manuals, application forms, posters, and materials that might not fall under the program's control but that do contain information released to employees. We gained experience in handling these procedures when we discontinued gifts to secondary schools in 1983.

Networking can also bring together corporate foundation administrators who are experiencing similar trends or concerns that could include potential changes in their programs and enable them to share information that could improve all their gift-matching programs. Meetings and informal lunches can provide an opportunity to exchange or brainstorm ideas in a nonthreatening, problem-solving atmosphere.

Several invaluable resources are available nationally to provide assistance on gift matching. The Council for Advancement and Support of Education sponsors the National Clearinghouse for Corporate Matching Gift Information. The Council for Aid to Education provides information concerning facts and figures on current and changing trends in the field of education. The National Association of College and University Business Officers is a source of assistance in cultivating beneficial relationships between the corporate sector and higher education's business sector. Each of these organizations provides useful publications on the subject of gift matching and can help you to develop a comprehensive reference library.

In 1989, corporate gift matching celebrated a thirty-five-year anniversary. Over 1,043 companies currently are active participants. The Council for Aid to Education estimates that close to $1 billion in educational assistance have been provided through matching-gifts programs since 1954 (*Matching Gift Notes,* 1989). Alcoa Foundation's program alone has generated over $11,000,000 since its inception in 1963. We are proud to be a part of this significant form of support for American colleges and universities.

References

Matching Gift Notes. 7 (2), Winter 1989, p. 1.

Chapter Nineteen

Contributions Programs
for Smaller Companies:
Why and How

Iris J. Krieg

"Major funding for this program was provided by the Amoco Foundation" or "by the General Mills Foundation" or "by General Electric." We have all heard a tag line like this at the end of a program on PBS. These are big corporations making major gifts to projects of national scope. Is this the only model for corporate philanthropy? Is there a place for modest-sized or even small companies to engage in meaningful philanthropy?

Growing numbers of small companies are realizing that they too can participate in philanthropy; gain the same benefits that large companies receive; and, at the same time, help their communities and causes that are important to them, their employees, and their shareholders. However, while small companies can learn from the experiences of large corporations, their contributions programs are not just down-sized versions of large companies' programs but have unique characteristics.

249

This chapter will describe how and why smaller companies can effectively operate a contributions program that distributes less than $1 million per year. If even this sum seems daunting, do not be discouraged; a small company can begin with less than $100,000 per year.

The terms *corporate contributions* and *giving programs* will be used interchangeably in this chapter. A distinction should be made between these concepts and *charity*. Charity is impulsive, often emotional, giving. In contrast, corporate contributions is a planned and budgeted activity, and it has intentionality, a unifying perspective, a concern for outcomes, and a structure within the company.

Corporate contributions programs encompass only those contributions recognized by the Internal Revenue Service as deductible as charitable expenses and exclude membership dues, contributions to fraternal organizations, and gifts that result in direct benefits to companies or employees.

Smaller companies tend to make charitable gifts rather than operate a corporate contributions program. In such cases, gifts are usually made at the request of the CEO, often because he or she has personal involvement with an organization or because a business colleague or friend requests that a gift be made.

The scope of corporate philanthropy can be broad or narrow. It can include cash only or any of the following: matching employee gifts, in-kind items (such as used furniture or machinery), product donations, use of space and other facilities, and services provided by employees at no cost (such as design of brochures or copying of materials). Employers may allow employees to serve on nonprofit agency boards during work time or loan staff for more extended periods.

Reasons to Start a Giving Program

Today, business schools are teaching students that they have five publics to which they are responsible: shareholders, employees, customers and potential customers, business associates, and the general public. A corporate contributions program is one way of responding to all of these publics. Among the reasons that companies both large and small engage in corporate contributions are:

1. *Community service.* A company can help improve its community and help find solutions to issues of public concern.
2. *Customer expectations.* Within the last few years, the public has come to expect companies to make contributions. Increasingly, consumers are purchasing products from companies that are socially responsible, and philanthropic contributions rank high on the scale used by the public to assess social responsibility.
3. *Community recognition.* A company can have a higher profile and better image when associated with corporate contributions. Very often, recipients of a company's contributions will list its name in newsletters or annual reports or announce the contribution through news releases or at luncheons.
4. *Employee relations.* Employees who know that their employer is making contributions may feel more positively about their company, especially when the contributions are for issues of concern to them.
5. *Reduced pressures on corporate officials to secure contributions for friends' causes.* Members of the board of directors, the CEO, and other officials can distance themselves from unwanted solicitations by referring persons making requests to guidelines and procedures established as part of the contributions program.
6. *Improved climate in which to do business and for employees to live.* A company does not operate in isolation from the social ills that plague our communities. Reducing problems such as illiteracy and lack of child care and fostering arts and culture will improve the local business climate and help attract and keep qualified employees.
7. *Good citizenship.* Companies are residents of a community; they share the obligations of all citizens to work to better their community.
8. *Knowledge and fulfillment.* A corporate giving program can be fun, energizing, and fulfilling for employees and provides the company with knowledge of important issues. Employees of a company actively engaged in philanthropy will have increased

opportunities to interact with government, business, and civic leaders.

Operating a contributions program will entail more effort by a small company than simply making charitable gifts, but the benefits of such programs are greater for both the company and the community.

Importance of Small Contributions

In communities where a small company is the sole donor or one of a few donors, the importance of its contributions to community groups is clear. For small companies located in an area with larger corporate donors and foundations, smaller contributions may appear to be raindrops in the sea of grants from much larger donors.

Fortunately, this conclusion is not inevitable. A small gift can be important to a large organization, even if it is a very small part of an organization's overall income. Many nonprofit organizations depend on a broad base of small contributions for most of their funding. Since large grants are often restricted to specific purposes, organizations of all sizes are hungry for unrestricted contributions, the glue that holds the organization together over time.

A small contribution can also allow a large organization to do something special. For instance, a few hundred dollars may allow an organization to hire a consultant to provide needed training to the board of directors. With $1,500 a social service agency could form a small loan fund for low-income job applicants who need to buy interview clothes. A grant of $2,000 could enable an arts group to put on performances at local schools or nursing homes. A grant of $5,000 could be used by a day-care center to buy play equipment.

When used for awards or scholarships, small contributions can highlight a particular need and attract favorable publicity for the company. Awards may be made at special events to which award winners and local dignitaries are invited. Some companies seek and receive much publicity for their awards, the winners, and the company. For example, a company might make an annual award of $10,000 to a selected agency for community service or for management excellence. The company could establish an awards committee and hold a presentation event. As an alternative, the company could make its award through a nonprofit, allowing the nonprofit to give the award in the company's name. This approach is especially useful if the individual receiving the award is a community organizer or if a scholarship is to be given to a student.

Small contributions to small agencies can be as meaningful as a large grant to a large agency. When an agency has a total annual budget of $100,000, $5,000 is a significant contribution.

Selecting Issues to Support

A contributions program is a reflection of a company, its employees, and its directors. A company should select issues with which it feels comfortable. After all, no objective source of information can rank one issue above another. All issues—whether of poverty, maintaining our environment, or strengthening the arts—need to be addressed if we are to have a better society.

Companies in small towns with few other philanthropic sources may want to have a wide scope of funding interests. However, a company in an area with many funders and nonprofits may wish to focus on a few issues to prevent being overwhelmed by requests. In this way, the company can become more knowledgeable about the issues and agencies it funds, have a ready rationale for declining prospective applicants, and, by publishing its interests, keep the number of applicants to a manageable number.

Small companies often restrict contributions geographically to the communities in which the company is located, has offices, or does business. Frequently, these companies include in their contributions programs issues of relevance or special concern to their business interests. For instance, a manufacturer of industrial equipment might support mathematics and science education at local public schools, or engineering at local colleges. Or, it might support activities of particular interest to employees, such as a theater for which many employees volunteer. Employees' interests could be easily determined by a poll. Sometimes pressing needs are evident, such as inadequate public schools or a particular public health problem. Contributions in such areas can be exciting or effective as long as faddism is avoided.

Elements of a Successful Small Program

To achieve the benefits described above, a small company must view corporate philanthropy as part of its regular operations and as a legitimate corporate function. Approval of the chief executive officer and board is essential.

A contributions program incorporates many of the same ways of doing business that other company departments or functions utilize. For instance, a contributions program must be a planned activity with some goals. A system must be established for making contributions, for obtaining required information from applicants, and for keeping records. Since contributions programs entail communicating with individuals outside of the company, it is essential that all dealings with applicants and recipients be handled in a professional manner.

Even with these elements, a corporate contributions program can be operated simply so that its major cost is the cash value of contributions. A more complicated program may contain many more components and elaborate systems. No matter how simple or complex a contributions program is, it must have at least the following elements.

Goals. A corporate giving program must be based on goals. These can be broad or narrow but must provide overall direction and coherence. A broad goal might be to strengthen communities in which the company does business. A company with this goal might support a wide range of activities, from economic development to the arts. A more circumscribed goal might be to help prepare young children to succeed in school. A different type of goal would be to reinforce the image of the company as one that is concerned with our society. A company might have more than one goal for its program. A program could include both a goal related to how the community might benefit (such as strengthening educational resources) and a goal related to how the company might benefit (such as creating a higher company profile in the community).

Annual Budget. A targeted amount to be spent should be established for each fiscal year. The budget may be a single amount, or it could be divided into line-item expenditures by category such as matching gifts and contributions by issue of concern. Determining the annual amount of the budget is discussed in a later section.

Decision-Making Structure. A program is more likely to be consistent and objective and involve employees if decisions about the program are made by more than one person. Some companies form small contributions committees composed only of senior management; others draw committee members from throughout the company. The CEO is generally included to ensure decision-making authority. Committee size most often is between three and nine members. Some companies are pleasantly surprised to find that employees generally want to participate in the contributions committee.

Decisions about the program should be made at special meetings called for this purpose at fairly regular intervals throughout each year. Minutes or notes should be kept of each meeting's proceedings.

Guidelines. Whether distributed to the public or kept as internal documents, written guidelines describing the company's contributions interests, policies, and procedures establish a framework for decision making. Decisions are much more likely to support the giving program's goals if guidelines exist.

Making guidelines public can reduce the number of unwanted and inappropriate requests and provide an easy explanation to organizations whose requests are rejected. Published guidelines also attract organizations that the company might like to support. Guidelines can be duplicated by photocopying, or they can be professionally designed and printed.

Record-Keeping System. Some basic records must be kept to comply with IRS regulations. Records for each recipient should include the letter of application; a copy of the IRS letter issued to every nonprofit agency attesting to its nonprofit status; information on agency contact; and date of contribution, amount, and purpose. Records may be kept entirely on paper or partially on computer files. Computer software is available to companies that prefer this approach, although commercial computer programs are generally more complicated than small corporate contributions programs need. An adequate program can be devised on a spreadsheet.

Applicant Response System. Through a contributions program, a corporation interacts and communicates with the public. All responses to applicants should be timely and professional. Responding to mail inquiries can be routinized to some degree by using preprinted postcards or standardized form letters. Many companies do not respond to mass mailings at all.

Staff. One person should be identified as responsible for the contributions program. If staffing is to be primarily a clerical function, responsibilities include responding to telephone and mail inquiries, setting up decision-making meetings and taking minutes, transmitting information to the contributions committee, and maintaining files and financial records. Most companies expect the staffing duties to go beyond a purely clerical function. Decision making is facilitated when staff members review requests, obtain additional information if needed, and make recommendations to the contributions committee.

     The following elements are optional. A well-run corporate contributions program may, but does not have to, include them.

Employee Matching Gifts. The company may match monetary gifts that employees make to eligible agencies. Often, restrictions are placed on the types of agencies that are eligible and the sizes of gifts that will be matched. Most companies only match employees' gifts to institutions of higher education or to cultural organizations, although, increasingly, companies are matching gifts to a broader range of organizations. Matching-gifts programs require more staff time, forms, and procedures to assure that gifts are made only to eligible organizations.

     Companies operate such programs because employees like them. Through these programs, employees feel they have a voice in determining how corporate contributions will be made, and they appreciate having additional gifts awarded to organizations that are important to them.

Information to Employees. Informing employees about the activities of the contributions program can improve employee relations. Employee newsletters and special announcements or memoranda are commonly used vehicles for information.

Public Relations. Companies can issue their own news releases or describe their contributions in the company's annual report to obtain positive publicity. A company might sponsor special events such as the performance of a play or underwrite a benefit for a nonprofit group to receive publicity. Another way to receive public notice is for the company to host an event at which contributions are announced, usually contributions in the form of an award or scholarship.

Product and Service Donations. Many companies have products that can be utilized by nonprofits. These can be current inventory, obsolete merchandise, or returned or slightly damaged goods. Used office furniture and equipment are welcomed by nonprofit organizations. Nonprofit agencies can also benefit from services provided by a company or its employees such as printing, legal representation, or publication design.

Employee Volunteer Programs. Employees are often eager to assist nonprofit agencies but may need help and encouragement to find an appropriate agency. A company might host a volunteer fair at which different community agencies are encouraged to describe their programs and volunteer needs to employees. Space may be made available on company premises for such activities as tutoring illiterate adults.

Since cash contributions of smaller companies will be modest, donated services and in-kind items can add substantially to the company's contributions program. Additionally, the cost of such donations to the company is generally less than their value to the recipients but easier for a smaller company to absorb.

Cost of a Giving Program

The total cost of a contributions program stems from three general sources: direct cash gifts and lost revenue from donated merchandise; time of the decision-making committee and of supporting staff; and overhead items such as telephone, postage, paper, filing space, office rent, and utilities. Actual cost relates to the scope and complexity of a program. Most small programs operate without employing new staff. Decision makers may meet three or four times each year for an hour or two, with an additional few hours needed for reading materials. Mail and phone inquiries may be handled routinely. The significant costs of this type of program are the amount of cash contributions and possibly product donations.

Some small companies take a different approach and do employ a part-time or full-time person to operate their program. For these companies, the time of the staff person is viewed as part of the contribution. The staff person is expected to be visible in the community and knowledgeable about community issues. This person serves on a variety of task forces and committees seeking to solve community problems, assists nonprofit organizations directly, and provides more in-depth review of requests. The staff member may also develop a volunteer program at the company to match employees with the volunteer needs of nonprofit agencies, organize benefits or special events for nonprofits, collect gifts from employees for the needy at holidays, manage the United Way campaign, assist the CEO in carrying out volunteer and nonprofit board activities, and arrange for product donations or donations of employee professional services. If a staff person is hired, the company's costs are significantly increased, but the benefits would also be increased.

Process of Making Contributions

The contributions process has only a few steps. How complicated each step is depends on the type of program the company wishes to operate and the available staff support. The following steps occur in every contributions program.

Step One: Getting Appropriate Applications. Contributions should only be made in response to a written request from a representative of an organization. A company may take the initiative if it wishes to consider a particular organization that has not applied by contacting the organization and discussing its interest. Similarly, if too few requests are being received, the pool of applicants can be built through informal contact with nonprofit agencies, word of mouth, news releases, or letters announcing the availability of funds sent to selected organizations.

Step Two: Evaluating Each Applicant Organization. Evaluation can be done by staff, contributions committee members, or both. At some companies, staff does initial screening and only eligible requests are brought to the contributions committee. In other cases, all requests are seen by the committee. The process may be restricted to a review of the written request submitted by the organization, or it can include additional written materials, telephone conversations with the applicant, meetings with the applicant at the company's or at the agency's site, and discussions with others who may be knowledgeable about the applicant.

It is essential that applicant organizations be evaluated on their merit and against the company's guidelines or goals. Personalities of nonprofit board and staff members, except in so far as they affect the ability of the organization to carry out its program, should not be discussed. Other criteria to consider are:

1. Does the applicant meet IRS requirements?
2. Does the project appear reasonable? Is there a logical relationship between the identified problem and the solution posed in the application?
3. Does the applicant have experience with the program it is proposing? Has it been successful in the past?
4. If the company would not provide the full amount needed for a project, does the agency have adequate plans for raising the rest? Can a challenge grant from the company assist the applicant to raise the balance?
5. What is the overall financial health of the applicant? Is the agency generally able to balance its budget?
6. Who will benefit from the activities of the applicant?
7. Does the agency have an active board? Is it representative? Is the staff adequate, and does it appear to be competent?

Step Three: Selecting Applicants to Receive Grants. The contributions committee should receive and review relevant materials in advance of the meeting to select applicants. Generally, each committee member should get some information generated by the applicants such as the letter of application, a list of board members, and a budget. Decision making can be facilitated if the materials also include a summary listing of the applicants, the purposes of their requests, and the amounts requested. Again, committee members must make decisions according to the guidelines. To do otherwise will ensure that the contributions program will not meet its own goals and will accomplish little for the company and community.

Step Four: Communicating with Applicants. All applicants, whether or not they receive a contribution, should receive a written response. Form letters may be used for much of the correspondence.

Step Five: Following Up. Most contributions programs do not require reports from recipients. If interested, a company can find out about what has been achieved with grant money through unsolicited materials sent by the recipients or through inquiries to the recipient when the group reapplies. However, if staff time is available, a year-end report from the recipient helps the company learn more about recipient agencies and issues. This information aids future decision making.

Contributions Program Policy Issues

Contributions programs must make several policy decisions. Among the key ones are the following.

How Much to Budget. Currently, a standard for corporate contributions being promulgated throughout the country is 2 percent of pretax corporate income. Giving clubs or associations of companies that promise to contribute 2 or 5 percent of their pretax income to nonprofit groups are flourishing in many areas. However, most companies give significantly less than these amounts. Donations by a company of less than 1 percent of its income are common.

One way for a contributions program to begin is with a small amount that is scheduled to increase over the years. Since the contributions budget will generally come from profits, building it up over time is sometimes more acceptable to stockholders than beginning with a large sum. This approach also allows the company to develop management expertise as the contributions program develops.

Types of Contributions. A company may mix types or restrict contributions to one type. Capital contributions are usually larger and sometimes paid over several years for such purposes as building construction or renovation. Usually a company receives quite a bit of recognition for a capital gift. Operating contributions are used by the agency for its general purposes and demonstrate a company's interest in the agency's overall purpose. Project contributions are targeted to a particular project of one or more agencies. This type of contribution provides the greatest accountability to the company as it is easier to gauge the impact of a project than of the overall agency.

How Long to Support an Organization. Some companies prefer to support many of the same organizations over several years because these organizations are known to the company and because they meet the company's giving objectives. The case for more flexibility is based on two issues. First, organizations that receive funds regularly may become dependent and lose their creative spirit. Second, by allowing new agencies to receive funds, the company may be perceived as more responsive to real and changing needs.

Foundation or Direct Giving. Most small companies choose to make their contributions directly rather than through company foundations. Operating a foundation has more start-up costs and more operating costs because a foundation is a legal entity. Among these costs are compliance with IRS regulations and regular reporting to the IRS and to the state. Company foundations increase the public profile of company contributions. They also allow a company to build up funds in good years to allow the flow of contributions to remain steady in bad years.

Centralized or Decentralized Program. A company with multiple sites or holding companies might centralize its program and funnel all requests through a single process. Alternatively, the company could allow each office to establish its own contributions program or could reserve portions of the central budget for recommendations from each office. A decentralized budget gives more recognition to and requires more involvement of the local company or office. A centralized program gives more control to the main office.

What to Expect

A small company that operates a contributions program should gain all of the benefits realized by a larger company operating such a program. Fortunately, the costs are significantly less as the scope and complexity of a smaller company's program will be less.

Most of the drawbacks result from more mail, more filing, more friends and business associates asking for contributions for their favorite organizations, and the actual costs of contributions.

Among the benefits of a good contributions program operated by a small company are: more knowledge about the community; more knowledge about issues; enthusiasm of involved employees; improved employee relations; higher company profile, better image, and more goodwill; increased opportunities to interact in positive ways with other companies, community leaders, and government officials; offset of certain costs due to tax deductibility; and ability to make an impact on agencies and issues of importance to the company.

Sources of Help

Corporate contributions is one area of business practice where no trade secrets are kept. Most companies are eager to share their knowledge and experiences with other companies. As a result, there are many free or low-cost sources of information, beginning with other companies in your area. Other sources include the following.

Council on Foundations. Despite its name, this national organization includes both corporations that have foundations and those that give directly. It is a source of technical and general information. It offers many publications that can aid companies with their contributions programs, and it provides many opportunities for all types of contributors to get together nationally and throughout the country. The council has a special interest in small corporations (Council on Foundations, 1828 L Street, N.W., Washington, D.C. 20036, 202-466-6512).

Regional Associations of Grantmakers. In many areas throughout the country, corporate contributors and foundations have joined in associations with the purpose of sharing information and promoting philanthropy. These associations are good sources of advice on everything from how to start a program to substantive information about issues. The Council on Foundations can provide information about these associations.

Publications. Many organizations publish materials that are particularly helpful to corporate contributors, including the Council for Advancement and Support of Education (Suite 400, 11 Dupont Circle, Washington, D.C. 20036-1207, 202-328-5900) for matching gifts, the Council on Foundations, and INDEPENDENT SECTOR (1828 L Street, Suite 1201, Washington, D.C., 20036, 202-223-8100).

Associations of Commerce and Industry. Many chambers of commerce have special philanthropy committees, some of which operate 2% or 5% clubs. These may be sources of information on local issues or on how to operate a contributions program.

Community Foundations. Community foundations are special types of foundations that make grants within a limited geographic area. They exist in many communities throughout the country and can often provide information or even staff support. Local United Ways, regional associations of grantmakers, or the Council on Foundations can identify a local community foundation if one exists in your region.

United Ways. These agencies are good sources of information on human social problems and agencies.

Get Started!

More and more small and medium-sized companies are replacing their scattershot approach to charity with a corporate contributions program. They are reaping many of the same benefits that large companies get from their programs. Establishing a program does take energy, resources, and planning, but a program can be phased in over time and made as simple or as complex as management wants.

Since there is no single model for corporate contributions, each company is free to design a program that meets its own goals and corporate culture. To get started, what is most needed is foresight, enthusiasm, and creativity. The rest will follow.

Chapter Twenty

Monitoring the Results
of Grantmaking

Sibyl Jacobson

Grantmakers are often asked what their dollars accomplish. It is not unusual for skeptics to ask whether grants might be "throwing money at a problem" or "down a bottomless hole of need" or to challenge grantmakers by asking, "Couldn't the company put the dollars to better use in some other way—in advertising, research and development, or salaries, for instance?" The grantmaker's answers to such questions depend on the person's ability to explain the purpose and results of grantmaking and to understand what is perceived as appropriate corporate activity.

This chapter approaches the results of grantmaking in two parts. The first part examines the relationship of corporate perspective to articulating grantmaking objectives. The second part suggests ways that the outcomes of grants might be measured.

Identifying Objectives

Determining Point of View. The approach a company takes to grantmaking derives from the nature of the company and its business. A company's point of view determines what it seeks to achieve through grants. Making grants is one of the ways a company can articulate and demonstrate what it thinks is important.

The following list suggests things that can shape a corporation's perspective and form the basis of its approach to making grants. An analysis of these factors can help the grantmaker anticipate what the corporation is likely to expect from its grant and provides a backdrop for developing their program rationale.

> Nature of business
> Structure and governance
> Product or service
> Method of selling
> Corporate self-image and desired public image
> Public perception
> Regulatory environment
> Competition/cooperation (internal and external)
> Centralization/decentralization
> Company/product orientation
> Customer/public/stakeholder/employee emphasis and relationships
> Delivery (distribution) system
> Geographic emphasis
> Control/entrepreneurshp
> Degree of readiness for risk
> Expertise and knowledge base
> Strengths/weaknesses (traditional and emerging)
> Reactive grantmaking/intentional or planned grantmaking
> Time frame
> Leadership/lack of leadership (internal and external environment)
> Attitude toward and extent of position as flag bearer for corporate involvement
> Corporate history and attitude toward the past

Examining Language. The language used to describe grantmaking creates expectations and conveys a point of view. How grants are explained to various publics, inside and outside the company, is important. This is especially so when resources become scarce; when there is a change in business direction, organization, or management; and when the grantmaking field begins to talk and behave differently.

Recently, corporate grantmakers have begun to borrow freely from the language of business to explain grantmaking. Thus, grants may be called *investments*. Such a change in nomenclature introduces the expectation of return on investment and with it a longer time horizon. Likewise, a list of grantee organizations in a field becomes a *portfolio* to be *managed* by the program officer. In many cases, however, the terms are being used not in their technical sense but in their metaphoric sense. A grant may be similar to an investment in many ways, but it is not one. If the comparison is carried to its logical conclusion, it breaks down. Thus, you should be aware of the credibility gap that could occur when applying such terms to grantmaking and remember that as figures of speech they serve best as illustration and least as logic.

Then, too, there is the language of an industry and of a particular corporate culture. This "corporate speak" can help create a common ground and communicate ideas and expectations by linking them to commonly held values, traditions, and judgments basic to the way the company sees itself and conducts its business. Such language can help give authority and resonance to concepts.

Analyzing Intent. How a company perceives itself and wishes to be perceived by others will guide its grantmaking. Grantmakers translate corporate point of view and ethos into rationale and program. In this regard, much of what is done in a grantmaking program may be seen as "packaging" activities so that they demonstrate a coherent approach that complements or illustrates the company's voice or philosophy (which, of course, can and does change).

A grant can be made for various reasons including to benefit the recipient organization or those served by it, to please the requestor (who may not be the grantee), or to reflect well on the giver. Some common reasons grants are made include to:

Match expectations and broad-based support—the bandwagon phenomenon

Be on the side of the angels—the halo effect
Help make something happen
Build awareness or bring attention to an issue
Support the provision of a service
Complement employee interest
Show business support of an issue, approach, cause, or
    organization
Create goodwill
Promote the common good
Meet a need
Demonstrate leadership
Help government fulfill its responsibility
Improve amenities and services
Create a healthy climate conducive to business and free
    enterprise
Make systemic change
Respond to a crisis
Encourage cooperation

In most cases, however, grants serve a number of objectives that are agreed upon as important by the company. The objectives are likely to express interest in certain populations, geographic areas, issues or needs, mechanisms or approaches, and activities or services.

The first level of analysis of a grant involves answers to the basic questions: What? Who? Why? Where? How? When? The second level of analysis examines the grant's relation to the expressed grantmaking mission and determines whether the grant can serve as a center of influence to foster an idea or demonstrate an approach. That is, such analysis goes beyond the specific grant to explore such things as experimentation, systemic change, transportability, and usefulness. It examines whether the grant can have effects beyond its immediate locus. In fact, some grants are made for what could be termed a second-order objective. This is the case, for example, when one funds a workshop to share a particular approach with other organizations.

Looking at Context. The objectives of corporate grants go to the heart of a company's values, view of itself, and relationship to the communities of which it sees itself a part. Thus, one company may measure success by the number of lines of coverage the project receives in the newspaper, another by the number of people who participate in the project, and still another by the achievements of a nonprofit organization in fulfilling its avowed mission. Others talk in terms of specific populations and see their grantmaking emphasis as a niche in which they can have an impact.

With all this said, what seems to work well—perhaps because it is so basic (some might say organic)—is to use a contextual approach to elucidate the objectives that will determine results. A contextual approach sees the objectives of an organization or project as deriving from the relationship of the activity and its various contexts. The goals are inherent in the effort and subject to discovery, design, and explication. This approach is used after the need for the organization or activity is established.

Much of what grantseekers and grantmakers do is to give definition to nonprofit activities so that they have a better chance of being understood, implemented, and funded. In this approach to grantmaking, one tends to avoid the question of which organization's purpose is primary, the grantor's or grantee's. Rather one analyzes the groups as a system and achieves a blending: first, by examining the characteristics of the activity and, second, by defining the activity's relationship to the grantmaking purpose and corporate perception. However, nonprofit activities are most successful if the corporate purpose is simply an overlay or translation of program design, rather than the engine driving the organization or project.

Tracking Results

Keeping Score. Many things need to be mapped, collected, counted, and compared to help explain the results of grants and how they relate to objectives. It can be useful to think in terms of equivalents to standard units of measurements when talking about the results of a grant. The following list suggests possible ways of thinking about and counting aspects of grants.

Measurement Units	*Possible Equivalents*
Length	Reach, duration, continuity
Area	Extent, scope, region
Volume or capacity	Quantity, likelihood, density
Weight	Critical mass, force, frequency

Whatever units are appropriate for the nature of the grant can be adapted and applied to the key questions: What? Who? Why? Where? How? When?

Touching Base. Was the check for the grant received, cashed, used as intended, and acknowledged? This question suggests results so basic that they tend to be overlooked in discussions on monitoring and evaluation. Lost, old, and uncashed checks can cause substantial problems for grantmakers in bank reconciliations and audits. And checks go awry more often than one might expect, particularly when the check goes to another party to present or forward to a nonprofit. So, too, periodic fund-raising efforts that rely heavily on volunteers may not have procedures to ensure that a check is immediately deposited. But large and sophisticated institutions such as universities also may fail to cash checks in a timely fashion.

Sometimes misunderstandings and misplaced or unacknowledged grants can be avoided by adequately informing the appropriate offices and executives. If local company representatives present checks, include a report form with the check to be returned to the contributions office when the check is forwarded or delivered. Although such a procedure does not ensure that the organization will cash the check, it lets the office know when the check becomes the nonprofit group's responsibility. If a volunteer fund raiser, often a corporate CEO, solicits grants for a charity and the contribution is sent to the volunteer's address (either because that is requested or because it is politic), it is a good practice to inform the chief staff officer or development officer of the nonprofit. In this way, the appropriate people are alerted to look for the check. If a grant is made to a national organization, say the American Red Cross, but local presentations and acknowledgments are desired in the company's home city and also in the city served by the chapter where the event occurred that prompted the grant, then letters about the grant should go to all parties and appropriate executives. Before writing the letters, bases should be covered to indicate intent and to ask if, and how, it can be accomplished.

Instituting Controls. The problem of outstanding and lost checks can be managed by controls to follow up uncashed checks in a predetermined amount of time. How such controls are instituted will depend on a company's organization and division of responsibility. In some cases, staff members charged with bank relations and reconciliation will develop a list of outstanding checks to trace. In some companies, the follow-up is done by financial departments, and in others, jointly with the contributions department or by the contributions department alone. Some contributions officers routinely telephone organizations to which they have made grants that have not cashed the checks in a specified amount of time (some at two months, others longer). In some cases, the check has not been received. Since the organization is not usually aware that a check is in the mail, the recipient does not know that a check has been lost. Potential problems can be mitigated by early follow-up of uncashed checks and by alerting the organization that it will be receiving a grant.

The way an organization handles its finances is one indication of its management capability. This is no less true of charitable organizations than it is of businesses. The impression created by an organization that does not deposit grant checks promptly can be that it is financially irresponsible and does not need the money. The explanation sometimes given by an organization that the check was kept intentionally so as not to spend it on immediate expenses does not instill confidence in the organization's business judgment or stewardship of funds. Such weaknesses in procedure should be brought to the attention of the nonprofit. In most cases, the organization will welcome such advice and correct the problem. Guidance in this area can be as important to the financial health of the organization as the grant may be.

The extent to which the use of the grant is of concern to the grantmaker varies with the nature of the grant. With a large project grant (large as defined internally as relative to a company's giving practices rather than an arbitrary dollar amount), periodic narratives from the nonprofit group or financial reports or other information may be a stipulation of the grant. If there is a payment schedule, the requirements—whether performance thresholds or time—should be defined as well as the action needed to trigger release of payment on the grant. Grant requirements can be documented in (1) a letter that cites the nonprofit's proposal as submitted (or as modified by mutual agreement and explained in the letter) as that which is being funded (this incorporates by reference the intentions detailed in the proposal); (2) a transmittal letter that gives the grantmaker's expectations and asks for a response in writing within a given period of time if the requirements set forth present a problem; (3) a letter of agreement signed by executives of the grantee and grantor organizations that gives the terms and conditions of the grant and situations that would lead to some change in payment or the return of the entire grant or an unspent portion of it; or (4) a formal contract (appropriate when supporting, for example, the development of a particular product, real estate venture, scholarship program, or series on public television).

The nonprofit group may need to make changes between the idea as proposed and as executed. Therefore, it is good practice to ask that any midcourse changes in the project as proposed and funded be submitted as written requests to the grantor. In this way, the changes can be tracked and recorded as the project is implemented. Such communication also improves the chances of a project's success by letting the grantmaker and grant recipient know what went awry with the original plan, knowledge that can inform both parties in their future work.

Monitoring such project grants takes time. Many techniques can be used; the following list is just a sampling.

Managing the Grant

Keeping in touch by telephone on progress
Conducting site visits
Reviewing narrative and financial reports
Obtaining copies of any product produced by the grant
Interviewing those involved in developing a report

Requiring evaluation data from participants

Getting counts of measurable units

Conducting cost/benefit analysis, such as cost per booklet or cost per client reached by information or service

Maintaining a call-up file or tickler mechanism to monitor progress on the agreed-upon time line, submission of reports, expenditures, and the like

Seeing that the proposed project is executed according to the plans and agreements

Determining that crediting is accurate and follows agreements

Collecting Data

Using a third-party evaluator

Analyzing self-reported information

Soliciting participant reactions directly

Seeing, touching, reading, attending, or photographing the sponsored project

Asking the opinions of experts in the field, those served, or the general public (as appropriate)—this can be done by the grantee, grantor, or third party

Assessing Influence

Tracing influence of the project through networks, presentations, citations, references, replications, adaptations, and use

Examining the project's place in a field—acceptance, duplication, competition, and synergy

Determining that the funds were segregated and used as designated

Determining that crediting is accurate and follows agreements

Comparing anticipated results with actual results

Conducting surveys

Using formal review panels of experts

Comparing data and using baselines

Analyzing responsiveness to change, adoption of programs, and institutionalization

Using Measurement Instruments

Giving pretests and posttests

Using double-blind studies, testing instruments, and control groups

Employing focus groups, opinion polls, and response mechanisms

Monitoring a nonrestricted or general operating grant is usually much simpler than monitoring one intended for a specific project. The grant transmittal letter may ask for updates and the organization's annual report, audit, or other information. This material, together with information from other sources, can form the basis for a periodic review of the organization. The file can be reviewed to see that there has been adequate correspondence to evaluate the grant and the potential for renewed support. It is disheartening to find that some organizations only communicate once a year and then only to request a grant. A corporation should use several of the techniques previously enumerated to evaluate an organization's work and the appropriateness of supporting it and to ask for whatever additional information is needed to adequately conduct a review. The extent of the review may depend on the amount of the grant, the type of organization, the program area or category, time, and geographical considerations.

Monitoring Finances. The following approaches should be used for financial monitoring, as appropriate:

- Verification of eligibility to receive a grant under IRS guidelines and the company's guidelines
- Review of audited financial report, project budget and expenditures, Form 990—Income Tax Return of Organization Exempt from Income Tax
- Auditor's confirmation letters to grantee organizations
- Spot checks of employee matching-gift and volunteer grant programs, including confirmations and verifications by the employer, employee, and the recipient organization

- Site visits by auditors to review books and fiscal management in accordance with grant stipulations

By demonstrating vigilance, the last two approaches may serve to deter abuses. This policing effect may be as important to the integrity of a company's program as actually identifying wrongdoing.

Checking Acknowledgment. A company should check to see if it has been correctly acknowledged in a listing of donors. An incorrect listing should be brought to the organization's attention by a telephone call and corroborating letter. Organizations all too frequently make mistakes in acknowledging the source of the gift, mixing company and foundation, for example, or getting the name wrong. They may mix up companies in the same industry and ascribe to one the programs or grants of another.

Occasionally a company is listed as a contributor in an organization's annual report or program when no grant has been made. Most often, employees bring such situations to the attention of the grantmaking office. The error should be promptly investigated and corrected. In a slight variation on the theme, organizations may list a company as one that matches all employee contributions to a particular type of organization although the company has a more restrictive matching program and such organizations would not be eligible for grants. These errors persist and are troublesome because similar organizations (public television stations, arts organizations, religious groups) may "borrow" the same language from another institution or organization without verifying its accuracy. So it happens that even clergy may announce erroneously that ABC company matches employee gifts to XYZ charity.

To avoid the appearance of implied corporate endorsement of an organization when the grant was made under an employee gift-matching program, some grantmakers ask that such grants be so identified in any listing. However, since such contributions tend to be numerous and reporting practices vary, it is difficult to determine if the grantor's request is honored. And, of course, it raises the question of whether a change in reporting style can be urged for a modest grant, particularly when it may be in the organization's interest to list the corporation or corporate foundation as an unqualified donor.

Evaluating Change in a Nonprofit's Program. If a company makes an operating grant to an organization because it serves a specific population at a given frequency, then a dramatic change in the organization's mission or operating procedure might change the grantor's measure of the organization's success. Therefore, grantmakers should periodically test their initial assumptions (the reasons the grant was made) with the present realities of the nonprofit's situation. In a sense this is a pre-grant/postgrant comparison that looks at present performance in relation to the funding objective. Some hypothetical changes in nonprofit organizations follow.

> A grant is made to a performing arts organization in large measure because of its national tour. Subsequently, the tour is discontinued and the organization performs only at one site with a shortened season.
>
> A grant is made to a social service organization on the basis of the comprehensive services it gives at no charge to a large number of poor adults with multiple problems. Subsequently, the pressure to document successful intervention and to produce revenue leads the organization to take on a less troubled client base and to serve those who can pay a fee.
>
> A grant is made to a college. Subsequently, it loses accreditation.
>
> A grant is made for a youth organization's program of after-school and weekend activities. Subsequently, visits and records show that few young people attend the program and that the organization consistently closes its doors earlier than publicized.
>
> A grant is made to a health education organization on the basis of the high-quality materials it produces and distributes at low cost. Subsequently, the organization decides to spin the educational materials program off as a separate

for-profit corporation and offer only consulting services through the nonprofit entity.

A grant is made to an organization that develops educational films and videos that reach large numbers of people. Subsequently, their pricing and rental arrangements for the material prices them out of the market, and use of their products decreases dramatically.

The cases above are examples of situations that call for careful review by the grantmaker, since there have been changes that may test the original rationale for the grant. The grantmaker's response, of course, varies with each situation and with the understanding (in writing) between the grantor and grantee organizations. Certainly dramatic changes may affect the willingness of a corporation to continue funding in the future. Yet, funders should realize that an organization or project may face unanticipated problems. Understanding by the corporation and disclosure on the part of the grantee organization are best. Changes that may make an organization no longer eligible under a company's program guidelines would argue for a careful check of the situation to see that requirements can be met before making a future grant.

Gathering Postgrant Information. The reason the organization or project was funded is the place to start in determining whether objectives were met. Postgrant analysis will be easier if ways to track results and feedback mechanisms are incorporated into the project design—either in the proposal as submitted or as eventually funded. Such information is also useful in planning. A weakness in many projects is that they do not provide a way to listen to those they serve so that changes can be based on "customers' opinions." Identifying any unintended consequences or secondary results is also important.

Gathering postgrant information can be helpful in determining what was achieved; learning from experience to inform future efforts; communicating, internally and externally, what the grant accomplished; documenting process and results for replication and influence; and validating an approach. The following examples show how information important to determining the extent to which a grant's objectives are achieved can be gathered.

Through a seed grant for a university and public school to develop a plan to retain students, a school reduces its dropout rate by 54 percent, greatly exceeding its goal. The program is chosen as an exemplary rural school project and receives state and federal funding to continue work with at-risk students. The program method is documented, published, and presented at conferences.

A site visit to a program in a troubled section of a large city aimed at likely junior high dropouts (those held back two years from their original grade level) finds teachers and counselors enthusiastic and students actively participating, with attendance much improved. A meeting with parents, who are poor and have language difficulties, is well attended and many parents arrive early, some carrying young children. When asked to express how they feel about their children being in a program that is specifically for students that are considered "failures," several parents smile and say they are proud. Asked why, one parent (whose English is very limited) says tearfully that if it had not been for the program, her son would most likely be on drugs, in jail, or dead. She adds, "This program has given us all hope. My son is doing better than even he expected."

Use of a film sponsored by a grant is tracked by number of bookings, showings, and total audience. The report breaks down viewership by location, date, type of organization, and numbers of adults and children by sex. This information is used to determine cost per booking, showing, and viewer and to determine geographic penetration.

A simple assessment form accompanies each free loan of a film designed for grade schoolers on alcohol and drugs. The teacher fills out the form, signs it, and returns it with the film to the person coordinating the loan. Information includes the date, grade, school, school system, number of students, and number of adults viewing the film. Teachers circle their responses on a scale for a number of questions. The following is asked: (1) What is your reaction to the drug education pamphlet series accompanying the file? (2) Was the film helpful in teaching the dangers of drug abuse? (3) Compared to other films on the same subject, how would you rate this film? (4) Did the film give new information to students? (5) Did the film evoke a good discussion from your students about drug use? (6) Would you use the film again for drug education? (7) In your opinion, for which grades are the drug education resources most helpful? (8) Please comment about the film and the resource materials. A final report compares viewers documented by response forms with the total possible target populations by project city for children, teachers, and parents.

A scholarship program analyzes the number of recipients by school and major. The selection procedures are documented as well as the number of applicants. Scholarship and fellowship winners are followed to see if the award is used for the purpose intended and whether the recipient's performance fulfills expectations.

A publication for teachers working with adolescents reading two or more years below grade level includes a postage-paid response card giving: reactions, grade level taught, percent of students reading two or more years behind grade level, educational setting (classroom, small group, one-to-one), name and address. A report on the grant's distribution of the publication includes number of copies, target audience (junior high and senior high teachers by type), geographical coverage by state, and analysis of response to survey cards, including percentage of return and comments.

Sometimes an anecdote is the best way to convince people that a grant can really make a positive difference because it is human and immediate. This is true whether it is a grantee explaining the results of a project to the grantor or the grantor describing the grant to people within the organization. For example, after presenting impressive statistics on the use of a drug prevention film supported by a grant, the grantee told the story of a telephone call from a mother to a local television station that had aired the film. The mother reported that her daughter had said, "Mom, that's my problem and I need help, too"—a breakthrough of recognition and communication that the mother said would never have happened without the film. This incident served to illustrate results and give flesh and blood to the statistics, and it found a ready audience within the corporation.

Maintaining Balance. The challenge for grantmakers is to maintain a healthy balance between accountability and flexibility. Although good management and program design are important, grantmakers still need to refrain from being intrusive, disruptive, and overweening. The best way to remember this is to expect the same level of accountability from both sides of the equation—the grantee and the grantor. Accountability, when tempered by insight, is good for the health and discipline of both.

Grantmaking is an art, not a science, and it succeeds best when conveying not only the quantifiable elements of a grant but also the human dimension—the potential to care and to reach out and, by so doing, to transform. Much of what nonprofits do every day defies business analysis. Many would have closed their doors long ago if they looked only at the numbers to measure their accomplishments. To translate the nonprofit world to the corporate world and vice versa and to formulate grantmaking objectives demand creativity and an appreciation of the grantmaker's role as conduit within a corporation.

PART FIVE

Achieving Success
in Corporate Contributions

Chapter Twenty-One

Total Resource Leveraging and Matching: Expanding the Concept of Corporate Community Involvement

Alex J. Plinio
Joanne B. Scanlan

Some people respond well to challenges. But when assigned the establishment of a corporate contributions program or the management of one already underway, they might not immediately see the task as a creative opportunity and as a chance to expand the concept of corporate-community involvement far beyond its traditional definition. In this chapter, we would like to show how corporate-community involvement (CCI) can be an exciting arena for executive creativity, with the potential to have an impact on all aspects of the corporate culture while creating a positive influence outside of the corporation.

A lot of the trouble with corporate *giving* is that name. It does not seem to make sense in a business environment. And corporate *philanthropy* is not much better when you are giving the twenty-five-second elevator speech on what you do in the company. We are all part of some larger set of functions that are running under the title of "corporate-community involvement" and that can include marketing, issues management, direct contributions, foundation management, employee matching contributions, scholarships, and external communications, just to keep the list short. Of all of these functions, though, direct contributions may seem furthest removed from the heart of the corporate enterprise.

But, in fact, creative corporate-community relations is composed only in part of corporate contributions. The other part—which is too often neglected by contributions program staffers—is *getting* substantial services and assistance from the community to assist the corporation. *Community*, for corporate-community relations, can be defined as certain geographic areas, such as metropolitan areas near the corporate headquarters, or as groups of stakeholders in the well-being of the corporation. The term can also encompass all aspects of the public and private nonprofit sector that have a natural interdependence with the corporation: local, state, and national government; school systems; health care facilities; transportation providers; and so on. Corporations can find valuable assistance from these community resources to help achieve their own business goals and help achieve the corporation's social goals.

Total resource leveraging and matching (TRL&M) is a practical way of obtaining valuable resources needed by business while at the same time enhancing the social structures that make business possible. Using the concept of TRL&M enables corporate staff to move away from the "we give—they get" definition of corporate contributions. The concept enables the staff responsible for many of the functions of corporate-community involvement to understand and assist in the nurturing of multidimensional partnerships that are central to successful corporate-community relations.

Approaches to Corporate Contributions Programs

The "Star Turn" and "Chamber Music" Approaches. Many top entertainers put together performances that allow the star to showcase his or her talents, supported by a small back-up group. In corporate contributions, some CEOs have shaped their "star turns" by placing themselves firmly in the center of all creative effort, backed up by a small group of other senior executives and one or two designated staff. Other contributions programs may follow a "chamber music" structure, with a committee of senior executives sharing control of the decision-making process under the general— but not necessarily autocratic—guidance of the CEO.

Both of these approaches may parallel private nonprofit foundation activities: an annual budget or income from an endowed foundation is allocated, applications come in and are investigated and considered, and a check is sent to the groups that meet the criteria of the corporation. The few people in the corporation who know about the giving program may think quite highly of its efforts. Should the CEO leave, these kinds of contributions programs may disappear.

The "Symphony" Approach. Some of the larger corporations have developed a "symphonic" approach, devising more elaborate and extensive programs and reaching employees with matching contribution programs, scholarships, and so on. The program's diverse staff is assembled or borrowed from other departments, resulting in many interdepartmental meetings and the commitment of more people in the corporation to the programs that they see as worthwhile charitable efforts. The corporation is often better known and more positively seen by its relevant communities and key audiences than corporations using the previous two approaches.

But with this approach and the previous two, a definite line is drawn between the corporation and the community, the one as the benefactor and the other as the recipient, just like the line between performer and audience. Each group has its defined role that makes the relationship work.

The "Alleluia" Approach. A fourth approach blurs the line between benefactor and recipient and depends on much more than cash. To follow our analogy, we call this approach the "Alleluia" or *A* approach because, like the ever-popular performances of Handel's *Messiah* that occur in most of our cities each Christmas, it can bring together the corporation and the community in joint efforts that benefit all concerned. In these performances, full orchestras and professional choruses are joined by hundreds of amateur singers. Everyone participates, and everyone enjoys the result, as the line between performer and audience is erased. In just such a way, the line between the corporation and the community can be erased so that the natural matches of resources and needs can be more easily made and maintained.

A fully developed *A* approach has these characteristics:

1. The corporation uses all of its resources—money, people, facilities, services, and so on—as a portfolio available to corporate interests and community needs.
2. The corporation seeks out resources from community nonprofits and for-profit groups and government to meet needs that are usually met only from for-profit sources.
3. The corporate giving program becomes an orchestrator for both the purchase and supply of services and assistance for the corporation and for the community, helping the various divisions and departments of a corporation to participate in strengthening corporate-community relations as they conduct their daily business affairs.
4. The giving program staff marshals corporate resources to develop new community services as the need for them is identified within corporate operations, thus integrating the giving program policies with general corporate objectives.
5. The approach fits well with a fundamental goal of corporate-community relations—to be constantly in touch with the environment surrounding the corporation, to feel the pulse of internal and external stakeholders, and to translate knowledge of the environment and the stakeholders into workable corporate strategies.

Why should you consider the *A* approach to help shape your work? First, many people find themselves in corporate-community involvement as part of their progress through the corporation. We think that even if all you can do is set some of your work objectives with this approach in mind, you can effect positive changes in a wide circle within the corporation and can be an extremely effective executive. Second, you will be able to meet specific corporate objectives by putting your knowledge of the community's assets at the service of your colleagues. Third, your company already works with the community, and by simply improving how the two work on shared goals you can add value to the efforts. Corporations have been making more than cash contributions for years, and yet few have realized that with minimal orchestration the various resources that have been put to the use of the community could be developed into major corporate-community endeavors. Finally, most people in your corporation like helping others, and you can provide them with a means to do so. The *A* approach is a classic win-win strategy.

How are you going to finance the *A* approach? You need to apply the same creative effort to gaining support for the *A* approach as it takes to implement this style of corporate response. Many corporate giving programs are being reduced. You may soon face demands to justify the costs of even modest giving programs during annual budget sessions. You need the support of the CEO if you want the company to rethink its more narrowly defined giving program and to initiate the *A* approach. Support of allies in other departments and your own expertise in interdepartmental negotiations are also critical. Base your community involvement program on the solid business reasons for meshing community interests with all aspects of corporate life, research the bare minimums needed to coordinate the endeavor, and set out a time line for measurable results. (We mentioned that this is an intriguing challenge.)

A Way to Think About Corporate Citizenship

The *A* approach is based on some simple assumptions, best articulated by Andrew C. Sigler (1982) in a speech to INDEPENDENT SECTOR's annual meeting of members. Mr. Sigler argued then that all aspects of business should be carried out with the attention to the responsibilities of corporate citizenship. He described his philosophy thusly: "What we do in the process of making a profit is the true measure of a corporation's overall responsibility. That's why we've tried to define a corporation's responsibilities to include 'How the whole business is conducted every day.'" The *A* approach makes the CCI office the primary location for following through on that definition of corporate responsibility. As such, the contributions program becomes more than a traditional giving program. How much more will depend on the circumstances of each corporation and the entrepreneurial skills of the contributions staff.

Some of the strongest proponents of corporate citizenship programs that encompass all aspects of the corporate structure have been service and retail companies. For these businesses, knowledge of public opinion and interests is vital. William Andres, former CEO and chairman of the Dayton Hudson Company, credited the knowledge gained from corporate-community activities with much of his company's success in the late 1970s when he accepted Columbia University's Lawrence A. Wien Prize in Corporate Social Responsibility in 1982: "The quality and effectiveness of a management team goes up as it becomes really involved in the community, as its members think more broadly about the world around them, and about the issues of the day; and as the corporation backs up that awareness and personal commitments with philanthropic dollars. The talents we develop, the skills we develop, the special sensitivities we develop, all carry over to help us meet the business challenges that confront us every day. We think they certainly help us to manage better in this rapidly changing world. At Dayton Hudson, we are thoroughly convinced that involved management is more effective, and that enlightened management and enlightened giving are two sides of the same coin" (Andres, 1982).

For companies that have few relationships with the broad public, it may be more difficult to see the value of well-orchestrated total resource giving, but it is certainly not impossible. Corporations contribute to maintaining and improving our society in a variety of ways. There is the contribution resulting from what might be called the "economic engine" functions of business enterprise. These functions include: producing and providing good quality products and services at fair prices, providing jobs in a nondiscriminatory manner, paying taxes, making a reasonable profit and investing funds to expand the economy, and fostering the growth and revitalization of our communities. But the function of business is not just economic with some minor, incidental social responsibilities. Business is a large and powerful force in our society. The price of such power—whether it is political power or economic power—is a responsibility for the public good.

"Doing good" as a responsible corporate citizen is not incompatible with doing well financially. Each is dependent upon the other, and both are essential to any organization's long-term success.

The corporate contributions staff of any company can become the orchestrator for helping all parts of the business to conduct its work in line with a philosophy of corporate citizenship. A corporate contributions program is legitimately concerned with meeting internal (corporate) as well as external (societal) needs. Corporate contributions programs hold a unique place in organized philanthropy. Charitable investments made in the name of the company are investments in the social and economic environment affecting future business success. Such a perspective does not limit the scope of corporate contributions to those projects that have an immediate and easily perceived effect on business.

At a day-to-day level, the role of corporate contributions manager requires the ability to see value in excess inventory, opportunity in positions that cannot be filled from local applicants, and fulfillment in the borrowing of a delivery truck by a nonprofit. It also requires an ability to retain respect for both the community and the corporation as potential contributors and benefactors in every negotiation between the two.

In 1982, a CORO Foundation study, CORO Foundation Fellows in Public Affairs, 1981–1982, surveyed California companies that had established community relations programs that included, in part, inventory contributions, loaned executives, and employee volunteers. The executives of these companies cited five aspects of the programs that were most appealing and generated excitement in executives' meetings. Compare these aspects with the characteristics of a traditional program that only gives monetary grants.

1. Low cost. Inventory and equipment were at low market value when contributed, and distributing them cost next to nothing.
2. Creativity. The staff members culling inventories for useful donations and performing volunteer service were prodded by these tasks to think creatively. Some of the executives felt renewed by their community contacts.
3. Cooperation. The company staff liked being part of something that contributed to the community, whether it was making the arrangements for a community organization's board meeting at corporate headquarters or helping a job-training instructor learn the newest machinery.

4. Potential for high visibility. A company may get a short story
    in the local papers for cash contributions but will generate
    much more visibility when it sponsors a picnic for local dis-
    abled kids or opens the office on holidays so nearby elderly
    persons can use the telephones to call distant relatives.
5. Increase in employee morale and productivity. Study after
    study shows that attending to the emotional needs of employees
    pays off.

Limits of the View from the Corner Office

If you are involved in a more traditional giving program, you are
typically located at corporate headquarters, and you work with senior staff more often than lower-level managers. No one would
suggest that it is not good to be near the CEO's suite, but the CCI
executive needs to remember that, to be successful as an orchestrator, the CEO's backing is only one of the critical components. The
other critical components are a strong understanding of the community and an equally strong understanding of the evolving operational needs and plans of the corporation. More often than not,
CCI executives find themselves spending a lot of time trying to get
the attention of the CEO and trying to find some free time from the
constant appeals of the community and hardly any time at all keeping abreast of the concerns of the corporation at a level of detail
necessary for making appropriate connections.

For example, what if the corporation has been criticized for
its statistics on minority hiring? After the company has responded
publicly, what are you going to do about the problem? As a member
of the office responsible for corporate citizenship, what can you do
to affect hiring? Looking at the statistical reports of departments
may indicate some areas for further investigation. One CCI executive approached the problem of minority hiring by focusing on the
company's printing department, where skilled production workers
were in high demand and where attracting and retaining minority
employees was difficult. The executive orchestrated a specially
funded scholarship and job training program through a local community college, tied to a summer job program in the corporation,
in which the printing department supervisor counseled and super-

vised the trainees. The program resulted in more trained minority workers, more minority workers familiar with the company and interested in working there, and a printing department with more knowledge of the backgrounds and styles of its new recruits. This program required commitment from the top management, but it worked because someone walked the production area with the supervisor, communicated that the company cares about his problem of hiring and keeping good workers, and got a commitment from the supervisor to try something new. And finally, it worked because the CCI executive's reputation in the community convinced the community college to follow through with its resources.

The *A* Approach and Corporate Goals

The kind of leadership illustrated by the printing department example relies on interpersonal skills, knowledge of needs, and an ability to draw people into teams. Another necessary skill for making the *A* approach work is strategic thinking. Strategic thinking is particularly important if you hope to transform a current "chamber music" giving program into a more participatory and wide-ranging effort.

Alison Coolbrith was the head of the Aetna Life and Casualty Foundation for a number of years. This foundation is one of the new fully endowed corporate foundations and, thus, does not need to rely on annual profits to conduct its business. But Coolbrith, now a senior officer in the Aetna company, believed strongly that the foundation needed to relate to the corporate culture and set about relating the two. Her guideposts in this were (1) to determine just how much change the company could accept and to take incremental steps toward change rather than to attempt a complete overhaul and (2) to analyze the corporate culture and identify changes in the corporate contributions program that could eliminate weaknesses and build on strengths.

Coolbrith used teams of managers from several divisions to review past operations of the contributions program and recommend new priorities for the program. Her comments on this project, recorded in a 1984 *Foundation News* article on setting priorities, are worth noting: "Setting priorities has many values: it brings attention to the giving function in an organized manner, allowing reconfirmation of values and integrating giving programs with the strategic goals of the company. This will give the program a relevance and utilitarian value. Setting priorities also allows you to involve many other persons who do not normally work in giving programs. You can use it as a mechanism to motivate employees to participate. In addition, setting priorities will give new strength and direction to your contributions staff and reduce the time spent processing paper. Overall, it will strengthen your role in the company. And lastly, you will achieve greater leverage of resources and demonstrate corporate responsiveness to shareholders, regulators, employees, and the public" (Coolbrith, 1984).

Does setting priorities that emphasize corporate objectives eliminate corporate assistance to community activities that do not directly relate to corporate operations? Not at all. When you set priorities, you will include a review of the corporate mission statement and a thoughtful action plan that shows the CCI program's relation to corporate identity and philosophy. Corporate values and social values generally have common themes, and a creative CCI executive can help to join those themes. A wonderful congruity of philosophy occurs when a home-construction supply company that identifies itself and its products as enhancers of family life supports a residence for hard-core juvenile delinquents who have no homes and no family.

The Start-Up of The *A* Approach

Mary Pickard has headed the St. Paul Companies giving programs for almost a decade. Several years ago, she was faced with streamlining the numerous kinds of corporate-community activities that the St. Paul Companies have participated in since 1952. Coordinating the reporting on the many kinds of equipment and inventory contributions made to community organizations was only a first step in the work. Most of Pickard's work has been devoted to drawing the various departments together to draft workable policies and reporting procedures and to work with her office to carry them out. For example, the personnel department agreed to handle the executive and employee volunteer program, matching organizations' requests for people with certain skills to the lists of willing volunteers at the company. Pickard's office supports the personnel office by screening the organizations so that services are delivered to organizations that fit into the corporation's giving priorities.

Pickard took several steps to develop a more unified CCI program out of separate noncash and cash grant programs and to make the A approach work for her corporation (personal communication with authors). You may be able to use the same steps when starting the A approach at your company.

1. Analyze the priorities of the cash contributions program and determine if they are still appropriate. If so, use them to guide priorities in noncash giving.
2. Conduct an inventory of noncash giving to date, including a review of the tax consequences of various contributions.
3. Decide if the noncash giving program needs to be changed, and determine the level of centralization of control if changes are warranted. The program needs to have some kind of workable control, perhaps in the form of established policies, that can shape noncash contributions without severely restricting those individuals who are already making them.
4. Set a dollar limit on noncash giving to serve as a goal and as a control.
5. Develop outcome evaluation measures. Are the contributions succeeding in meeting certain needs, and is the company content with the level of success, visibility, impact, and so on?
6. Educate those employees authorized to approve grants so that they embrace one general policy for giving.
7. Try to coordinate contributions of similar products and large-volume contributions.
8. Decide what the goal of any program will be, especially volunteer programs. If greater involvement throughout the company is the goal, then the direction or focus of actual volunteer activity may not be too important. If the corporation's interest is in marshaling volunteers to help with particular causes or issues, different approaches are required. With either type of volunteer program, it is important to establish two-way com-

munication with the recipient agencies and to listen to the expectations and interests of those involved.

Resources for the Corporate-Community Involvement Executive

If you want to audit the current status of your corporation's total corporate-community involvement—cash, volunteers, equipment, inventory, joint investments, vendor contracts, and so on—you might call in the development directors of your community's most successful nonprofits. These individuals may know more about working with your corporation than you do, and you may be surprised to find that the formal grants program is perhaps third or fourth on their list of preferred contacts in the company. Information about nonprofits' contacts in the company will help you to identify valuable allies within the corporation who are already committed to corporate citizenship. Be mindful to work toward maximizing the efforts already made by people in the corporation, not merely controlling them.

You can also learn about both the capacities and the needs of your corporation by developing an internal resource guide. This guide may be nothing more elaborate than notes from meetings with various department heads, although large corporations have developed profiles on key departments. The goal of the resource guide is to give the CCI office a quick reference on what is available in the company and how to access it. For example, a reference guide entry on the design department in a manufacturing firm might include a few notes on past community involvement and the kind of assistance that the department head feels can be provided. Can the department staff offer some advice on appropriate office furniture for workers with physical handicaps being hired by a community center? Can they provide names of distributors for this furniture? What is the procedure for getting the department involved? How the department answers these questions will depend on how well you can respond to the design department's concerns such as getting more creative challenges into their work and learning more about the end users of their products. In fact, what you pick up as concerns within the corporation can be extremely useful for shaping your giving policies.

Everyone Can Sing with This Choir

In 1985, we listed forty-seven ways—besides cash—that a corporation could provide resources to a community in *Resource Raising: The Role of Non-Cash Giving in Corporate Philanthropy* (Plinio and Scanlan, 1986). We did not itemize the ways communities can provide assistance to the corporation, and perhaps we should have, if only to reinforce the concept that everyone has something to offer and that total resource matching assumes that the community can help to meet corporate needs. Here are the major resources that you have at hand right now and that can be utilized to further corporate goals and community interests:

> *Facilities and services.* You can use your company's facilities and services in ways ranging from lending your corporate dining room for a fund raiser to taking cancer patients for treatment on the corporate jet.
>
> *Public relations.* Public relations can involve everything from cause-related marketing to completely behind-the-scenes help with a special event.
>
> *Loaned talent.* Within every department, corporations have found top people willing to help on special projects for community groups.
>
> *Products, supplies, and equipment.* These are the resources that everyone thinks about first, and they are very visible and important resources.
>
> *Program-related investments.* Your corporation can purchase from nonprofit organizations as well as invest in community development programs.
>
> *Employee volunteers.* The list of successful programs using employee volunteers is astounding, with everything from side-by-side training of community personnel with company personnel at basic employment law seminars to formalized time-off programs that let employees work at nonprofit organizations that match their interests.

It Works and It Is Fun, But Is It Ethical?

Whenever corporate-community involvement discussions begin to veer into the debate of philanthropy versus corporate needs, two topics usually spring up: cause-related marketing and product dumping. The CCI executive who tries to follow the *A* approach and extend corporate citizenship to all business functions is in a somewhat better position to discuss these topics than most executives.

A frequent criticism of cause-related marketing is that it emphasizes upbeat issues at the expense of other worthy, but difficult, issues. If you are following the *A* approach to corporate contributions, you may well find some of your most enthusiastic partners in the marketing department, particularly if you can bring them positive-image community or public issues that need publicity. Those issues will have been selected by you as the most appropriate ones for helping to meet corporate objectives, and you will have also considered the myriad ways that your corporation can provide assistance to several other marketable issues.

However, it is quite likely that while the marketing department is creating the next Hands Across America for a need that relates to your corporate objectives, you have also arranged with the personnel department to provide ten tutors to a local literacy clinic. You may have also recommended a local nonprofit organization to your personnel department as a reliable vendor of stop-smoking clinics for your employees. The list of corporate-community connections can go on and on. Cause-related marketing may be one of the most visible ways of helping the corporation and the community, but it is the CCI executive's job to be sure that highly visible programs are not the only programs.

The primary criticism of any noncash contributions program is that it can easily be used to dump unwanted products or inventory. In some cases, products have been pulled from U.S. or European markets and distributed to Third World countries where consumer laws are loose or nonexistent. Otherwise intelligent businesses have unloaded useless items as unsolicited contributions to nonprofit organizations and then have been surprised at the lack of warmth from the recipients.

Responding to the criticism of product dumping is simple if

you have adopted the *A* approach: Do not dump products knowingly. If you find that it has been done, do not call it philanthropy, and do all that you can to prevent it from happening again. Andrew Sigler's words (1982) bear repeating in these instances; "how the whole business is conducted every day" is the CCI executive's responsibility. If you respect the community as a resource for corporate needs, you cannot also see it as a dumping ground. The United Way of America's Gifts in Kind organization can help corporations to think more carefully about the kinds of products or equipment they intend to give away. Rather than deal with past abuses as ethical issues, a CCI executive may be able to use this program to educate overly enthusiastic donors without calling their motives into question.

Leading the Choir in a Rousing *Amen*

Most corporate-community involvement officers are in their positions for only a few years and sometimes less. To install a full *A* approach to giving, auditing all ways the corporation can help the community as well as matching community resources to corporate needs, can take all of that time.

You will need the support of the most powerful people in your company in order to introduce the approach. You may need to slowly redefine an existing narrowly conceived program. But you have at least three strong incentives for trying. First, this approach can do more with less cost, except for your staff time. In good times or bad, cost-efficient measures are welcome. Second, interest in business ethics never really disappears, although corporate attention intensifies whenever scandalous behavior reaches public notice. The *A* approach takes ethics off the shelf between crises and provides a way of shaping daily routine more ethically and for the common good. Third, once corporate-community resources are linked, they can promote themselves through the grapevine. You have the chance to affect the style and culture of the corporation for the better.

If you can succeed in beginning this effort, it will follow you throughout the company. And how pleasant it will be for you, as you move on through the corporate ladder, to meet with your corporate-community involvement successor and help this person to update the resource guide entry on your new department, and to say, "And now can *you* get me . . . ?"

References

Andres, W. A. "Corporate Responsibility: The Mark of Professionalism." Speech given on accepting the Lawrence A. Wien Prize in Corporate Social Responsibility, Columbia University, Oct. 27, 1982. Text distributed by the Dayton Hudson Corporation, Minneapolis, Minn.

Coolbrith, A. "Setting Priorities: Why and How." *Foundation News*, Jan./Feb. 1984, pp. 48-49.

Plinio, A. J., and Scanlan, J. B. *Resource-Raising: Non-Cash Giving and Corporate Philanthropy.* Washington, D.C.: INDEPENDENT SECTOR, 1986.

Sigler, A. C. "Business and the Common Good." Address to INDEPENDENT SECTOR membership meeting and assembly, Oct. 26, 1982, Washington, D.C.

Chapter Twenty-Two

Building Relationships
with Grantseekers

Donna L. Cummings

In the mid to late 1970s, corporations began to feel comfortable enough about their participation in philanthropy to openly reveal it. The sensitivities about an economic unit "giving away" its profits started to fade, and corporate CEOs began to tout what their companies were doing in the community beyond their contributions to the local and national economy. Corporate foundations and corporate giving programs began to put out annual reports, and it became acceptable, and perhaps fashionable, to talk about the company's social contributions.

Although today corporate giving is discussed in many circles, and corporations are visibly contributing to the social well-being of communities where they reside and to the nation, corporations still remain aloof in their identification with social programs and other noneconomic causes and activities. Perhaps they fear diverting too much of their resources to nonbusiness activities and losing sight of business's primary purpose—shareholder profits. Or perhaps corporations fear being so closely aligned with the nonprofit sector that they could risk losing their "holier-than-thou" self-perception. Whatever the reason, corporations still tend to shy away from truly letting the community in and becoming an integral part of shaping the social fabric of communities and the country.

Corporations do not seem to recognize the significant contributions they are capable of making, beyond what they are currently doing, to finding solutions to the social needs and dilemmas confronting our society. As a result of this aloof position, too many corporate giving programs are managed outside of the company's prevailing management system. Although the giving function sits within the corporation, the time and attention given to managing and integrating other business functions into the strategic plans of the corporation are not likewise given to the contributions program. Rather, the contributions program is held almost as an addendum to the rest of the organization. This attitude is often manifested in the positioning, staffing, and funding of the program. Consequently, too little time is spent on developing an understanding of the needs and problems of the community. Community needs and how the corporation can play a role in fulfilling those needs can only be determined through the establishment of relationships with those people on the front line in the communities, managing the problems and responding to social needs as best they can.

The corporate grants officer is one of the focal points for building relationships with the community. This person is the most frequent contact between the corporation and the community. The grants officer creates the first brush stroke for the picture being painted of the company and its presence (or lack thereof) in the community.

Given the significance of the grants officer to the company's community image, it is important that these officers be supported in their efforts to create and build good working relationships with grantseekers. This means, among other things, that grants officers must be given the freedom to understand, interpret, and translate the community's needs to the corporation in an informed and sensitive way, so as to shape giving decisions that are rational for the company and that meet the needs of the community. This freedom can only be realized when grants officers have a clear sense of the mission of the giving program and are open and sensitive to the needs of the community.

Characteristics of Good Relationships

The grants officer, the corporation, the grantseeker, the prospective donee organization and its beneficiaries, and the community all benefit from good working relationships between grants officers and grantseekers. Not only does a good relationship qualitatively enhance the grantmaking process, it also assures an informed decision. In this era of mergers and acquisitions, downsizing and restructuring, and cost reduction and cost effectiveness, relationships (that is, partnerships) have emerged as an important strategy for delivering services and effecting positive change.

A good relationship, however, does not happen by itself. In the past, grantseekers tended to initiate and nurture the relationship, and grants officers expected them to do so. But grants officers cannot afford to take a passive approach in building the relationship because the grants officer is just as dependent on the grantseeker as the grantseeker is on the grants officer. Each party involved must actively participate in building a good relationship.

To start, the grantseeker must have contact with the appropriate corporate representative, the grants officer. The two must come together as equals in mutual respect for one another, open to the possibility of heightening each other's awareness about the other and about the organization or opportunity each represents. The exchange must be one of honest exhortation and truth as each knows it. One grantseeker characterizes the ideal exchange as one where neither talks "stink." "Never talk stink," he says. "We must learn how to give our candid opinions without putting other people down. Trust is the real relationship" (personal communication with author). Trust will not emerge at the initial meeting, but if the interaction has been one of honesty and truthfulness, trust will inevitably develop over time.

Keep in mind the following characteristics of good communication between grants officer and grantseeker.

- Communication between the grantseeker and the grants officer flows freely. Sharing occurs in both directions.
- The two parties trust each other and communicate openly and honestly. Each knows what to expect of the other.
- Different points of view are tolerated and respected even if they are not fully reconciled.
- Each party attempts to understand each other's goals and objectives.
- Each party withholds judgments until after all pertinent and available information is reviewed.
- The exchange process is flexible.
- A fair evaluation is made of the potential fit between the grant-seeking organization and the corporation.
- The grants officer provides assistance to the grantseeker in understanding the corporation, its modus operandi, and its interests.
- The grantseeker helps the grants officer to understand all aspects of the nonprofit organization or cause.
- Each party is patient.
- Each party respects the other's time and resources.
- Each party displays genuine interest and concern throughout the grantmaking process.
- Both the grants officer and the grantseeker feel important to the process.
- There is no negative tension in the interaction. Tension is centered around the myriad possibilities each interaction offers.
- Each listens to the other.
- The relationship is a learning process for everyone involved.

What can the grants officer do to build trust? To begin with, the grants officer must be known and must be available to grant-seekers. It is imperative that grantseekers know whom to make contact with for funding consideration. I do not know of a corporate giving program that is not understaffed, so do not get immobilized by feeling you must meet in person with every grantseeker who approaches the corporation with a request for funding. Instead, find ways of acknowledging the grantseeker through information and a responsive attitude.

One of grantseekers' frequent complaints is that many corporations do not provide any or enough information about their programs to allow grantseekers to make efficient decisions about the prospective corporate donor. Grantseekers do not like to waste their time anymore than grants officers like their time being wasted. Providing information about the corporation's grantmaking mission and goals and its programmatic and geographic interests can save time, effort, and resources, as well as eliminate a potentially bad experience for the grantseeker approaching the corporation.

The more accurate the information disseminated about your program, the fewer inquiries you will receive because it becomes clear to the grantseeker what kinds of programs the company is interested in funding. Making available annual reports, giving guidelines and limits, the grantmaking procedure, and other descriptive materials about your program helps the grantseeker to determine whether an approach to your corporation is potentially fruitful.

Another frequently cited concern is the inability of grantseekers to get an audience from the corporation. Most grantseekers feel they can make a more effective case for their organizations in a person-to-person contact. An opportunity to meet with the grants officer is desired and welcomed. A visit by the grants officer to the organization is most grantseekers' dream. Absent either of these contacts, however, an attentive telephone conversation that imparts some level of knowledge of and interest in the request can suffice.

Grantseekers desire the interaction to be "authentic," that is, an interaction in which the grants officer exhibits unbiased interest in the grantseeker and the cause. Grantseekers wish to be respectfully acknowledged and listened to. They want the grants officer to learn enough about their organizations to be able to make judgments about their "fit" with the corporation's giving goals and objectives. They want the grants officer to be interested in their organization even if it is small, not very visible, or unglamorous. They would like the grants officer to have some appreciation for what the organization is doing, even when the officer has had no prior exposure to the nature of the work of the grantseeking organization.

American Honda Foundation learned through a survey ("Feedback," 1987) that if basic courtesies are not extended by the corporation the development of good relationships with grantseekers will be hindered. These courtesies include: the opportunity for grantseekers to talk personally with the grants officer, prompt response to telephone calls, prompt response to written correspondence, and reasonable length of time for a decision on a grant request. In addition, American Honda learned that other factors will serve to distance the grantseeker or weaken the relationship: inability to determine who the grants officer is, inability to determine the corporation's grantmaking interests, insensitivity to the grantseeker's organization or cause, ambiguity in communications, and condescending attitude by a grants officer toward a grantseeker.

I believe the degree to which a relationship is formed between a grants officer and a grantseeker is highly dependent upon the level of knowledge and sophistication of the grants officer. In my experience as a corporate grants officer, the more I came to know and understand my organization—its mission, values, and motivations—the better I was able to influence the system to effect meaningful grantmaking decisions. Concomitantly, the more knowledgeable I became about the concerns and needs of the community and society, the better positioned I was to see opportunities the company could use to carry out its grantmaking mission.

I also believe it is the grants officer who is best positioned to determine whether a fit exists between the goals and objectives of the grantseeker and the goals and objectives of the corporation. Grants officers are in a powerful position when they have a good understanding of their corporation as well as an understanding of community needs and issues. They can make or break the relationship with a grantseeker and the person's organization. I have been impressed and humbled by this position. But I have also seen it abused.

I believe it is incumbent upon all grants officers not to be too impressed with themselves because of having what I call "power by default" but rather to recognize and appreciate the seriousness of the responsibility that is placed on them. This means that they must not succumb to a superiority complex in their relationship with grantseekers but must relate to them as partners in an exploration of potential mutual benefit. I believe you have arrived as a full-fledged professional grants officer when you are proactive in your approach to grantmaking—proactive in understanding and analyzing community needs and issues, locating organizations and people who can positively influence those needs and issues, collaborating with others to shape a strategic plan for addressing the need, and moving your corporation to a position of vested interests in addressing public needs through thoughtful deployment of its resources.

Formulating a mission and goals for the grantmaking program and then communicating these to grantseekers are good investments of a company's time. Well-communicated goals along with any focused interests that the corporation might have can eliminate unwanted requests, save time, and avoid negative feelings. Clear boundaries and limits deter unrealistic expectations and save time. Being clear about the limitations of your program is equally or more important than having clarity about what it is you want to accomplish.

A structured grantmaking process organizes the work flow and can help keep the decision-making process on track. In addition, it gives clear direction to grantseekers about the procedural elements of your program.

Access to the grants officer saves the grantseeker time, eliminates frustrations, and avoids residual negative feelings. The name of the person responsible for your corporation's grantmaking needs to be available for public consumption, so that every grantseeker gets led in the same direction. It is confusing to the grantseeker and it clouds the grantmaking process when grantseekers either approach the wrong person in the organization because of misguided information or attempt to circumvent the system.

An information system that can report the status and disposition of a request without undue delay communicates to grantseekers that their request is being or has been given full and serious consideration. Timely responses to inquiries save everybody's time and help to create a good public image for the corporation.

Outcomes of Good Relationships

In my experience, endless "ripples" can result from the grantmaking process. The process in and of itself has a catalytic quality to it that mirrors no experience I have ever had before. This catalytic quality reinforces the value of making the process a good experience

for everyone involved. Here are two examples of my experience of
ripples that were created as a result of establishing good
relationships in the grantmaking process.

> A local plant manager whose company had been acquired by
> a foreign corporation was concerned that the foreign par-
> ent would not want to remain in the community. After
> sharing his concern with the executive director of a grant-
> seeking organization the company had supported over the
> years, the manager was able to formulate an appeal to
> keep the plan in the community. The appeal showed the
> foreign parent that the local plant had been a positive
> force in the community through its support of the com-
> munity-based organization and had in turn benefited from
> that relationship by being able to function in a supportive
> community environment. The plant manager made his
> case, and the local operation remained in the community.
> A grantseeker went through a corporate grantmaking process
> that did not result in funding to the organization she rep-
> resented. However, during the interaction with the grants
> officer, she learned about a special program emphasis the
> corporation had for that year. She took it upon herself to
> communicate the corporation's special program to other
> appropriate grantseekers who were working in that area,
> resulting in funding to those organizations. Thus, the
> grantseeker became a catalyst for the corporation's grant-
> making interests.

In addition to the serendipitous nature of grantmaking, you
can expect some things to occur as a result of establishing good
relationships with grantseekers. For example, the quality of the
decision making about which groups to fund will improve because
the grants officer will be in a better position to make a case when
presenting pertinent information to the corporate board or decision
makers. Out of good relationships flows good information and a
greater understanding of the issues associated with the request for
funding. Grantseekers will make every effort to provide you with
enlightening information because they know the closer they can

bring you to understanding their area, the better their chances of receiving support from your corporation.

The old adage "It's not what you do, it's the way that you do it," certainly applies to the grantmaking process. As I have shown through one of the examples of unexpected outcomes, grantseekers who have been turned down by your company are apt to make positive representations about the company if they have had a good experience in their contacts with you. How you interact with a grantseeker becomes an effective public relations tool for the corporation.

The grantmaking process can be an environmental scanning tool for the corporation. It is a way of learning what is going on in the community from those people who are closest to the issues. Done effectively, the grantmaking process can become the corporation's eyes and ears.

Both grants officers and grantseekers have the opportunity to broaden their knowledge of community issues and improve their human interaction skills. The eagerness of grantseekers to enlighten grants officers about the issues they focus on, in the hopes that a contribution will result, places grants officers in the enviable position of being able to gather information of all sorts just by expressing a sincere interest in the subject.

Grants officers accumulate knowledge for the corporation about community issues and about ways of resolving those issues. Grantseekers probably interact more closely with grants officers than they do with their own colleagues. A grants officer is in a position to act as a catalyst for bringing people together around issues of common interest, either inside or outside the corporation.

Challenge to Grants Officers

Whether they consciously acknowledge it or not, grants officers are in service to two constituents: the corporation and the grantseekers. They act as the corporation's agent in seeking out, evaluating, and recommending grantmaking actions that are in concert with and supportive of the corporation's mission and goals. In fulfilling this responsibility, they must interpret the grantseeking organization's mission and goals to the corporation and demonstrate that the prospective donee's mission and goals are compatible with the corporation's when they recommend a grant be given or not compatible when they recommend declining to give a grant. These dual constituencies place the grants officer in a position of conflicts and challenges. Conflicts occur when grants officers consider whether to confine themselves to the boundaries of corporate policies and guidelines or creatively stretch the boundaries to accommodate a community need. Representing dual constituencies is always a challenge, even when their interests are mutual. Questions always arise, for example, over who has preemptive authority in the case of opposing viewpoints on strategy, donor or donee?

Do not trap yourself into believing that the carrot (funding) you hold as a grants officer elevates you to a position of authority over grantseekers. You are just as dependent upon them for your success as they are on you for their success. When you view the grantmaking process as collaborative and become fully aware of the give-and-take required to make it a successful process, the one-upmanship position of the grants officer quickly fades away. As the pressure increases to align giving activity with corporate goals, grants officers will increasingly welcome the partnership approach to grantmaking as a means of discovering new ways for corporate resources to address community needs.

Challenge to Corporations

Fully engaging in problem solving, shaping solutions, and developing and implementing strategic plans is becoming a requirement for participation in the life of communities today. Participative management is crossing all sectors of society. Social issues have become too complex for corporations to view monetary contributions as an acceptable way of satisfying corporate citizenship responsibilities. Strong partnerships must be forged to tackle the complex issues our society faces, and corporations must be fully participating members in these partnerships.

How well a corporation forges relationships with grantseekers is dependent on how committed the corporation is to providing the necessary support to effectively carry out the grantmaking function. Corporations may need to rethink their grantmaking program with respect to the potent role it plays in shaping the corporation's public image. The basic requirements of mission and goals, process, procedures and staff, along with accessibility to information about the corporation's grantmaking program must be carefully established before the contributions staff can develop meaningful relationships with grantseekers and their organizations.

Building relationships with grantseekers is a natural outcome of the grantmaking process. The relationship steadily emerges between initial contact and final disposition. The challenge to the grants officer is to ensure that the interaction is a positive one, in which all parties involved have good feelings about the quality of the process. To do this requires the creation of an atmosphere of care and respect in which open and honest communication abounds.

References

"Feedback: Negative and Positive, A Key Policy Determinant." *Foundation Focus* (quarterly newsletter of American Honda Foundation), Fall 1987.

Chapter Twenty-Three

Encouraging Company Employees
to Volunteer

Sheryl Wiley Solomon
Barbara O. Ragland
Eugene R. Wilson
Myrna Plost

Editor's note: A word of explanation is in order concerning the structure of this chapter. Each of the other chapters is a self-contained essay on a single topic or theme. In Chapter 23, however, we asked four executives to describe the elements in the employee volunteer program of their respective companies. The diversity of corporate employee volunteer programs is so great that a single chapter would not do justice to the richness of this field of enterprise. By asking Sheryl Wiley Solomon to describe the employee volunteer program at Ralston-Purina, Barbara Ragland to outline the Corporate Neighbor Program of Federal Express, and Eugene R. Wilson and Myrna Plost to write on Atlantic Richfield's corporate employee volunteer program, we hope to convey to our readers the enormous range of options available to them when they fashion or fine-tune such programs in their own companies.

Ralston Purina's Volunteer Program

When I was first asked to write a section on Ralston Purina's volunteer program for this book, I declined, citing what I thought were valid reasons: our program is small, it is not unique, and any company can start a program like ours. I was persuaded, however, that information about our program would be useful to other firms that were considering launching volunteer efforts precisely because of these reasons. Upon reflection, I agreed that many companies delay plans to start volunteer programs because they are short on manpower, money, and time. Moreover, my message is that it does not take a lot of any one of these resources to run a successful volunteer program.

The task does require a staff person to develop the program, publicize it to employees, and implement it on an ongoing basis. It also requires some money—but program costs can vary greatly. Most of my expenses are incurred in sponsoring special events (volunteer fairs, walk-a-thons, rallies), and in creating the employee communications pieces that promote our program activities (posters, fliers, table tents). Moreover, a quality program can be tailored to fit any budget, especially if in-house creative services are available.

I will present an example of what any company can do to start a volunteer program with limited staff and budget. Our program is based on the clearinghouse model, which provides employees with information about volunteer opportunities available in the community and refers them to appropriate nonprofit agencies. I have implemented this model at two very different corporations. The concept is simple and, with a little nurturing, it does work.

First Steps. Once your company decides to launch a volunteer program, the first step is to determine what form it will take. Establishing program goals helps determine the program format. For example, Ralston Purina's program objective is to promote voluntarism in general and to match the volunteer interest of employees with community needs. For this reason, we designed our program using the clearinghouse model as described above.

How do you find nonprofit agencies seeking corporate volunteers? I contacted the Volunteer Action Center of the local United Way. They provided me with a list of 250 agencies that met the minimum United Way standards. After reviewing the list, I selected twenty to twenty-five agencies in each of six categories: youth, health and welfare, education, senior citizens, crisis services, and other. When selecting agencies, it is important to include a good cross section of organizations to appeal to diverse employee interests. Also, remember to choose agencies located in different geographic areas of your community.

A letter and application form were sent to each organization to determine its interest in participating in the newly created Ralston Employee Volunteer Network (EVN). The only requirements for participation were that agencies have flexible hours for volunteers and a volunteer coordinator on staff.

Agency response to our invitation was very good. We began to build a data base directory of EVN organizations that later would be distributed to employees who joined the network. The directory included each agency's location, telephone number, contact person, and service areas. The document was compiled using the dBase software package, which most companies have, but any similar software that allows for easy updating will do the job.

Employee Recruitment. The process of recruiting employees is fun and can be done in many ways. Special events help create enthusiasm for new employee involvement programs, so we staged an EVN rally to announce the program. The rally was held from 3:00 to 3:45 P.M. in the cafeteria, and refreshments were served. Information was provided about the goals of the program, the need for community volunteers, and upcoming EVN activities. Employees were asked to sign up as EVN members, automatically placing their names on the mailing list for future newsletters. The *EVN Agency Directory* was also distributed.

To publicize the event, I wrote an article about the joys of volunteering for our employee publication. I included a survey, asking employees to tell us about their volunteer activities. This gave us an idea about the current level of employee involvement. A special written announcement was sent to all employees explaining the new program and inviting them to the rally. Posters, banners, and table tents also promoted the activity.

Communications. Every program manager needs a vehicle for communicating with members on an ongoing basis. The most popular medium is a volunteer newsletter. Through our EVN newsletter, I provide members with information about upcoming program activities and include any recent volunteer opportunities submitted by agencies. Ideally, the newsletter should be produced regularly so that you keep in touch with members and they anticipate hearing from you. However, do not be discouraged if you cannot produce a monthly or even a bimonthly publication. Quarterly newsletters or even periodic memos will maintain employees' awareness of the program, especially if other program activities are in progress.

To achieve strong program identity, I recommend creating a distinct logo and newsletter masthead. Costs can be contained by using standard size paper stock in an attractive color that can double as stationery. The newsletter can be produced on your department computer or word processor, using special fonts to give it a professional look.

Develop a close working relationship with your company's communications staff so that you can promote program events and employee volunteers with them throughout the year. By featuring a volunteer every month in the employee newsletter, we focus attention on community agencies, heighten awareness of the need for corporate volunteers, and salute our employees.

Program Activities. Initial program plans should include several activities to bring employee volunteers together soon after the program is launched. This will help keep enthusiasm and interest high. One program event that attracts employee volunteers during the workday is the Brown Bag Lunch. At these events, we provide dessert and beverages, and employees bring their lunches. I use these forums to invite guest speakers to discuss their community programs and volunteer opportunities. For example, a Red Cross official has presented the pros and cons of volunteering as a disaster relief worker. A hospital representative has covered the variety of volunteer positions available in the health field. I have also invited

my corporate colleagues to discuss the various employee volunteer
programs and activities they administer.

In the early days of corporate volunteer programs, volunteer
fairs were favorite events for bringing agencies and employees together. Although these fairs are less popular now, I have sponsored
them with good results. Fairs are an efficient way to link large
numbers of employees with agency representatives who can take the
mystery out of volunteering and provide specific information about
what their organizations do.

Fairs are usually held during the workday, making it easier
for employees to attend. I schedule them to be held outdoors in very
pleasant surroundings during the lunch period. My company is
fortunate in being located in a park setting with three small ponds
around which we stage our fair. Each agency is provided with a
table, chairs, a banner, and balloons. We promote the event heavily
with fliers, posters, table tents, and articles in the employee publication. I also write about it in our EVN newsletter. Volunteer fairs
are a good tool for recruiting new volunteers. However, employees
generally do not make commitments at fairs. Agencies must follow
up to get commitments.

Long after the fair is over employees continue to ask for
information about the participating agencies. It is wise to keep a file
on each organization and, as much as possible, maintain a relationship with representatives of nonprofits who participated.

There are many opportunities to bring program members
and nonmembers together for company-sponsored volunteer projects. The EVN sponsors Red Cross blood drives, Goodwill household item drives, and holiday food drives. These events can be
structured so that different departments, divisions, or business units
compete to collect the most donated items for a particular cause.

Volunteer Telethon. The launching of our employee volunteer network in 1987 coincided with a major media event to promote voluntarism in the greater St. Louis area. A local television station, the
United Way, and the Corporate Volunteer Council (of which I am
a member) joined forces to sponsor the city's first-ever "Volunteer
Connection Telethon." The purpose of the two-hour prime-time
event was to encourage viewers to call in and pledge hours of ser-

vices to more than 200 agencies. Member companies of the Corporate Volunteer Council planned internal prepledge campaigns, inviting employees and their families to donate hours that company representatives announced during the live broadcast.

At our initial EVN rally, I gave employees information about the telethon and encouraged them to get their families and friends involved. Several weeks later, we began to publicize the event, sending announcements and prepledge forms to all employees. By writing articles in Ralston's employee publication explaining the need for increased voluntarism and through campaign publicity materials, we raised employee interest in both our program and the telethon. Ralston employees pledged 17,793 hours of volunteer service and helped the community double its telethon goal to nearly 500,000 hours. After three successful years, the telethon will be replaced this year with a prime-time television special, hosted by Miss America, that highlights local agencies and volunteers.

Team Projects. Team projects, which involve a group of employees tackling a volunteer effort together, are another sure way to spark participation. Team projects appeal to many people who do not want to make a long-term commitment because they usually have a set beginning, middle, and end. We have recruited employees to participate in the March of Dimes, United Negro College Fund, and Cystic Fibrosis walk-a-thons as Ralston team walkers, checkpoint hosts, and record keepers. When the requests for walk-a-thons began to multiply last year, I recruited an employee to be chairman of an event because I did not have the time. I provided staff and monetary support and hosted a collection/victory party for participants.

Another successful EVN team project tapped employees to serve as case screeners for our community's annual 100 Neediest Cases program sponsored by the United Way and the *St. Louis Post-Dispatch* newspaper. Through this project, social service agencies submit brief case reports of families in the metropolitan area in dire need of medical, housing, clothing, food, or financial assistance. Cash donations are solicited from the public in December to help these families have a happy holiday.

Each year, over $1,000,000 is donated to more than 12,000 families, so the United Way must have hundreds of volunteers to respond to these requests. To address this need, our EVN sponsored its first lunchtime team project. Fifty volunteers were recruited to screen 500 cases. Because these cases depicted tragic human situations that were emotionally difficult for volunteers to review, employees worked in teams in three conference rooms. We created a positive environment for the volunteers by providing pizza, sandwiches, and salad while they worked. Holiday decorations added a reminder of the brighter season others would have through their efforts.

Another type of team project familiar to many companies is Junior Achievement (JA). In one JA program, volunteers serve as business advisers to high school students who learn about the American economic system by running their own minicompanies. Students are recruited by Junior Achievement staff and assigned to JA Centers throughout the community.

Ralston sponsors two JA companies. I enlist the aid of employees who work with young adults on business projects from September through February. The companies identify products they will sell, devise business plans, sell stock, set up operating units, pay debts, make profits or losses, and then liquidate. Advisers often meet on company time to plan their sessions with the students, which are held at night once a week. Each Christmas, the EVN sponsors product sales days at Ralston to encourage employees to buy our JA companies' products. I also invite interested employees to JA adviser recruitment lunches in July to explain program goals and hold in-house training sessions for new advisers in September.

Board Bank. One program component that nonprofit agencies and employees alike find helpful is the Volunteer Board Bank. Community agencies are always seeking qualified people to serve on their boards of directors, and they welcome any organized means of locating volunteers with skills in fund raising, public relations, or other specializations. Employees often want to volunteer as board members but lack the initial contacts to get involved. This is especially true of lower- and middle-level managers who have not yet had much visibility in their companies.

Whether or not you have a formal board bank, your company will probably get requests from local organizations to provide candidates for board positions. One easy way to facilitate this match is to develop a list of employees who have expertise in certain areas and are willing to share it with others. Inserting a survey in your company newsletter is an effective way to elicit responses from interested employees.

Most local United Ways offer training for board candidates throughout the year. They often will conduct these sessions at company facilities for the convenience of employees. Once volunteers have completed this training, they usually are eligible to become part of the United Way's board candidate data base. Board banks also prove useful in providing management with a suggested list of employees for special assignments or loaned executive positions.

Summary. The program I have described is comprehensive, but very flexible. Each of these components can be implemented on either a large or small scale. Remember: you can start a volunteer program using as many or as few program elements as is feasible for your company. Many programs start small and expand to meet demand. Do not worry if you lack a few resources. Some programs may be blessed with good staff support, strong top management involvement, and big budgets, but you can succeed with limited resources. Of course, challenges always exist. But help can be just a telephone call away. The United Way's Volunteer Action Center, managers of other corporate volunteer programs, and national organizations like The National Volunteer Center and INDEPENDENT SECTOR (both located in Washington, D.C.) are eager to provide assistance.

So, you want to start a corporate volunteer program? Although it is a project that requires an initial investment of staff time, creativity, and money, the payoff for your community and your company and its employees will be well worth the effort. My best advice: Go for it! You hold the key.

The Federal Express Corporate Neighbor Program

The Federal Express volunteer program is founded upon some very basic principles that have propelled the organization to be nationally heralded as a model corporate volunteer program. The premises are quite simple and not in the least original. However, in the fast-paced, complex corporate arenas within which we operate, with primary emphasis necessarily on increased profitability and market share, the simple approaches can sometimes be overshadowed. . . . Get the people to become a part of your story by becoming a part of theirs; create an environment that welcomes input and interchange; listen to their ideas; state the general objectives and desires, and let them design program specifics and take charge of the implementation. . . . The success of the Federal Express Corporate Neighbor program, which has received White House recognition five times over the past several years, is largely a result of this mindset.

Organized corporate volunteerism is an excellent complement to corporate grantmaking, and in times of tight money, it can provide an invaluable alternative to grantmaking. The Federal Express Corporate Neighbor Team (CNT) program was introduced in 1983 by a large-scale promotional campaign that featured an eighteen-minute videotape of executive and senior managers espousing the significance of the program from a corporate, community, and personal perspective. Federal Express bases its operations on a three-prong philosophy: people, service, and profit. With the emphasis on people embedded within the "soul" of the corporation, official endorsement of an employee volunteer program was seen as a natural extension of the corporate philosophy.

The CNT program was designed to facilitate employee participation. Under the CNT umbrella nine teams operate year-round. Each team is unique in the type of service it provides. The specialties of the teams are evident in their titles: Arts Services, Children/Youth Services, Educational Services (Junior Achievement and Adopt-a-School), Handicapped Services, Health Services, High Tech Services, Senior Citizens (fondly referred to as Expressly Gray) Services, United Way Services, and the Federal Express Pilots' Wives Association. Employees select the team or teams of their choice based on expertise or interest.

A cornerstone of the CNT program is management of the individual CNTs by employees. Team operations are guided by a handbook presented to annually elected officers at mandatory orientation sessions held at the start of each fiscal year. Teams have the authority to select community service projects and estimate the budget and other resources necessary to perform them.

Team officers have the responsibility of ensuring that all activities are consistent with CNT program guidelines. Within a prescribed period of time, team officers and project leaders must complete standardized project completion reports. In essence, CNTs are treated as business units. CNT membership is open to all employees, their families, and friends; however, only employees can hold offices or serve as project leaders. By design, employees develop a strong sense of ownership for the program and are truly committed to the success of the program. Clearly, organized corporate volunteerism provides a means for employees to maximize the impact of their individual efforts.

Based on a survey taken several years after the start of the CNT program, we were able to document the many benefits to the corporation that result from the program. Survey results confirmed that employee participation contributes significantly to career development and job productivity. This is especially so for volunteers in leadership positions. Enhanced skills development was cited in eight assessed job skills. The following list gives each job skill and the percentage of employees surveyed who thought their volunteer work improved the skill.

Job Skill	Percent
Teamwork	67
Ability to motivate others	57
Organization	55
Leadership	53
Listening	48
Decision making	45
Speaking	43
Writing	28

Enhanced job skills contribute to employee job satisfaction and productivity. The ability to act as company representatives trained and authorized to complete specific missions generates a strong sense of loyalty and pride in a corporation. The improved employee attitudes ultimately have a favorable impact on the bottom line. The positive attitude of active volunteers serves to attract new volunteers to the program, particularly employees whose jobs offer few outlets for creativity, self-expression, and variety. Although the survey results did not constitute news to the veteran volunteers nor to the community relations staff, they did help the professional staff in securing increased budgets and use of other company resources for community involvement projects.

It is important to administer volunteer programs with the same management techniques commonly used in other areas of the business operation. The success of too many corporate volunteer programs depends heavily on the "decency" and conscience of upper management to motivate them to "do the right thing." However, the "right thing" can change in times of economic uncertainty. Volunteer managers need to operate their programs with a business perspective. Some suggestions for doing so follow.

Operating Manuals for the Program. Volunteer programs should have a charter that is very specific about the purpose, goals, and objectives of the program and a clearly defined organizational structure. In our case the charter includes the team concept, the composition of the teams, membership requirements, offices, and officer responsibilities and authorizations. You should clearly state the staff support that will be available to assist the volunteers with their projects and to intercede on their behalf to upper management. Establish channels through which you can be most effective in your liaison role. For example, under the umbrella of the CNT program, we established the CNT Community Relations Council. This council is composed of the officers of each of the CNTs and the volunteer staff, and it meets monthly at the lunch hour. Meeting monthly at, for the most part, a brown bag lunch avoids use of the one-hour-per-month work release time allotted by the company, which was established to allow individual teams time to plan project strategies. (With the exception of the Adopt-a-School and Junior Achievement CNTs, the volunteer projects are generally conducted after work hours on the employees' time.)

Knowledge of the Company. As a corporate volunteer program manager, you must recognize that you have internal constituents who are just as important, if not more so, as your external ones. This realization, then, requires that you stay abreast of the current events in your company. For example, what are the employee-related problems that managers are encountering? Are these problems related to boredom or low morale? Is the company or any particular division suffering from some sort of image-related problem? What are the key concerns now facing your corporation?

Corporate volunteerism can boost the morale of employees as well. Some years ago, the illegal activities of several employees at a particular location were discovered. This discovery received great attention within the corporation; although only a few employees were involved, most employees at the location felt tremendously stigmatized by the events. They felt a certain dignity was lost, and morale was low.

The location was targeted for CNT start-up. Management approved the plan, and presentations soliciting employee involvement were made. The response from employees interested in participating in this company-endorsed program was high. Concurrently, management stepped up its efforts to reinforce and reward positive performance in the targeted area.

On one occasion, a CNT meeting was interrupted in order to read a letter of commendation for extraordinary workgroup performance. The employees interjected cheers at several points during the reading, and when the manager finished, he exclaimed, "We are back!"

That CNT developed into one of the our strongest employee volunteer groups. Today, the team continues to receive high internal and external recognition and commendation for outstanding employee volunteerism.

We credit the partnership of our corporate neighbor program and division management with having laid the foundation for this success at a time when it was critically needed. Volunteer program administrators must be alert for such factors so that they can propose volunteer opportunities to offset negative occurrences such as these. Volunteer managers who approach their job from this perspective will surely capture the attention and ultimate support of upper management.

Integration of Programs into the Corporate Culture. The positive survey results mentioned earlier were used to get commitments from upper management to "adopt" a Corporate Neighbor Team. We initially disclosed survey results in a meeting with the chief operating officer that concluded with our request that he make a presentation to his peers at the next meeting of senior managers. At the conclusion of the chief operating officer's fifteen-minute presentation to his peers, each of the teams was "adopted" by a senior officer, and a few teams had multiple "adopters." The direct ownership of the CNTs by senior management provided a tremendous boost to the program. The morale of the volunteers improved markedly, and the growth of the overall program surged. Of course, we had given considerable thought to and had fully discussed the responsibilities of the adopters.

Managers of volunteer programs must continually search for ways to facilitate management support of the programs. At Federal Express, individual adopters are requested to divert little time from their busy schedules. However, with prior approval, their names are used a great deal—for endorsements and commendations, for example. Approximately once a year, adopters are requested to attend a CNT meeting and give brief but spirited remarks of encouragement. Some adopters attend more frequently. Adopters are kept on the automated mailing rosters of all teams and receive regular communications of team activities. They appreciate being kept apprised, and the volunteers are encouraged by the knowledge that the adopters follow their activities.

Study your employees as well as the current events in your company. Why do they volunteer? What types of projects interest them? With what frequency do they volunteer? What are their strengths and weaknesses? Who are the planners versus the hands-on implementers? A wealth of information such as this can be obtained through project reports, surveys, observation, and conversation with volunteers.

It is important to note that the majority of the volunteers will not be interested in project planning. Volunteer managers should not be discouraged by this. In fact, projects are better planned by a small core group of people who have access to a large pool of volunteers who are generally happy to accept and perform specific assignments when asked to.

Promotion of Programs and Participants. Do not allow your group's hard work to be the company's best kept secret! Tasteful promotion of community service projects is not only appropriate but essential to the long-term health of your volunteer program. Program exposure can be accomplished a number of ways: mention in the corporate annual report; publication of an annual social responsibility book; articles in departmental, divisional, and corporate newsletters; and letters, certificates, and plaques of commendation signed by officers of the corporation and presented at staff meetings, team meetings, and recognition receptions.

Thank-you letters, with copies sent to management several levels above the volunteer, are very effective. Many times, such letters precipitate additional commendations directly to the employee from upper management. The employee receives the workplace recognition that is essential to the longevity of the program, and management's position that the program serves a real need (in this case, that of keeping employees motivated) is reinforced. Behind the scenes, of course, volunteer managers should be equipped with a ready supply of such letters of recognition and commendation.

In these times of economic uncertainty, volunteer program managers face enormous but surmountable challenges and opportunities. Managers who continually strive to understand and make better use of corporate cultures may reach a level of internal and external effectiveness not yet known to us.

The ARCO Volunteer Service Program

Out of the blue, we received a call from another large California oil company seeking to start a volunteer program. In response, the director of Atlantic Richfield's (ARCO) volunteer programs met with the vice president of communications of this company, an enormously busy woman concerned about the need to initiate a companywide program with little staff support. What had attracted her to corporate volunteer programs?

Without question, support from the top—even from the

White House in recent years—has had strong positive impact on the trend toward these programs. At ARCO, over 2,000 volunteers are working to solve community problems through a program sponsored by the company. This volunteer program has been and remains at the core of ARCO's community involvement efforts.

"What do I need as essential ingredients to make a successful volunteer program—such as ARCO's—work?" she asked. "What's the best role for the corporate foundation in providing grants to volunteers? How did you involve your CEO, which would be critical to the success of our program—as it must be for yours?"

Companies large and small feel the need to answer these questions and establish volunteer programs. Every American has been reminded by President Bush that any definition of a successful life must include serving others. A corporate volunteer program is an important way to unleash the power of service represented by willing employees and retirees who want to work in behalf of others in need.

ARCO's volunteer program may not work totally for another company without some changes. But the essentials run like a thread through most corporate volunteer programs. These are: support from the CEO; recognition of outstanding volunteers; and ongoing promotion, communication, and placement.

Support from the CEO. ARCO's CEO and chairman, Lod Cook, stated at the 1988 Chairman's Award Dinner that "We believe a corporation must be responsible not only for a satisfactory level of return on investments, but also to improve the society in which we all live. That's why the spirit and tradition of volunteerism at ARCO runs so strong and deep. Our employees and retirees are the heart and soul of our efforts to help build better communities. We encourage our people to give their time and talents to community organizations of their choice. By giving of our individual time and resources, we can make a difference." At the annual Chairman's Award Dinner, ARCO's top volunteers throughout the country and sometimes from overseas are recognized by the chairman. This is the high point of the Volunteer Service Program's recognition effort— the Community Service Awards. The process begins with several hundred nominations from ARCO's facilities throughout the country. Each local ARCO operating division and corporate headquarters then selects its own finalists. These finalists are involved in activities as diverse as mentoring low-income children in inner-city schools, running foster homes, caring for terminally ill patients, delivering meals to shut-ins, repairing homes of low-income elderly people, serving in volunteer fire departments, ushering for a theater group, or coaching in the Special Olympics.

Local volunteer winners receive a $500 foundation grant for their nonprofit agency, unless they go on to become the winner in their specific operating division or corporate headquarters unit. In that case, they receive a grant of $1,000 for their designated nonprofit group, usually presented by the president of their ARCO business unit. The ARCO Employee Volunteer of the Year receives a $2,500 grant for his or her nonprofit organization and an elegant clock from Tiffany. ARCO retirees are given similar recognition, with the Retiree Volunteer of the Year selected from winners at the local level. ARCO's most distinguished volunteers are honored each year at a banquet at the company's headquarters in Los Angeles, hosted by Lod Cook. The most outstanding volunteers are chosen from employees in ARCO operating divisions in California, Alaska, Pennsylvania, Texas, Colorado, and Washington, and retirees from these same areas. The National Volunteer Center based in Arlington, Virginia, actually makes the final selections. "I'll never forget those three days in Los Angeles. My treatment, from the time I stepped off the plane, was truly royal," stated a drilling superintendent and Volunteer of the Year from ARCO International, at the Chairman's Award Dinner in 1989.

Communication. Communication is critical to maintaining programs. It was particularly critical several years ago after the company had restructured and significantly reduced the number of employees. At that time, the company newspaper went from a weekly to a monthly. With support from several senior public affairs executives, the volunteer program was assigned one or two pages of coverage in each monthly edition of *The SPARK,* ARCO's internal company paper, and that was a strong start to promoting volunteerism again.

Additionally, a monthly newsletter was initiated at several

ARCO locations. Volunteer opportunities from helping redecorate a New Year's parade float to working with child-abuse victims are advertised. Group projects are announced, and they sometimes draw several hundred volunteers. One-on-one volunteer placement opportunities are also advertised.

Local Volunteer Action Centers provide volunteer counseling to interested ARCO employees and retirees. ARCO traditionally supports these Volunteer Action Centers, which in turn provide the kind of counseling a limited corporate staff cannot. Some centers are excellent; others need help to improve and can improve with corporate assistance. ARCO staff have played a significant role in supporting the Volunteer Centers of California and in the statewide volunteer awards effort, with strong participation by many other corporations.

A Central Program. An important volunteer program supported by ARCO is the Adopt-a-School program, or Joint Education Program (JEP). ARCO was one of the first companies in Los Angeles to establish school partnerships when it joined the Adopt-a-School movement in 1975. That program now includes over 700 Adopt-a-School partnerships. As a result of its long involvement, ARCO received the Presidential Award for Excellence in Private Sector Initiatives in 1987.

JEP sends over 100 or more volunteers each year to ten inner-city schools to provide one-on-one tutoring or weekly courses in the classroom. These ARCO volunteers, or "JEPers," get company released time of one-and-one half hours per week, and frequently also work with parents after school. Six greater Los Angeles elementary schools, one junior high school, two high schools, and a special education school now benefit from ARCO employee involvement.

Recently, the ARCO Foundation provided a grant to bring the "Writing to Read" computer program to the first grade students and parents learning English at one predominantly Latino inner-city elementary school near ARCO's corporate headquarters. ARCO volunteers have new opportunities to work in the area of literacy with these youngsters and with the adults in their families.

Employee-Directed Programs. Volunteer programs have few limits in what they can do to inspire and place employees in areas of critical need. The only real limits are of staff time to coordinate these efforts. Sometimes employee initiative can help; employees can provide coordination of fellow volunteers. For example, one ARCO employee is strongly committed to aiding abused children with a program called Free Arts for Abused Children. She brought two actresses—Ali MacGraw and Rita Moreno—to ARCO to present an appeal not for employee donations of money, but for their volunteer time. It worked. Since that initial presentation, fifty volunteers spent one Saturday at the Hathaway House, a shelter for child-abuse victims in Los Angeles. Volunteers learned a lot about child abuse, and more important, they learned how they could help. ARCO volunteers work with children as young as two years old to teenagers on art projects and show the youngsters that people really do care about their future.

ARCO has discovered that local employee coordinators at the work site make a significant difference in leveraging the abilities of time-limited staff. The Junior Achievement program, which enables company volunteers to help elementary, junior, and high school students learn economics, has had the commitment of one dedicated ARCO employee for the past twelve years. He is currently coordinating three separate Junior Achievement programs, with some forty ARCO volunteers. Hundreds of young people are helped—a task he alone could never achieve.

ARCO Foundation Volunteer Grants Program

When the ARCO Volunteer Service Program was initiated in 1980, ARCO management realized that the company's contributions resources would not ever be sufficient to provide major financial support to all of the nonprofit organizations in which ARCO employees and retirees were likely to become involved. To make best use of limited contributions resources, the ARCO Foundation decided to focus its grants in a few program categories for specific kinds of activities that changed over time as educational, community, arts, and environmental needs changed. Included in this focus, however, is the objective, as stated in the 1989 ARCO Foundation Annual Report, "to support efforts that encourage individual giving and volunteer involvement in support of the philanthropic nonprofit sector in the United States" (p. 42).

ARCO management recognized the merit of providing incentives for encouraging its employees and retirees to volunteer their own time after working hours in behalf of nonprofit organizations of personal interest. The solution to the problem of insufficient funds seemed to lie in the ARCO Foundation, and the answer was a new Volunteer Grants Program.

For many years, the ARCO Foundation had matched the individual financial contributions of employees and retirees to colleges and universities. In 1980, the types of nonprofit group that could receive a matching gift from the ARCO Foundation were significantly expanded beyond just higher education groups. In that year, the foundation began matching employee and retiree contributions to any nonprofit "public charity" (as defined in Sections 501(c)(3) and 170(b) of the Internal Revenue Code). The only caveat was that recipient groups could not be religious or political.

Through this expanded policy, ARCO had decided not to prejudge the kinds of nonprofit groups that its employees should support but to foster among its employees and retirees the spirit of pluralism on which our free democracy was established. The expanded policy also is a subtle reminder to ARCO employees and retirees that if their communities are to continue to be fit places to live and work, individual residents must take responsibility for them. ARCO management believes that no company or government agency alone can create effective communities.

Standards and Rules. The Volunteer Grants Program was a logical extension of that concept of pluralism. Through the Volunteer Grants Program, the ARCO Foundation implemented a policy of offering grants of up to $500 per year to any qualified nonprofit organizations for which any ARCO employee or retiree devoted significant amounts of his or her own time on a consistent basis. That requirement has since been made more specific, based on the findings of the Gallup surveys of giving and volunteering behavior in America that the Gallup organization (1988, 1990) conducted for INDEPENDENT SECTOR.

To qualify for a Volunteer Grant from the ARCO Foundation, an ARCO employee or retiree must complete a Volunteer Grant Request Form documenting that a minimum of three-and-a-half hours per week, twelve hours per month, of the employee's or retiree's own time (not released time during working hours) is devoted consistently to a nonprofit organization. The time standard was established because this amount of time was discovered in the Gallup surveys to be the average amount of time given by Americans who do volunteer. Long-term volunteer involvement is the objective of the program. Short-time or one-time volunteer service does not qualify for an ARCO Foundation Volunteer Grant.

Qualifying nonprofit groups are defined according to the same Internal Revenue Service rules for public charities as are applied in the foundation's matching-gifts program. Only religious and political groups are excluded. Any given nonprofit organization may receive up to $2,500 in Volunteer Grants per year. Few employees qualify for more than one Volunteer Grant in a year because of the average monthly volunteer time required for a specific nonprofit group.

Procedures. The employee or retiree fills out a Volunteer Grant Request Form and presents it to the nonprofit organization. The manager of the nonprofit group prepares an accompanying letter and forwards the form and letter to the appropriate ARCO regional public affairs office to ensure a local ARCO tie-in. The letter attests to the number of volunteer hours claimed by the employee or retiree. The letter also explains the specific nature of the volunteer services that the applicant is providing.

The public affairs staff in the regional office usually includes the local Volunteer Service Program coordinator. That staff person validates the information from the employee or retiree and the nonprofit organization, then forwards the Volunteer Grant Request package to the ARCO Foundation for approval and for awarding of the Volunteer Grant. When approved, the Volunteer Grant check is mailed to the employee or retiree volunteer to present in person to the nonprofit group for which the individual volunteers.

Results. Over 4,000 Volunteer Grants have been awarded to a wide variety of nonprofit groups since the inception of the program.

Approximately 300 Volunteer Grants are awarded each year by the ARCO Foundation, totaling some $250,000. This relatively low cost makes the Volunteer Grants Program one of the most effective vehicles for motivating and supporting ARCO employees and retirees to become involved in meaningful ways in their communities. Consistent with the Gallup surveys (1988, 1990), ARCO volunteers also tend to be very active contributors of their own financial resources as evidenced by their participation in the Foundation's Matching Gifts Program.

The human impulse to serve others is expressed through the ARCO Volunteer Service Program and the ARCO Foundation Volunteer Grant Program. While no formal measurements have been made, employees and retirees who do volunteer seem to have discovered that their volunteer service brings fulfillment and satisfaction as an enriching complement to their work-a-day jobs.

INDEPENDENT SECTOR encourages all Americans to give 5 percent of their income to charity and to volunteer five hours each week in service to others. ARCO promotes this national Give Five program of INDEPENDENT SECTOR, and the ARCO Foundation uses the Give Five logo and message in its Matching Gift and Volunteer Grant Request brochures. Many of the winning local volunteers in the ARCO Volunteer Service Program already exceed the standard of devoting five hours per week in voluntary service to others. They represent the model of committed volunteerism for other ARCO employees and retirees.

These individuals have become an important part of an ARCO tradition. ARCO now recognizes that its employees and retirees will volunteer—especially if they are given opportunities to do so and then are asked to serve. And when they do volunteer, they represent a proud symbol of ARCO to the organizations and communities in which they are involved.

Any corporation studying how best to initiate or expand a program of community involvement probably will find that a carefully conceived volunteer program for employees, and perhaps also for retirees, will bring highly leveraged returns from only a modest investment of staff time and financial resources. The power of committee people, as Alexis de Tocqueville observed in the early nineteenth century, and as business and political leaders are recognizing anew, is a very worthwhile source of energy with many mutual benefits to the corporation, the community, and the nation.

References

The Gallup Organization. *Giving and Volunteering in the United States.* Washington, D.C.: INDEPENDENT SECTOR, 1988.

The Gallup Organization. *Giving and Volunteering in the United States.* Washington, D.C.: INDEPENDENT SECTOR, 1990.

Chapter Twenty-Four

Being Ethical and Accountable in the Grantmaking Process

Robert H. Dunn
Judith Babbitts

Corporate grantmakers have one of the most difficult jobs in the philanthropic world. To begin with, they perform a function that is antithetical to the business environment in which they work: they give money away rather than make it. As noted earlier in the book, this can make them "marginal" employees, neglected and ignored by those who carry out the "real" purpose of the corporation. No less difficult, on the other hand, is to be seen as the ethical conscience of the company. Because grantmakers are not responsible for the bottom line, they may be dubbed the company's moralists and asked to preserve a good community image for a company that may be careless about ethical business practices.

Grantmakers who dispense both corporate funds and corporate foundation funds face more difficulties. Although it is appropriate to use corporate funds to support nonprofit organizations that provide direct marketing, public relations, or other benefits to the company, it is illegal to use foundation monies for such purposes. This distinction is not readily understood or always popular with company managers, and grantmakers may frequently find themselves justifying their decisions to dissatisfied corporate employees.

Grantmakers must not only be adept at resisting pressures to use philanthropy to increase corporate profits but must also be visionary enough to see opportunities to harness the special resources businesses can offer nonprofit organizations. Corporate grantmakers can multiply the value of grants they make by considering the full range of company assets—the time and talent of company employees, the disposition of investments, and the donation of goods and services. Grantmakers may find themselves called upon to assess the publicity benefits their corporation can derive from funding a particular group, or they may be able to persuade their company's computer department to adopt a grantee and help it solve its most troublesome systems problems.

Some corporate grantmakers believe that their role includes raising questions about how a company's decisions affect its responsibility to the general public. Most corporate managers, however, do not regard community members (excluding shareholders) as legitimate stakeholders in the decision-making process. As a result, grantmakers' insistence on socially responsible business conduct can lead to complaints that they are being nuisances, moralists, or naive do-gooders.

Even the seemingly straightforward process of making funding decisions is different for corporate grantmakers than it is for other grantmakers. Each funding decision requires that corporate grantmakers consider a hierarchy of stakeholders in the grantmaking process. The list of stakeholders includes the grantmaker, investors, senior executives, all other company employees, customers, vendors, opinion setters, community leaders, neighborhood residents, and grantseekers. The corporate grantmakers' challenge is to be mindful of the philanthropic intentions of their donor company, wary of corporate interests that cannot be accommodated, and creative in devising and administering a program that meets legitimate community needs.

Like all grantmakers, corporate grantmakers must be ethical in presenting their programs, judging grant requests, monitoring projects, and reporting the results back to their board, company employees, and the community. This array of considerations and demands makes the position of corporate grantmaker one that tests the mettle of even the most seasoned professionals in the philanthropic arena.

Ethical Problems Faced by Grantmakers

To speak of ethics in corporate grantmaking means to examine the full range of decisions grantmakers face every day. Some ethical decisions are potentially a part of every funder's process in administering a grant program. Others arise because of a relationship between philanthropy and business. A few examples may highlight the ethical dilemmas that occur when philanthropy and business converge.

Suppose a grantmaker receives a special request from a senior manager in the company to review a proposal. The senior manager's interest is sparked because he has been personally solicited by a close friend who chairs the board of a local nonprofit agency. The proposal arguably fits within the corporation's general funding guidelines, but the grantmaker learns that the organization is not widely respected, does not have adequate financial controls in place, uses a disproportionate percent of its revenue for administrative costs, and fails to provide representation on its board for the community it serves.

What does the grantmaker do? Is the solution to simply inform the executive of what the grantmaker has learned and explain why the foundation would hesitate to fund the organization? In most circumstances, yes. Sometimes, as in this example, an organization fails to satisfy the tests a grantmaker must apply in making a funding decision. Ethically proper decision making is then clear and straightforward. But sometimes grantmakers must also deal in shades of gray. Is it ethical to consider the rank and influence of the senior executive requesting the funding? Is it ethical to consider the extent to which this same manager has been a critic of the company's philanthropic efforts and to try to appease him by funding his proposal? Is it ethical to be swayed by an interest in a promotion within the company to a position that has a reporting relationship to the senior executive?

Consider yet another grantmaker's dilemma. Company X is a major employer in a rural county with inadequate public services. The local government adopts a plan that will significantly enhance the health, education, or recreational benefits of its citizens, but the proposed program is to be financed by taxes levied against area businesses. Company management believes that business is being asked to carry a disproportionate share of the proposed taxes and opposes the initiative. The vast majority of employees overwhelmingly favor the measure and think the tax burden is being fairly distributed. The employees seek foundation funds for a community organization conducting a public education campaign that would likely generate support for the ballot measure. The company has a tradition of supporting employees and similar educational campaigns in the past. What does the grantmaker do?

Or suppose Company Y has historically supported a worthy organization that suddenly finds itself at the center of community controversy. As emotions around the agency's work rise to a feverish pitch, a group of activists announces that they will launch a boycott of any business that supports the embattled nonprofit agency. The president of Company Y calls the grantmaker to confirm his assumption that the foundation will cease funding the agency immediately. What does the grantmaker do?

Situations such as these probably cannot be handled without sacrificing some benefit to the corporation, disappointing an individual's personal desires, or subjugating the grantmaker's own interests to a larger philanthropic goal. But it is possible for grantmakers to avoid many difficult situations altogether, or if they do arise, to mitigate the risk they pose and ensure outcomes that are fair and ethical.

Perhaps the single most important ethical decision grantmakers must make occurs before they actually accept their position in corporate philanthropy. Potential grantmakers must determine if they will be asked to operate a program that reflects generally accepted standards of what is fair and proper. They should raise issues in the hiring interview that have ethical implications such as: Does the company view its philanthropic program as independent or as a servant of business objectives? What is my authority to make final funding decisions? What recourse do I have to deflect pressures to deviate from funding guidelines? Does the company take its responsibility to the community as seriously as its duties to other corporate constituencies, that is, shareholders and customers?

If grantmakers fail to learn about the values and ground rules of the corporate and philanthropic culture they enter, they may find themselves in situations that rule their conscience and erode their own sense of integrity. Skeptics may doubt whether company representatives will be forthcoming in hiring interviews about any dubious business practices or about a pattern of ambiguous funding decisions. But by merely asking such questions, future grantmakers reveal their own values and allow employers to know whether there is a match between the individual's and the institution's ethical framework.

Most of the troublesome ethical issues that arise between grantmakers and others in the corporation occur because funders and their sponsors fail to agree upon a clear statement of purpose for the philanthropic goals of the corporation, articulate the criteria that will be used in decision making, and communicate these policies and procedures effectively to their business colleagues. The first responsibility of corporate grantmakers—whether they are starting a new funding program or joining a well-established one—is to examine these issues.

The most important perspective grantmakers should acquire early in their tenure is to see the foundation as an independent and separate entity from the corporation. Failing to insist upon a distinction between the interests of the giving program and the interests of the company, places the funding program and the company in legal and ethical jeopardy. In their zeal to establish or increase their philanthropic budgets, grantmakers may be tempted to make ambitious promises about what their programs can contribute to the short-term interests of the business enterprise.

Grantmakers should be aware that laws prohibit "self-dealing" on the part of corporate foundations. Although it is appropriate for corporate foundations to make grants to schools, hospitals, or symphony orchestras, the benefits to the company and its stakeholders must be incidental. It is altogether inappropriate to make such grants if the only people who benefit from them have connections to the company. Other issues, while not necessarily issues of legality, pose equally unpleasant choices if sharp distinctions do not exist between philanthropic and corporate goals. They include the use of contributions to place company executives on prestigious nonprofit boards, obtain significant benefits for customers or employees, promote research biases in favor of important business interests, or pressure community organizations to make a place for a retired company executive.

Whenever these or other issues arise, grantmakers should remember that ethical dimensions are inherent in the process used to reach a decision as well as in the outcome of the decision itself. For example, excluding a particular group of stakeholders from the decision-making process may simplify the procedure but ultimately may not be fair. In addition, stakeholders who are excluded from an opportunity to influence the process or who feel themselves ignorant of the outcomes, are not likely to be bound by the results. Grantmakers planning a new direction for their giving programs, for example, will be wise to discuss their intentions with both the source of their funds, the corporation, and those who may benefit, community organizations.

Every grantmaker, at one time or another, will be forced to consider the ethical dilemmas presented earlier in this chapter—the repercussions of refusing to fund the pet organization of a senior executive or making the decision to support one group of stakeholders over another. But these situations occur relatively infrequently. More troublesome are the countless small daily decisions and simple acts a grantmaker executes that often go unexamined or, if noticed, are not seen as ethical problems.

Ethics in the Daily Routine

But are all of the decisions that grantmakers wrestle with concerned with ethics, or are we simply dealing with a matter of definitions? Are some decisions just bad and not unethical? Where do we draw the line? Examined carefully enough, all decisions have an ethical component. Consider the following list of questions about the funding process in which all grantmakers engage. At one level, the questions point to sloppy managerial habits or misguided ideas about efficacy in expediting the paperwork and funding requests that engulf all grantmakers. But on another level, they suggest an ethical dimenision to procedures and practices that appear routine.

1. Does your foundation have clear guidelines for you, your staff, and your board to prevent the real or apparent conflicts of interest that can develop when someone associated with your program also has a special relationship with a potential grantee?

2. Are your guidelines sufficiently straightforward so that neither you nor your grantseekers can manipulate them to suit the situation of the moment? Conversely, are your funding criteria broad enough to avoid forcing grantseekers into impossible and unethical positions, causing them to distort their program objectives or promise unrealistic results in order to receive funds?

3. Do you collect enough information and the right kind of information before you make a funding decision? Do you call the grantseeker to verify information you have gathered from other sources or to clarify ambiguous portions of the grant proposal before using those reasons to turn it down?

4. Do you give privileged information to some grantseekers about the board's preferences in making funding decisions so they can tailor their proposals to fit the board's inclinations?

5. Do you respond to proposals in a timely manner and avoid putting grantseekers in untenable positions waiting for a reply?

6. Are you truthful in telling a rejected agency why they were not granted funds? Do you justify providing false reasons by saying the agency does not need to know the truth and that a short answer will avoid prolonged dialogue between you and the agency staff?

7. Do you monitor the progress of the projects you fund, not only holding organizations accountable for the money they receive but also for achieving their objectives?

8. Do you honestly and fully report the results of your funding decisions to those who have a need to know about them?

9. When the board members are considering a shift of the company's funding focus, do you make them aware of any grantees who are counting on continued support to ensure an orderly transition?

10. Do you invest your financial resources to maximize the dollars available for your giving program? Do you explore opportunities to manage your assets in ways that reinforce and support the objectives of your program?

11. Are you satisfied that staff salaries and benefits, office rent and furnishing, printing costs, and other operating expenses are at an appropriate level given the size of your funding program?

12. Do you speak up publicly when you believe other funders are engaging in unethical practices, or do you regard your obligation to colleagues as outweighing your responsibilities to the community or to the attainment of high professional standards in philanthropy?

You can diminish the ethical problems you face in daily routines. Publishing clear guidelines and only deviating from them for very considered reasons is one way. Guidelines that reflect your program's interests and respond to grantseekers needs in the chosen field take time and effort to develop. They should be as explicit as possible and state if preference will be given to one activity or group over another, to rural over urban organizations, for example.

Guidelines that unrealistically demand that grantseekers include a myriad of program components, serve an unusually large number of participants, adhere to a time line that is too short, or promise extraordinary results, often reflect grantmakers' ignorance of the field or the community. Not doing your homework in designing a funding program can invite unethical behavior on the part of those seeking funds. The grantmaker is no less culpable than the proposal writer in this case. The grantmaker also has an ethical responsibility to present the community's case to its board when the board applies unreasonable criteria in making its decisions or setting policy.

At times, grantmakers may feel that they just do not have enough information to decide whether or not to fund a project. What kind of information is legitimate to use and how far should you go in search of it? Is it ethical to call up grantmakers in other foundations and ask for their candid opinion of the organization? Many grantmakers do just that. Is it fair to include information you learned over drinks at the last Council on Foundations meeting? It would almost seem impossible not to recall those interesting observations made by a more experienced practitioner in the field when deciding whether to fund a group. The crucial issue, the point at which your conscience should begin to tug, is the importance you give to such extra data. Each element must be put in its proper place before the final decision is made.

Ethics and the Grantmaker's Values

What about the grantmaker's own values and preferences? Where do they fit into the grantmaking equation? Grantmakers must be wary about listening to their own desires in reviewing proposals, for the temptation to satisfy one's wish for personal gain potentially lurks behind every decision. Grantmakers have the kind of power that money can buy, and the rewards for using it are great: status, influence, self-satisfaction, or the heightened self-esteem that comes from believing you have helped alleviate a societal problem. Few grantmakers would fund a proposal mainly to advance their career within the corporation or to improve their standing in the community. Such obvious enticements clearly wave ethical red flags. However, other, less evident, advantages tempt all grantmakers at one time or another.

Probably most people would think it farfetched to say that funding a project that addresses an obvious community problem could be an abuse of power. But grantmakers who fund projects because they believe in the cause the project addresses even though the project is poorly conceived and appears to have little community support are misusing their power as grantmakers. They are breaking their board's and the community's trust that they will fairly and equitably disburse the funds in their keeping. And by giving to an organization that may not use the money wisely, they are shortchanging the community of a service it needs. If grantmakers abdicate their responsibility to evaluate a proposal objectively, they are accomplices to the broken promises, disappointments, and failed hopes a dysfunctional project invariably creates for community residents.

Some grantmakers give in to seemingly more innocuous biases or, at the least, biases they feel they can justify. Grantmakers may hesitate in deciding to fund a program sponsored by a police organization because they were on the other side of police lines in civil rights demonstrations in the 1960s, and they still harbor notions of the police as a repressive force in society. Or they might be more critical of a school dropout program because it will use church-based youth groups to recruit tutors, and the grantmakers have a personal bias against organized religion. You may ultimately fund proposals that you have a bias against, but not acknowledging the role your personal biases play in a just consideration of all the proposals that cross your desk invites unethical behavior somewhere down the line.

By definition, ethical dilemmas elude simple answers that are either right or wrong. Nor is every ethical problem of identical magnitude or consequence. Not every breach of what grantmakers regard as the best ethical practice warrants their outrage or resignation, but neither is it appropriate for grantmakers to respond to seriously unethical conduct with silence or acquiescence. If something bothers grantmakers, they should speak up. If the frequency or magnitude of less than ethical decisions makes grantmakers uncomfortable, they may need to consider whether the situation justifies resigning. Although it is the head and the heart that often yield good ethical decisions, it is the stomach that generally sends out the early warning signals that a grantmaker is in the wrong corporate setting.

Grantmakers have useful resources to draw upon when they are uncertain about ethical issues or when an ethical question is unfamiliar or vexing. They can speak about their concerns with those who share decision-making responsibility with them. They can consult other grantmakers and academic scholars, professional journals, or experts in regional and national grantmaking organizations. Sometimes, grantmakers have found that the most valuable insights come from someone outside the field of philanthropy itself, someone who shares the same ethical framework as the grantmaker and listens well.

Wrestling with outside pressures to engage in unethical funding procedures, learning to recognize the ethical dimension in seemingly innocuous everyday decisions, and clarifying your own ethical values make corporate grantmaking a difficult endeavor in a society that sometimes appears to be increasingly callous about ethical issues. Corporate grantmakers may often feel that their efforts to fund worthwhile projects are really only a front for a larger mission. If they don the many hats offered them by the corporation and accept their multiple roles, they will, however, find themselves shaping more socially responsible businessess and improving the quality of life for needy community residents. Whether the role of any particular grantmaker is narrow or broad, the exercise of his or her professional responsibility carries with it a special public trust. This trust can only be exercised if decision making and the decision-making process are characterized by high standards of ethical judgment.

Chapter Twenty-Five

Successful Corporate Grantmaking: Lessons to Build On

James P. Shannon

Building good programs in corporate grantmaking or in corporate community affairs is an art, not a science. The more than two dozen corporate executives who have written chapters for this book are recognized as successful practitioners of this art.

No perfect model for corporate grantmaking exists that can be copied by one company from another. Effective grantmaking and effective community affairs programs differ from company to company, depending on the maturity, history, product line, leadership, folklore, and profitability of each company. Serious corporate practitioners of this art will find much to admire and emulate in the chapters of this book, but it is up to each practitioner to write his or her own book, using some of the materials offered here. Good programs in this art are like corporate fingerprints. Each is different and because these programs are alive, they should be steadily changing as they grow and mature.

No other country has the range and variety of nonprofit agencies that we have in the United States. As we move toward the twenty-first century, our citizenry, often without knowing it, is steadily expecting more and better services from our nonprofit sector. Enlightened corporations have a window of opportunity at this time. If they understand our society's growing range of public needs and if they have a realistic view of how different corporate resources can address some of these needs, corporate America can have a larger leadership role in deciding how we shall match our finite private means with our countless public needs in the 1990s and in the new century.

In 1982 and again in 1988 the Council on Foundations commissioned the Yankelovich Group to conduct in-depth personal interviews about their corporate giving programs with more than 200 chief executive officers of representative large, medium, and small companies. In 1982, a majority of those interviewed candidly admitted that their giving programs were not as well managed as the rest of their company operations (Yankelovich, Skelly, and White, 1982). Why not? Reasons differed: The giving program had a low corporate priority. It had no full-time staff. It lacked an adequate operational budget. On balance, the grantmaking operations of most companies surveyed in 1982 got low marks on their management, effectiveness, and impact.

The good news in the 1988 study (Daniel Yankelovich Group, 1988) was that a majority of CEOs thought that their grantmaking programs had improved markedly, were more effective in reaching desirable targets set by the company, and were comparable to other departments of the company in the quality of their management. Close examination of the results of the 1988 study shows that many corporations in the 1980s gave a higher priority to their grantmaking programs, held their grantmaking staff to higher managerial standards, and expected greater cooperation and synergy between their grantmaking staff and the rest of the company.

Part of this change in the 1980s resulted from increased attention within the companies to the productivity and efficiency of every corporate department, and part of it resulted from greater emphasis by the Council on Foundations on how to help its members and other corporate leaders correct weaknesses in corporate grantmaking revealed by the 1982 Yankelovich study. This book is graphic evidence of the council's continuing resolve to identify and help replicate sophisticated corporate programs that bring the business community into a closer working relationship with the other two sectors of our society.

Grantmaking and the CEO

The grantmaking program in any company cannot flourish unless that company's chief executive officer has an abiding personal interest in the program. Studies over many years demonstrate that the grantmaking programs of most companies are both inefficient and ineffective. The single most basic reason for this state of affairs is that chief executive officers all too often do not consider their grantmaking programs an integral part of their long-range corporate plan and do not hold its administrators accountable to the same standards of performance as those that prevail throughout the rest of the company.

The chief executive need not, indeed should not, be involved in the day-to-day execution of the company's giving program. But this person must, at the very least, insist that the giving program have a clear mission statement, explicit strategies for achieving the mission, specific targets and written guidelines for grantmaking, and a person or staff accountable for regularly scheduled reports on performance against these objectives. If each of these simple procedures is in place in a company, the CEO can comfortably tell the corporate grantmaking officer, "Go till we say stop." Unfortunately too many CEOs follow the reverse rule, saying or implying to the grants officer, "Stop till we say go," thus assuring a mediocre grants program administered by an officer who has no authority and hence no sense of accountability or ownership for the program.

In 1988, I addressed a meeting of thirty-five CEOs of small companies in a middle-sized midwestern city. They had come together expressly to find ways to make their corporate grantmaking programs better. Most of them admitted they were not proud of the way their grants programs were being run (or ignored) by the CEO himself. Because they knew each other well and because no media representatives were present, their dialogue was disarmingly open.

One of them admitted that all requests for grants were stacked in a corner of his office and left there until the second Saturday in December, at which time he began to read them alone. He said that all year long the sight of that pile of unanswered mail made him feel guilty. The act of reading and evaluating these requests was for him a nightmare. His company had no mission statement and no guidelines for grantmaking. As a result, every file in that stack of proposals was a crisis for him. Every request seemed to have some merit. Many were from friends he did not want to offend. He shamefacedly admitted that he regularly chose to fund proposals that were close to the top of the pile, in order to get this unpleasant annual ordeal behind him as quickly as possible. After the meeting, some of his peers told me comparable horror stories about their companies.

Not one of us relishes doing work (or play) at which we are incompetent. The executive just cited is a highly successful and wealthy entrepreneur who knows very well how to finance, manufacture, and market profitably a respected line of precision tools. The same skills he uses to run his company would show him how to administer (or delegate the administration of) a comparably efficient grantmaking program. But first he has to spend time analyzing his problem and hammering out a business plan to address it.

Management of a Grants Program

Successful entrepreneurs who own and manage their privately held companies often find it difficult to make time to draft a business plan for their giving program. Like the guilt-ridden executive with the stack of requests piled in his office, these executives would be surprised to learn how easy it is to set up and manage a respectable grants program for a small or medium-sized company.

The first step in managing a grants program for any company, large or small, is to write a mission statement describing what the company wants to achieve by its giving program. This statement should be very brief. This is not an easy document to draft, but with a little editorial help from peers, employees, and friends, a respectable mission statement can be crafted in a short time.

The mission statement describes the generic categories of grants a company will favor. The grantmaking guidelines (step number two) will help the grants officers (or the CEO) identify specific grants to be funded within these generic categories. Guidelines explicitly tell grantseekers what a company is likely to fund. They should also implicitly tell grantseekers what a company will not fund.

The basic reason why most corporate grantmaking programs are not well managed is that they lack a set of printed guidelines and a clear-cut mission statement. It is the lack of these simple tools that made the executive cited above ashamed that he could not handle the stack of papers in the corner of his office.

In fairness to grantseekers, corporate mission statements and printed guidelines should not be changed at short intervals. But in fairness to changes within a company and within society at large, both the guidelines and the mission statement ought to be reviewed and, if necessary, revised or updated at least every five years.

Corporate Restructuring and the Grants Program

Some chief executive officers know all this when they take over as CEO. Working with them can be pure pleasure. The hard fact is, however, that many CEOs must learn on the job about the company's grants program after they take over as chief executive. Recent corporate mergers and acquisitions have put a premium on grants officers who know how to support their chief executives in this delicate learning process without seeming either haughty or aggressive.

Given the current rate of corporate mergers, grants officers of the future will likely be called upon more frequently to help senior managers in the company learn how their company's grantmaking program fits into the grand strategy of the company. To be effective in this mission, grants officers must understand their company's main business. Lacking such knowledge, they can easily be perceived by their new boss or bosses as peripheral employees presiding over marginal operations of doubtful value to the company.

How does a grants officer go about this task of educating the boss? Very carefully. And principally by supplying the boss with information and reports (and visits, if possible) that acquaint the boss with the rationale for the giving program and show how this program relates to the company business. Granted, in many companies it is still difficult for the grants officer to get the attention of the CEO for any sustained period of time. Nonetheless, grants officers must realize that it is imperative for them to find ways to reach the boss and to earn and keep the continuing respect of the boss for the company's giving program. Without the enthusiastic endorsement of the CEO and of the senior management team, any corporate giving program will languish, drift, and eventually sink. At several places in this book, grants officers describe how they have creatively solved this age-old problem of getting support from the top down in the company. It is up to each corporate grants officer to find avenues or persons or procedures within the company whereby the grants program can be or become a companywide project with high priority in the eyes of the chief executive.

For grants officers, one of the most painful corollaries of the current wave of corporate restructuring or mergers is that in a span of five years, some of them have had to learn how to live and to deal with two or three new CEOs in succession. Instead of looking on this trend as a problem, grants officers with a good outlook see it as a challenge to their administrative and political skills. Every CEO wants the company to be successful on as many levels as possible. Successful corporate grants officers of the future will be those who see themselves as team players, obligated and privileged to teach their companies and their chief executives more about the dynamics of the independent sector of our society, the sector that differentiates corporate culture in the United States from corporate culture everywhere else in the world.

Involving Employees in the Program

Getting (and keeping) the chief executive on their side is only half of the job of grantmakers inside the company. The other half is to win the allegiance and respect of as many employees as possible. Most employees think of the company foundation or contributions program as a mystery or a black box. But in their hearts, employees, from the top down, really want to know more about the company giving program. They also want to be invited to be part of its in-house support network and to experience personal pride in their company's record as a good corporate citizen.

There are dozens of ways to involve employees in the giving program. Dale Carnegie learned a long time ago that you can make friends more quickly by asking others to help you than by offering to help them. Take your fellow employees into your counsel. Tap their professional expertise in marketing or sales or communications or finance. Corporate grants officers have an enormous in-house advantage. Dozens of talented fellow employees need only to be asked to help on worthy projects that benefit the company and the community.

Power of Grants Officers

The corporate giving office and the office of community affairs usually have a low position on the corporate totem pole. They are not on the "fast track," not "in the loop." But an imaginative and visionary executive in charge of these offices can have genuine power within the company. This is the power of putting together a team of dedicated fellow employees whose cumulative energy and influence are beyond the imagination of persons who have never been grants officers. The regular exercise of this in-house power enables grants officers to whistle on their way to work. A newly appointed grants officer in a company receives a very limited amount of authority merely by being named to this post. But the appointment only starts the process whereby that officer could steadily augment power by gaining what is call the "authority of service." That is the kind of authority that is conferred on any person by colleagues, partners, or clients after they observe a grants officer in action and conclude that the person is both competent and trustworthy.

This authority, earned by good service to the company and to the clientele, gives some senior grants officers a great deal more credibility and trustworthiness than junior grants officers have in this business. Credibility and trustworthiness, in the company and

in the community, must be earned. How? By doing one's homework, by telling the truth, and by meeting one's deadlines.

Concerns About Site Visits

At this writing, almost two years have passed since my retirement
as director of the General Mills Foundation. In that time, I have
been amazed and humbled by the candor of conversations I have had
with friends who were grantseekers when I was a grantmaker. They
tell me things now they would never have said then. Some of their
concerns are these: Why do grantmakers fail to return telephone
calls? Why do grantmakers send us "canned" declination letters?
Why are those letters not candid in giving us reasons for the declination? Why do grantmakers fail to make site visits? The list is
longer, but these four queries are the most frequent.

A respected school of thought in our line of work holds that
the single best indicator of quality in any grantmaking program is
the quality of its site visits to the grantseeker's own turf. Sad to
relate, the staff cutbacks at corporate grantmaking offices resulting
from current corporate mergers and voluntary restructuring are seriously eroding both the quantity and the quality of many corporate
grantmaking programs today.

In 1987, Brian O'Connell, president of INDEPENDENT
SECTOR, conducted a survey of staffing patterns in family (that is,
endowed) and corporate foundations. O'Connell's greatest surprise
in conducting this survey concerned the small size of corporate
grantmaking staffs.

> Given the rapid and significant growth in the size and breadth
> of corporate public service, it is to be expected that some
> strains are evident. Some of these are internal, relating to the
> ability to manage the enterprise, and some are external, in-
> volving growing expectations and misunderstanding. In my
> view, one of the most serious problems is the degree of signif-
> icant understaffing that exists in corporate philanthropy. For
> more than ten years, I've regularly visited private foundations
> and corporate grantmaking offices and have often been struck
> with how very much smaller the corporate staffs are. Other

than some random inquiries and comments about this seeming disparity, I've never really focused on it. Lately, however, the dilemma of corporate efforts compared to staff capacity has seemed to reach crisis proportions, so I decided to test my impressions. I've now compared a random sampling of the staff sizes of approximately 75 private foundations and 75 corporate grantmakers. While I don't pretend that this has been a scientific study, I'm now absolutely satisfied that my impressions are borne out. In these 150 programs of equal grantmaking size, the private foundations have, on average, one professional staff person for each $1.2 million of grants and the corporations have one staff person for each $2.3 million of grants, a ratio of approximately 2 to 1. It is interesting that this ratio is about the same in all size programs [O'Connell, 1987, p. 4].

If it continues to be necessary for corporations to cut the size of their grantmaking staffs (and this is a reasonable inference), could grants officers recruit teams of knowledgeable fellow employees to make site visits to nonprofits? Even if these employees produced less than perfect reports, it strikes me that such reports would be vastly better than no reports at all.

The Grantmaker-Grantseeker Relationship

A grants officer is a link between the people in the company who approve the disbursement of company funds and the people who seek these funds in order to make good things happen in their communities. Both groups must be able to rely on the integrity of the grants officer to represent their best interests in any dialogue with the persons in the other group.

The grants officer is a translator who brings back from site visits with applicants a fair and accurate picture of the strengths, weaknesses, risks, and potential of nonprofit agencies seeking corporate support. These agencies must be able to trust the grants officer as their agent in this reporting process. Repeated evidence that a grants officer is trustworthy will in time confer on that person increased moral authority in the community and inside the company.

Conversely, the grants officer is honor bound to present to the grantseeking public a truthful and accurate description of what the company expects from an agreement it might make to help the nonprofit sector. It can be a delicate balancing act for a grants officer to be both truthful and candid about the company when hard-hitting grantseekers ask tough questions about the company, its past practices, its leadership, or its reliability as a partner. The grants officer who, in effect "keeps two sets of books" by telling different stories inside and outside the company will in time be discovered and replaced. The one who understands and covets the authority of service will be recognized as an honorable spokesman for the company and a trustworthy advocate for that company's grantseekers.

It is no secret in our line of work that arrogance is the greatest temptation facing a grants officer. Being in charge of a process that dispenses money to persons who need this precious commodity can turn the head of a grants officer whose ego needs to be bolstered or whose sense of power over others needs to be fed. In 1982, Roy W. Menninger, director of the Menninger Mental Health Clinic in Topeka, in an address to a group of chief executives of foundations, reminded them that "grantmaking can be harmful to your mental health."

The best way to avoid this pitfall is to endorse and habitually cultivate the conviction that grantmakers and grantseekers are indeed peers, deserving of the same degree of respect and courtesy from one another. Their relationship is one of equals, not one of servant and master. Good performance is demanded of each of them if the desired results of the grantmaking process are to be achieved.

Money, by itself, can do nothing. It can grow if wisely invested, or it can shrink if poorly invested. But in the grantmaking process, the donors of the money need competent and trustworthy partners who are capable of using the money to make something good happen in society. In the memorable words of Dolly Gallagher in *Hello Dolly!*, "Money is like manure. It doesn't do any good unless you spread it around." The spreading of money, in our line of work, is done by the nonprofit agencies who are our partners. They are also our equals, not our minions.

Cause-Related Marketing

At several places in this book, authors refer to the current trend of tying a company's grantmaking strategy to its marketing strategy. Ever since the American Express Company coined and registered the term *cause-related marketing* in 1981, there have been many variations on this theme, all intended ultimately to promote the sale of the company's products or services by means of the company's grantmaking.

Given the strict rules of the Internal Revenue Code prohibiting the use of corporate foundation funds to promote such sales ("self-dealing"), variations on the theme of cause-related marketing must be done with corporate funds, not foundation funds. Accordingly, an increasing number of companies are using corporate dollars, sometimes taken from advertising or marketing budgets, to underwrite their grantmaking program. This is a perfectly legitimate use of company money, even though several purists have charged that this kind of funding cannot seriously be called corporate philanthropy. Perceptive readers of this book have already noticed that most of the authors (and this book's title) do not speak of corporate philanthropy but of corporate contributions. This usage on our part is deliberate.

Part of the corporate management's duty in authorizing a company giving program is to decide where to position the company on the spectrum that runs between altruism and self-dealing. Every company has a position somewhere on this line, even though I know of no company that calls its grantmaking purely altruistic. Clearly the trend today is away from altruism and toward practices that tie grantmaking in some way to a company's marketing strategy. No perfect position for any company exists on this line. Unfortunately, in many companies, their position on this line is not the result of any deliberate decision on their part but is in effect simply assigned to them after the fact by the patterns of grants made yearly by the company.

In essence, cause-related marketing and its variations depend on closing the loop of self-interest between corporate grantmakers and outside grantseeking agencies. Some grantseekers express concern, especially advocacy groups and small or new agencies with low visibility, that it is impossible for them ever to match their services with any corporate product or service. Hence they claim that as this pattern of funding grows, their chances of corporate support will steadily lessen. Most often these voices are asking corporate grantmakers to balance their own self-interest with a broader interest in public needs. Often, these groups are also asking that corporate donors give greater consideration to general operating support grants and less attention to specific project grants that match identifiable corporate interests.

Views of Grantmakers

J. Irwin Miller, who is rightly regarded as a model for all corporate grantmakers (from his days as chairman and CEO of the Cummins Engine Company), once cautioned persons in our line of work not to call ourselves professionals (Miller, 1984). He would prefer that we see ourselves more modestly as craftsmen, ever trying to be better at these twin crafts of grantmaking and grantseeking.

Many businessmen believe persons working in the nonprofit sector, either as grantors or grantees, really could not "cut it" in the business world. To the extent that this view ever was correct, I submit that it is less so with every passing day. The third, or independent, sector is steadily recruiting well-educated and highly motivated managers and leaders, who have deliberately opted to work in the nonprofit sector because the work here is exciting, psychologically satisfying, and holds out to its practitioners the promise that they will be part of the solution, not part of the problem, in our complex, high-technology, and often troubled society.

Peter Drucker, who is known as "the father of modern management," recently announced as he approached his eightieth year, that he intends "to devote the balance of his years to helping all nonprofit organizations operate more effectively" (Goss, 1989, p. 16). This is wonderful news for the nonprofit sector. In Drucker's view, "Nonprofit organizations are leagues ahead of businesses in learning how to motivate people without the use of promotions or raises." It is important for persons in our line of work to pay attention to spokesmen like Miller and Drucker. Both of these wise men have "won their spurs" in the business world. But as they near the end of their long and successful careers in business, they both see the nonprofit sector, not business and not government, as the sector most likely to chart the course for survival of our heavily mortgaged, uncertain, and beleaguered democratic society.

Another light-giving leader of our time is Robert K. Greenleaf. In his long career as director of management research for AT&T, Greenleaf (1988) came to believe that the most effective leaders in all sectors are what he calls the "servant leaders." They are the people who spend their time and talent empowering other people to actualize their personal potentialities as active members of the human community. Like proud parents, servant leaders want their protégés to outstrip them.

Greenleaf does not confuse service with servitude. His now-classic work on servant leadership reserves the term *leader* for those persons who pledge and give their best efforts over a long term to help other people to grow and to advance a cause or an ideal that benefits community life. The persons he has known who exemplify this high standard were not primarily motivated by the personal rewards, raises, promotions, or golden parachutes that came to them for doing a good job. Rather, they were driven by a willingness to pursue worthy causes or programs that empowered others to measure up to their full potential as people working together in a collegial style. Greenleaf's heroes are persons whose power comes from the authority of service.

The Public Sector

It is ironic that our society has steadily increased its reliance on the nonprofit sector and raised its expectations from year to year for more and better services from nonprofit agencies but has not in the same span increased its knowledge of what sustains the nonprofit sector and makes it work. Our citizenry at large, and even great segments of the print and electronic media, do not really understand the history, the elements, or the important function this sector plays

in the day-to-day operation of our social, economic, and governmental systems.

One possible reason for this public ignorance of our sector
is that we made an error a long time ago in allowing it to be defined
by what it is not! We allowed the business sector and the governmental sector to be named by what they actually do. One does business and the other governs. But the third sector, we call *nonprofits*.
It is like saying, "I have three children. Two are girls and one is not
a girl."

David Mathews, president of The Kettering Foundation, has
written a thoughtful article on this topic. In this essay, delivered at
the Spring Research Forum of INDEPENDENT SECTOR in
March 1987, Mathews argues persuasively that what we now call the
nonprofit sector should be called the political or the public sector.
He specifically laments our tendency to define the nonprofit sector
by its relationship to government, either "as independent from it or
supplementary to it. . . . In either case that focus obscures the larger
political history of the Sector; and, more, it obscures its broader
political functions." A similar complaint can be made about our
ready acceptance of a negative definition of this sector as being
simply the "nonbusiness or nonprofit" sector when in reality it does
a lot of business and in recent years has even begun to create and
operate wholly owned for-profit subsidiaries.

It is clearly too late now for us ever to rename the sector. Too
many of us are confirmed in our usage, calling it either the nonprofit sector, the third sector, or the independent sector. In reality,
as Mathews argues so well, it should have been called the public
sector, both because historically it antedates the other two sectors
and because it was and is our original forum for speaking our minds
and for pleading our case as a new people in a new nation. This
is the large concept Abraham Lincoln advanced in the Gettysburg
Address when he called ours a "government of the people, for the
people and by the people."

This sector is also the fundamental predicate of the Mayflower Compact. Even before the *Mayflower* made its landfall on
what is now called Cape Cod, its goodly company mutually pledged
under God to do all in their power to create a new society in the
new world. When they landed, there was no business sector to meet

them, no governmental sector to welcome them. The new arrivals were, in their own persons, the first sector, the only sector—the public sector. Later they would form a government, "a civil body politic," to which they promised "all due submission" to such "just and equal laws" as the government they would set up might pass ("Mayflower Compact," 1985). They would also in due time enter into trade among themselves, with the Wampanoag Indians, and with the world, but on their arrival they were what the opening phrase of the Constitution of the United States would later so eloquently describe as "We the People," in a new world still to be fashioned by them.

It is of course too late for us to reclaim all the ideological ground that this sector has lost since the nation began. But it is not too late for those of us who are privileged to be in and of this sector to be more vigorous in our statement of the case in favor of the dignity, the stature, and the importance of this sector, call it what you will.

There is also mounting evidence outside the United States of increased interest in the role that the nonprofit sector plays as partner, critic, and connector with the other two sectors. The entry of more than 600 major Japanese corporations into manufacturing or distribution operations in this country in the last two decades has recently caused Japanese executives to pose for themselves the question: "How can we become and be perceived as good corporate citizens in America?"

In the Soviet Union, *glasnost* and *perestroika* have resulted in the sudden creation of several new foundations, a minuscule but rapidly growing nonprofit sector, and, most remarkably, a for-profit, private enterprise sector which looks increasingly to the United States for guidance or models on how to develop cooperative and productive public-private ventures between business and government and between for-profit and nonprofit enterprises.

In Hungary, Erno Rubik, the inventor of Rubik's Cube, has become a rich man by the worldwide sale of his invention. With part of his new wealth he has endowed a foundation committed to identifying and supporting boys and girls who show unusual promise in the study of mathematics or science.

These are exciting times for persons fortunate enough to be working in the field of corporate grantmaking. Enormous new possibilities for service to society are opening up within the United States and around the world. And although the United States at this writing is the leading debtor nation in the world, there is abundant evidence, as Peter Drucker has said, that the nonprofit sector has a unique opportunity to help this country chart its own course and to offer models for other countries that are striving to explore all the corollaries of what it means to be a free nation.

References

Goss, K. A. "Peter Drucker Wants to Move Charities 'From Good Intentions to Effectiveness.'" *Chronicle of Philanthropy*, June 13, 1989, p. 16.

Greenleaf, R. K. *Servant, Retrospect and Prospect*. Newton Centre, Mass.: Robert K. Greenleaf Center, 1988.

Mathews, D. "The Independent Sector and the Political Responsibilities of the Public." Address delivered to INDEPENDENT SECTOR Spring Research Forum, New York City, March 19, 1987.

"Mayflower Compact." *World Book Encyclopedia*, Vol 13. Chicago: World Book, 1985, p. 262.

Menninger, R. W. Keynote speech at a workshop for foundation executives, Hot Springs, W.Va., Mar. 7, 1982.

Miller, J. I. Address at a plenary session of Council on Foundations' annual meeting, Denver, Colo., Apr. 25, 1984.

"Morita Wants Japanese Companies to Increase Philanthropy in the U.S." *Japan Times*, Nov. 15, 1989, p. 3.

O'Connell, B. "Corporate Philanthropy, An Information Service." *The INDEPENDENT SECTOR Newsletter*, Aug./Sept. 1987, 7 (4), p. 4.

Daniel Yankelovich Group. *The Climate for Giving: The Outlook of Current and Future CEO's*. Washington, D.C.: Council on Foundations, 1988.

Yankelovich, Skelly, and White. *Corporate Philanthropy: Philosophy, Management Trends, Future and Background*. Washington, D.C.: Council on Foundations, 1982.

Resource A

The Council of
Better Business Bureaus'
Standards for
Charitable Solicitations

Introduction

The Council of Better Business Bureaus promulgates these standards to promote ethical practices by philanthropic organizations. The Council of Better Business Bureaus believes that adherence to these standards by soliciting organizations will inspire public confidence, further the growth of public participation in philanthropy, and advance the objectives of responsible private initiative and self-regulation.

Both the public and soliciting organizations will benefit from voluntary disclosure of an organization's activities, finances, fund raising practices, and governance—information that donors and prospective donors will reasonably wish to consider.

These standards apply to publicly soliciting organizations that are tax exempt under section 501(c)(3) of the Internal Revenue Code, and to other organizations conducting charitable solicitations.

While the Council of Better Business Bureaus and its member Better Business Bureaus generally do not report on schools, colleges, or churches soliciting within their congregations, they encourage all soliciting organizations to adhere to these standards.

These standards were developed with professional and technical assistance from representatives of soliciting organizations, professional fund raising firms and associations, the accounting profession, corporate contributions officers, regulatory agencies, and the Better Business Bureau system. The Council of Better Business Bureaus is solely responsible for the contents of these standards.

For the Purposes of These Standards:

1. "Charitable solicitation" (or "solicitation") is any direct or indirect request for money, property, credit, volunteer service or other thing of value, to be given now or on a deferred basis, on the representation that it will be used for charitable, educational, religious, benevolent, patriotic, civic, or other philanthropic purposes. Solicitations include invitations to voting membership and appeals to voting members when a contribution is a principal requirement for membership.
2. "Soliciting organization" (or "organization") is any corporation, trust, group, partnership or individual engaged in a charitable solicitation; a "solicitor" is anyone engaged in a charitable solicitation.
3. The "public" includes individuals, groups, associations, corporations, foundations, institutions, and/or government agencies.
4. "Fund raising" includes a charitable solicitation; the activities, representations and materials which are an integral part of the planning, creation, production and communication of the solicitation; and the collection of the money, property, or other thing of value requested. Fund raising includes but is not limited to donor acquisition and renewal, development, fund or resource development, member or membership development, and contract or grant procurement.

Public Accountability

1. Soliciting organizations shall provide on request an annual report.

The annual report, an annually-updated written account, shall present the organization's purposes; descriptions of overall programs, activities and accomplishments; eligibility to receive deductible contributions; information about the governing body and structure; and information about financial activities and financial position.

2. Soliciting organizations shall provide on request complete annual financial statements.

The financial statements shall present the overall financial activities and financial position of the organization, shall be prepared in accordance with generally accepted accounting principles and reporting practices, and shall include the auditor's or treasurer's report, notes, and any supplementary schedules. When total annual income exceeds $100,000, the financial statements shall be audited in accordance with generally accepted auditing standards.

3. Soliciting organizations' financial statements shall present adequate information to serve as a basis for informed decisions.

Information needed as a basis for informed decisions generally includes but is not limited to: a) significant categories of contributions and other income; b) expenses reported in categories corresponding to the descriptions of major programs and activities contained in the annual report, solicitations, and other informational materials; c) a detailed schedule of expenses by natural classification (e.g., salaries, employee benefits, occupancy, postage, etc.), presenting the natural expenses incurred for each major program and supporting activity; d) accurate presentation of all fund raising and administrative costs; and e) when a significant activity combines fund raising and one or more other purposes (e.g., door-to-door canvassing combining fund raising and social advocacy, or television broadcasts combining fund raising and religious ministry, or a direct mail campaign combining fund raising and public education), the financial statements shall specify the total cost of the multi-purpose activity and the basis for allocating its costs.

4. Organizations receiving a substantial portion of their income through the fund raising activities of controlled or affiliated entities shall provide on request an accounting of all income received by and fund raising costs incurred by such entities.

Such entities include committees, branches or chapters which are controlled by or affiliated with the benefiting organization, and for which a primary activity is raising funds to support the programs of the benefiting organization.

Use of Funds

1. A reasonable percentage of total income from all sources shall be applied to programs and activities directly related to the purposes for which the organization exists.
2. A reasonable percentage of public contributions shall be applied to the programs and activities described in solicitations, in accordance with donor expectations.
3. Fund raising costs shall be reasonable.
4. Total fund raising and administrative costs shall be reasonable.

Reasonable use of funds requires that a) at least 50% of total income from all sources be spent on programs and activities directly related to the organization's purposes; b) at least 50% of public contributions be spent on the programs and activities described in solicitations, in accordance with donor expectations; c) fund raising costs not exceed 35% of related contributions; and d) total fund raising and administrative costs not exceed 50% of total income.

An organization which does not meet one or more of these percentage limitations may provide evidence to demonstrate that its use of funds is reasonable. The higher fund raising and administrative costs of a newly created organization, donor restrictions on the use of funds, exceptional bequests, a stigma associated with a cause, and environmental or political events beyond an organization's control are among the factors which may result in costs that are reasonable although they do not meet these percentage limitations.

5. Soliciting organizations shall substantiate on request their application of funds, in accordance with donor expectations, to the programs and activities described in solicitations.
6. Soliciting organizations shall establish and exercise adequate controls over disbursements.

Solicitations and Informational Materials

1. Solicitations and informational materials, distributed by any means, shall be accurate, truthful and not misleading, both in whole and in part.
2. Soliciting organizations shall substantiate on request that solicitations and informational materials, distributed by any means, are accurate, truthful and not misleading, in whole and in part.
3. Solicitations shall include a clear description of the programs and activities for which funds are requested.

Solicitations which describe an issue, problem, need or event, but which do not clearly describe the programs or activities for which funds are requested will not meet this standard. Solicitations in which time or space restrictions apply shall identify a source from which written information is available.

4. Direct contact solicitations, including personal and telephone appeals, shall identify a) the solicitor and his/her relationship to the benefiting organization, b) the benefiting organization or cause and c) the programs and activities for which funds are requested.
5. Solicitations in conjunction with the sale of goods, services or admissions shall identify at the point of solicitation a) the benefiting organization, b) a source from which written information is available and c) the actual or anticipated portion of the

sales or admission price to benefit the charitable organization or cause.

Fund Raising Practices

1. Soliciting organizations shall establish and exercise controls over fund raising activities conducted for their benefit by staff, volunteers, consultants, contractors, and controlled or affiliated entities, including commitment to writing of all fund raising contracts and agreements.
2. Soliciting organizations shall establish and exercise adequate controls over contributions.
3. Soliciting organizations shall honor donor requests for confidentiality and shall not publicize the identity of donors without prior written permission.

Donor requests for confidentiality include but are not limited to requests that one's name not be used, exchanged, rented or sold.

4. **Fund raising shall be conducted without excessive pressure.**

Excessive pressure in fund raising includes but is not limited to solicitations in the guise of invoices; harassment; intimidation or coercion, such as threats of public disclosure or economic retaliation; failure to inform recipients of unordered items that they are under no obligation to pay for or return them; and strongly emotional appeals which distort the organization's activities or beneficiaries.

Governance

1. Soliciting organizations shall have an adequate governing structure.

Soliciting organizations shall have and operate in accordance with governing instruments (charter, articles of incorporation, bylaws, etc.) which set forth the organization's basic goals and purposes, and which define the organizational structure. The governing instruments shall define the body having final responsibility for and authority over the organization's policies and programs (including authority to amend the governing instruments), as well as any subordinate bodies to which specific responsibilities may be delegated.

An organization's governing structure shall be inadequate if any policy-making decisions of the governing body (board) or committee of board members having interim policy-making authority (executive committee) are made by fewer than three persons.

2. Soliciting organizations shall have an active governing body.

An active governing body (board) exercises responsibility in establishing policies, retaining qualified executive leadership, and overseeing that leadership.

An active board meets formally at least three times annually, with meetings evenly spaced over the course of the year, and with a majority of the members in attendance (in person or by proxy) on average.

Because the public reasonably expects board members to participate personally in policy decisions, the governing body is not active, and a roster of board members may be misleading, if a majority of the board members attend no formal board meetings in person over the course of a year.

If the full board meets only once annually, there shall be at least two additional, evenly spaced meetings during the year of an executive committee of board members having interim policy-making authority, with a majority of its members present in person, on average.

3. Soliciting organizations shall have an independent governing body.

Organizations whose directly and/or indirectly compensated board members constitute more than one-fifth (20%) of the total voting membership of the board or of the executive committee will not meet this standard. (The ordained clergy of a publicly soliciting church, who serve as members of the church's policy-making governing body, are excepted from this 20% limitation, although they may be salaried by or receive support or sustenance from the church.)

Organizations engaged in transactions in which board members have material conflicting interests resulting from any relationship or business affiliation will not meet this standard.

Resource B

Council on Foundations'
Principles and Practices
for Effective Grantmaking

As the contours of American society have changed dramatically, so has the breadth and nature of organized philanthropy. The philanthropic enterprise is more varied in geography and type. It is more complex. It has entered into many more diverse relations with other American institutions, including the corporate and governmental sectors. It is a more significant factor in forming and implementing public policy than ever.

In the course of this evolution, trustees and managers of many foundations and other grantmaking institutions have developed an array of operating principles. Principles have a two-fold advantage. They provide a framework for consistent, effective practice, and they afford the public a view of ethical and philosophical values on which grantmaking organizations base their conduct.

Note: Reprinted by permission of the Council of Foundations, 1828 L Street, N.W., Washington, D.C., 20036.

Organized philanthropy's voluntary efforts to set standards for accountability and openness follow in the tradition of other independent enterprises dedicated to the public interest. These self-determined measures strengthen, and assure public confidence in the distinctive purposes and practices fundamental to the pluralistic world of philanthropy.

The Council on Foundations has served as the primary forum through which grantmakers have debated their views and exchanged experiences. This dialogue led the Council's Board of Directors, in June 1980, to adopt a statement on "Recommended Principles and Practices for Effective Grantmaking." The purpose of the statement is to provide practical counsel to new foundations in establishing their operating guidelines and to existing foundations and other donor organizations that may be re-examining their policies and procedures. In form and substance the statement recognizes the pluralistic nature of organized philanthropy and affirms what has proved useful in the successful handling of grants and in the maintenance of good relations with various publics.

In preparing the principles, a special committee drew suggestions from a wide variety of grantmaking organizations. Extended discussions were held at a number of regional associations of grantmakers' meetings. In addition, open hearings were held at the 1979 annual meeting of the Council.

The resulting statement of Principles and Practices for Effective Grantmaking, to which Council members subscribe, therefore represents not only the action of a Board of Directors representative of Council members, but also any number of modifications that emerged from a wide process of consultation throughout the grantmaking community.

In subscribing to this statement, members of the Council affirm their belief in the principles and practices and their willingness to move toward implementing them. While some of the practices refer rather specifically to professionally staffed foundations, smaller foundations and corporate giving programs strive to achieve the spirit of openness and accountability which underlies their principles in a manner consistent with their size, scope and financial capacities.

Still, the statement is subject to further changes by later

boards, and the issues raised in the statement should be topics for an ongoing dialogue.

What is enduring, however, is the embodiment in the statement of the philosophy behind a rich tradition of American philanthropy as well as a set of sound practices consistent with the dedication of organized grantmaking to the public interest.

Principles and Practices for Effective Grantmaking

In subscribing to this statement, members of the Council affirm their belief in the principles and practices and willingness to move toward implementing them.

1. Whatever the nature of the entity engaged in private grantmaking, and whatever its interests, it should seek to establish a set of basic policies that define the program interests and the fundamental objective to be served.

2. An identifiable board, committee or other decisionmaking body should have clear responsibility for determining those policies and procedures, causing them to be implemented, and reviewing and revising them from time to time.

3. The processes for receiving, examining and deciding on grant applications should be established on a clear and logical basis and should be followed in a manner consistent with the organization's policies and purposes.

4. Responsive grantmakers recognize that accountability extends beyond the narrow requirements of the law. Grantmakers should establish and carry out policies that recognize these multiple obligations for accountability: to the charter provisions by which their founders defined certain basic expectations, to those charitable institutions they serve, to the general public, to the Internal Revenue Service, and to certain state governmental agencies.

5. Open communications with the public and with grantseekers about the policies and procedures that are followed in grantmaking is in the interest of all concerned and is important if the grantmaking process is to function well, and if trust in the responsibility and accountability of grantmakers is to be

maintained. A brief written statement about policies, program interests, and grantmaking practices, geographic and policy restrictions, and preferred ways of receiving applications is recommended. Prompt acknowledgment of the receipt of any serious applications is important. Grantseekers whose programs and proposals fall outside the interests of the grantmakers should be told this immediately and those whose proposals are still under consideration should be informed, insofar as is possible, of the steps and timing that will be taken in reaching the final decision.

6.   Beyond the filing of forms required by government, grantmakers should consider possible ways of informing the public concerning their stewardship through publication and distribution of periodic reports, preferably annual reports, possibly supplemented by newsletters, reports to The Foundation Center and the use of other communications channels.

7.   The preservation and enhancement of an essential community of interest between the grantor and the grantee requires that their relationship be based on mutual respect, candor, and understanding with each investing the necessary time and attention to define clearly the purposes of the grant, the expectations as to reports related to financial and other matters, and the provisions for evaluating and publicizing projects.

     Many grantmakers, going beyond the providing of money, help grantees through such other means as assisting in the sharpening of the objectives, monitoring the performance, evaluating the outcome, and encouraging early planning for future stages.

8.   It is important that grantmakers be alert and responsive to changing conditions in society and to the changing needs and merits of particular grantseeking organizations. Responses to needs and social conditions may well be determined by independent inquiries, not merely by reactions to requests submitted by grantseekers. In response to new challenges, grantmakers are helpful if they use the special knowledge, experience and insight of individuals beyond those persons, families or corporations from which the funds originally came. Some grantmakers find it useful to secure ideas and comments from a variety of

consultants and advisory panels, as well as diversified staff and board members. In view of the historic underrepresentation of minorities and women in supervisory and policy positions, particular attention should be given to finding ways to draw them into the decisionmaking processes.

9. From time to time, all grantmaking organizations should review their program interests, basic policies, and board and staff composition, and assess the overall results of their grantmaking.

10. Beyond the legal requirements that forbid staff, board members and their families from profiting financially from any philanthropic grant, it is important that grantmakers weigh carefully all circumstances in which there exists the possibility of accusations of self-interest. In particular, staff and board members should disclose to the governing body the nature of their personal or family affiliation or involvement with any organizations for which a grant is considered, even though such affiliation may not give rise to any pecuniary conflict of interest.

11. Grantmakers should maintain interaction with others in the field of philanthropy including such bodies as regional associations of grantmakers, The Foundation Center, the Council on Foundations and various local, regional, and national independent sector organizations. They should bear in mind that they share with others responsibility for strengthening the effectiveness of the many private initiatives to serve the needs and interests of the public and for enhancing general understanding and support of such private initiatives within the community and the nation.

Why the Concern with Principles?

To speak of principles is to speak of values and virtues which are presumed to be fundamental. At times the word is used literally to refer to rules of conduct, but the Council's statement of principles is much less prescriptive, referring instead to suggested guidelines in pursuit of what are deemed to be responsible and good foundation practices.

Given the ambiguity of moral language, some might argue that it is less than useful to marry the word principles with philanthropy. Yet, it is also possible that the word gives us a symbol with which to grasp and understand what is fundamental when we decide on priorities, choose among grantseekers, commit resources and otherwise serve a public good.

This use of the word principles makes it a relatively late-born child in the family of virtues in which words like duty, law, goodness and morality are its much older siblings.

Aristotle began his influential book on *Ethics* with the statement: "Every act and every inquiry and similarly every action and pursuit is thought to aim at some good." The concern with principles and practices in the foundation field is consistent with this claim in that it seeks to keep the eyes of grantmakers on purpose as well as process, on the responsibility *for* public benefit as well as the responsibility *to* private benefactors. And while cognate terms like "good" and "moral" might have been sufficient in the past to describe practices and values considered fundamental, we are likely to look for language which is more precise and definitive.

The most recent effort to engage foundation trustees and staff in a discussion of responsible foundation practices has brought to light the continuing tension between the unique priorities of each foundation and the larger mission shared in common with other grantmakers. Fortunately, this tension has enriched rather than stifled the discourse.

But given the difficulty of the task and the lingering uneasiness engendered by any effort to propose standards, it is appropriate to ask, "Why the continuing concern with principles?"

The first answer is that the Council's statement on principles and practices was—and continues to be—an affirmation of pluralism as an essential value. It affirms the freedom of each foundation to choose which public purpose it will serve, while at the same time, pointing to commonalities which go beyond our individual program choices.

It is our "public purpose" commitment which is the most persuasive in convincing critics and public policymakers that we should be permitted to hold philanthropic resources in trust for perpetuity.

A second answer is that the Council's statement affirms the goals to which most foundation trustees and staff already aspire. It is, therefore, a public acknowledgment of a private commitment, a demonstration to those who would further regulate an already over-regulated sector that additional government involvement is neither needed nor desirable. When self-regulation works, it is not only good private practice, but good public policy.

That reality took on new significance both within and outside of the Council when, in 1983, the Council's Board of Directors adopted a policy which makes endorsement of the principles and practices statement a condition of membership. The action proved to be a form of enlightened self-interest, given the subsequent interest of Congress in every aspect of foundation activity, but particularly in the public accountability posture of our sector.

The fact that the vast majority of our members had, indeed, affirmed the statement on principles and practices was not lost on our elected officials. No public presentation by the Council or other witnesses was as effective as this demonstration of commitment to responsible foundation practices in making the case for less government regulation.

While there was criticism from a few of our members regarding this policy when it was adopted, the positive response from most confirms that there is a broadly shared set of common values regarding our responsibilities to the public we serve.

In the end, the attempt to identify and affirm principles and practices constitutes a marriage of private and public values. This union preserves the social contract between private philanthropy and American society and protects the legal charter which makes each foundation a trustee of the public good. And that is the ultimate answer to the question, "Why the concern with principles?"

Resource C

Excerpt from
INDEPENDENT SECTOR's
"Profiles of Effective
Corporate Giving Programs"

Excellence in Contributions—A Description
of the Effective Program

There is no commonly accepted standard of excellence for judging the effectiveness of a contributions program: there is no equivalent to net profits or earnings per share. Data from the study suggest that excellence in this context has three components: the "mechanical" *management* of the program, the *character* and philosophy of the program as reflected by the nature of grants made, and program *size* in relation to the size and resources of the business. Cross-cutting the three components is the program's ability to reflect the needs and nature of the business while appropriately responding to the

Note: Knauft, E. B., *Profiles of Effective Corporate Grantmaking Programs,* available from INDEPENDENT SECTOR, 1828 L Street, N.W., 12th Floor, Washington, D.C., 20036.

374

needs of the communities where the company is located and the needs of the nation. The following discussion of excellence highlights program features and may serve as a guide for those who wish to evaluate their own program.

Program Management. The following items describe management techniques and performance objectives that apply to the contributions function. These items provide the base on which to construct the other two components of excellence.

1. *Total Level of Giving*
    a. Budget constructed at start of each year
    b. Numerical long range goal established for internal purposes
    c. Numerical long range goal publicly announced
2. *Program Operation*
    a. Written objectives and rationale of program are fully developed
    b. Areas of giving identified and clearly defined
    c. Special priority areas of giving identified and clearly defined beyond or within the broader categories of giving
    d. Areas of giving formally re-assessed at least once every three years
    e. Exceptions to defined areas of giving limited to no more than 10 percent to 15 percent of the total program
    f. The proportion of dollar value of grants in non-headquarters locations to total grants fairly reflects the representation of those locations in terms of number of employees, revenue produced, local needs, etc.
3. *Decision-making and Review Process*
    a. A contingency, discretionary or unallocated category representing at least 20 percent of the total budget included in the contributions fund
    b. Defined dollar approval levels set for unbudgeted grants at each organizational level
    c. The chief executive officer (CEO) is an active supporter of the contributions program
    d. CEO's objective is a contributions program comparable to or better than the best programs of peer companies

    e.   A formal mechanism established (such as membership on a contributions committee) to enable managers to have an impact on the contributions program

4.   *Grantseekers' Accessibility to Program*
    a.   Published statement concerning contributions guidelines, priorities and application procedures
    b.   Published grant list, including grant amounts
    c.   Grantseekers submitting formal proposals consistently given prompt response about the status of their request, including, as appropriate, the time frame for further steps
    d.   Grantseekers automatically notified of status of any grants still pending within three months after original response

Character of the Program. Program philosophy, character and content can be defined by these factors:

- Existence of a rationale for the program. The rationale should address such questions as: What is the program's basic purpose? How does the company want employees, community people and nonprofit organizations to view the program? What should be the content of the program five years from now? To what extent should the program actively seek and encourage grant requests in target areas?

- Existence of a process to involve company personnel in the program, thus encouraging feelings of ownership of and involvement with the program across the company.

- The program responds to the nature of the company's business and product lines by relating company interests or expertise to grantmaking. Examples include support of literacy training programs by a chain of book stores, or support for development and use of toys for handicapped children by the toy division of a corporation.

- The program responds to the needs of communities where the company is located. Examples include a bank's sponsorship of a "Handi-Van" that provides supplies and expertise for senior citizens to make home repairs, or a company's support for the formation of a community foundation in a branch office city.

- Concentration of a portion of the program in several major grants sustained for several years, as contrasted with scattering all funds in small grants to many organizations.

Size of the Program. The program's dollar size is its most objective characteristic, and possibly for that reason becomes an area of controversy among contributions professionals. Conventional management practice suggests that the contributions function should have long- and short-range numerical objectives like most other business operations. The clearest example is the 2 percent and 5 percent "giving clubs" that started in Minneapolis and later spread to a dozen cities. The corporate members pledge to attain a giving level representing 2 percent or 5 percent of their pre-tax profits. Most major corporations have resisted the clubs because they are perceived as imposing an external goal on management and would often result in doubling or tripling a company's giving. Currently, the corporate world has not accepted any "ideal" level of giving; even the advocates of the concept of a target agree that no single index or ratio (regardless of the exact number) applies equitably to all corporations at all times.

Recognizing the difficulty in establishing "reasonable but stretching" targets in this field, but adhering to the principle that "excellence" should include a quantitative objective, the following guidelines for program size are suggested:

• Companies should establish a dollar contributions objective that is carefully developed, approved and communicated to appropriate persons within the company. Final and intermediate target dates should be established. The goal should be developed after program purpose and content have been defined and should be accompanied by staffing and committee assignments to produce a program that will achieve both qualitative and quantitative objectives.

• Companies with highly erratic profits should strive for a modicum of consistency in their giving levels. Many local agencies supported by the company will experience an increase in case loads and a decrease in support from other sources during times of economic downturn. The experience of 1982 and 1983 suggests that companies with foundations were better able to sus-

tain their giving levels by drawing on foundation assets which
could then be replaced in years of higher corporate profits.

- The statement of a quantitative goal should specify the categories to be included in the goal. The first consideration should
  be achieving the desired level of *cash* contributions as distinct
  from (1) gifts of equipment to increase the company's market
  penetration for its products, and (2) the estimated value of employee volunteers and their services donated by the company.
  Such activities constitute important means of corporate involvement, but they should not substitute for a company's basic cash
  contributions program.

The Impact of Key Individuals

The Chief Executive Officer. As one part of the study, contributions
managers were asked to rank 18 factors in order of their importance
to a quality program. A primary factor was "The chief executive
officer is an active supporter of the contributions program." Interviews indicated that CEO support takes such forms as (1) encouraging the establishment of stretching objectives for the program; (2)
urging creative grantmaking that reinforces company objectives; (3)
placing "fast track" line managers on the in-company contributions committee to constructively challenge the thrust of the program; and (4) advocating a planned level of giving to the board of
directors. For example:

> Our new CEO wants the company to be perceived externally
> very differently from the way it has been. He feels it was re-
> garded as well-managed, but rather dull, bureaucratic and
> plodding. He wants it to become more dynamic, including the
> thrust of the contributions program. As a result, we're looking
> for innovative and creative programs in such areas as precol-
> legiate education, environment and conservation.
>
> At a retreat of the foundation board, our president
> pleaded with us to preserve 20 percent of our discretionary
> funds to take some risks. And he said, "Be sure you don't take
> the fun out of contributions."
>
> I was concerned that the new contributions budget

would be a tough sell at the board level. We were primed to discuss and justify why we were asking for all this crazy money. But at the board meeting, the new budget was introduced by the chairman, who said "I think it's up to us to make enough profits to cover those contributions," and that was the end of the discussion.

I'll give a recommendation to senior management and they may knock me down on the amount or raise the amount, but it's not their style to sit there and dictate which grants to make . . . They treat it very much as a business function . . . The key thing is that this area has the interest of the top people.

Managers in many staff functions tend to stress the importance of personal support from the CEO and the need for a reasonably close reporting relationship to him. However, because of its highly subjective and arbitrary nature, the contributions function especially benefits from senior management's thoughtful affirmation. Several contributions managers noted that board level support for the contributions function is especially dependent on the CEO. In most companies in the study, the board was clearly influenced by the CEO, with few instances of outside board members taking the initiative to affect the direction and scope of the program.

Contributions managers also emphasize that there is a thin line between a CEO's constructive support of the activity and domination of contributions decisions as an arbitrary expression of personal preferences. Frequent use of the contributions program as an executive "perk" reduces both the influence and the motivation of the contributions staff and sends a message throughout the company that the program is the private preserve of the CEO. But most importantly, the quality of grantmaking is likely to suffer because priorities are ignored. Managers throughout the company are denied the potential of a program that is responsive to corporate and community interests.

There are times when the CEO or another senior manager feels strongly about supporting a nonprofit organization or cause that it is at variance with defined giving objectives. Obviously, it is his prerogative to instruct that a contribution be made, but some companies have followed alternative strategies: (1) They set aside a stated percentage or dollar amount of the contributions budget as "senior management discretionary"; (2) they use operating funds from the CEO's own cost center; or, (3) the CEO makes contributions from personal funds.

Problems of arbitrary senior management intervention are minimized when the management of contributions is treated like any other business function. Application of conventional principles of management to the contributions function involves: (1) developing objectives and policies for the giving program; (2) establishing grantmaking priorities that track the objectives; (3) defining and following a decision-making process that most effectively carries out program objectives; (4) assigning levels of accountability to the individuals and/or groups that make decisions; (5) monitoring performance; and (6) assigning to the contributions function staff personnel and committee members that are creative, objective and results-oriented.

The Contributions Manager. The contributions manager performs a unique role in the company. The position is "one of a kind" and requires numerous contacts with a wide variety of community organizations and their leaders. The effectiveness of this manager is dependent upon his/her ability simultaneously to relate to community and company interests by operating a contributions program that is useful to both constituencies. In larger national corporations, the constituencies are enlarged to other communities where the company operates, as well as nonprofit organizations that are national in scope. While required to be sensitive to the "outside world," the contributions manager is charged with dispersing funds that rarely produce a measurable benefit for the company. As a consequence, the incumbent must perform a delicate balancing act in serving the interests of both the company and the community.

Several managerial styles observed during the study illustrate the skills employed by contributions managers. These descriptions are admittedly an oversimplification of the real world; most managers use a combination of two or more styles in varying proportions.

- *The loyal soldier* receives orders from above and faithfully carries them out. This manager is alert to any signals that may accompany grant proposals sent down from the executive office. Contributions priorities, if they exist, are broad and perfunctory, so that the program tends to be driven by requests received from outside constituencies or causes important to the CEO. If there is an internal contributions committee or foundation board, it tends to have brief meetings where grants are routinely approved because "everyone is on the same team." Similarly, there are no reversals of committee decisions by top management because orders have been followed to the letter.

- *The skillful tactician* is adroit at reading the mind of the CEO, but augments this skill by building a constituency of other company managers who have high credibility with the CEO. This constituency, in turn, gives credibility to the contributions program and may help to protect it in times of corporate adversity. Depending on the tactician's reading of the company culture, the program may reflect creativity, growth and reasonably wide involvement and support across the company. The tactician caucuses frequently with his boss and the CEO about individual grants and only rarely champions those that might encounter difficulty within the contributions committee or foundation board. For example: "When we go to the foundation board, the staff expects the board will endorse our recommendations because there has been some sampling of the water on each of these proposals before we get that far . . . There are rare times at a board meeting when I sense that if we called for a vote, they would vote 'no' on something that we were recommending. I then ask them if we can go back to the drawing board and they smile and say, 'Take it back and see us next time.' On three or four occasions, we have gone back and brought new evidence and gotten it approved, and several times we re-examined it and realized that the board was right and we were wrong."

- *The change agent* sees the job as an opportunity for moving contributions in new directions. Change agents vary in the relative emphasis they place on changes in the *content* of the program versus the *process* by which changes are made. Those oriented toward *content* take all available opportunities to move the program in the direction they desire. By contrast, those oriented toward *process* establish a climate and mechanism to produce consensus decisions, whatever the outcome may be. The true change agent introduces changes in process to bring about changes in content that reflect the thinking and support of the decision-making group. Programs managed by change agents are characterized by candid give-and-take in committee meetings and with no predetermined outcome, but with group support once the decision is made. The best of such programs creatively relate grantmaking to the interests of the business and the community and have reasonably wide support and understanding throughout the company. The change agent manager usually feels secure in the job and perceives the climate as supportive of risk-taking. "I could give you a whole list of things our committee turned down. It's important for several reasons. If we didn't do this, we wouldn't have ever changed anything we're doing. That's when change is introduced. Secondly, it tells us when the committee gets together for its annual review meeting what basic issues we should be talking about. It forces policy decisions. For instance, I said to them, 'I tried to bring you the Peace Museum last year. Are you telling me that nuclear arms and peace are really not issues you want to address?' "

- *The broker-advocate* is a person with a cause, acting to connect the company and the community. Beyond grantmaking, this manager mobilizes employees and other non-cash resources of the company to address those community needs he/she feels are important. However, the broker-advocate who fails to relate effectively to company managers and culture runs the risk of being a "do-gooder" operating outside the mainstream of the company. In its most effective form, this management style provides a bridge between the corporation and the community and helps create a favorable local impression of the company.

- *The technocrat* relies almost exclusively on a rigid application of the principles of planning, organization and control in the operation of the program. Requests for funding receive prompt reply via a form letter or a printed post card. The objectives and priorities of the program are spelled out, but may have been developed unilaterally by the contributions manager. The program will not be known for its creativity, but donees know where they stand and within the company, the contributions function is perceived as being under tight control.

Conclusion

The quest for the characteristics of the effective contributions program has included an examination of the decision making process, of individuals and committees in the company that play a role in contributions decisions and of three components of excellence: the management of the program, the character of the program as reflected by the grants made and the dollar size of the program relative to potential company resources. Overlaying those components is the impact of two individuals: the chief executive officer of the company and the contributions manager. The components of excellence can be most fully attained when they reflect the commitment and challenging support of the chief executive coupled with a contributions manager who structures a program reflecting the needs, culture and resources of the company while creatively responding to relevant public needs.

Resource D

National Charities
Information Bureau's
Standards in Philanthropy

PREAMBLE

The support of philanthropic organizations soliciting funds from the general public is based on public trust. The most reliable evaluation of an organization is a detailed review. Yet the organization's compliance with a basic set of standards can indicate whether it is fulfulling its obligations to contributors, to those who benefit from its programs, and to the general public.

Responsibility for ensuring sound policy guidance and governance and for meeting these basic standards rests with the governing board, which is answerable to the public.

The National Charities Information Bureau recommends and applies the following nine standards as common measures of governance and management.

Note: Reprinted by permission of the National Charities Information Bureau, Inc., 19 Union Square West, New York, N.Y., 10003-3395.

NCIB STANDARDS   *NCIB INTERPRETATIONS*
                                   AND APPLICATIONS

Governance, Policy, and Program Fundamentals

1. Board Governance: The   Fiscal guidance includes re-
    board is responsible for   sponsibility for investment
    policy setting, fiscal guid-   management decisions, for in-
    ance, and ongoing gover-   ternal accounting controls, and
    nance, and should   for short and long-term budget-
    regularly review the orga-   ing decisions.
    nization's policies, pro-
    grams and operations. The
    board should have
    a. an independent, vol-   The ability of individual board
        unteer membership;   members to make independent
                                   decisions on behalf of the or-
                                   ganization is critical. Existence
                                   of relationships that could in-
                                   terfere with this independence
                                   compromises the board.
    b. a minimum of 5 vot-   Many organizations need more
        ing members;   than five members on the
                                   board. Five, however, is seen as
                                   the minimum required for ade-
                                   quate governance.
    c. an individual atten-   Board membership should be
        dance policy;   more than honorary, and
                                   should involve active participa-
                                   tion in board meetings.
    d. specific terms of office
        for its officers and
        members;
    e. in-person, face-to-face   Many board responsibilities
        meetings, at least twice   may be carried out through
        a year, evenly spaced,   committee actions, and such ad-
        with a majority of vot-   ditional active board involve-

ing members in attendance at each meeting;

ment should be encouraged. No level of committee involvement, however, can substitute for the face-to-face interaction of the full board in reviewing the organization's policy-making and program operations. As a rule, the full board should meet to discuss and ratify the organization's decisions and actions at least twice a year. If, however, the organization has an executive committee of at least five voting members, then three meetings of the executive committee, evenly spaced, with a majority in attendance, can substitute for one of the two full board meetings.

f. no fees to members for board service, but payments may be made for costs incurred as a result of board participation;

Organizations should recruit board members most qualified, regardless of their financial status, to join in making policy decisions. Costs related to a board member's participation could include such items as travel and daycare arrangements. Situations where board members derive financial benefits from board service should be avoided.

g. no more than one paid staff person member, usually the chief staff officer, who shall not chair the board or serve as treasurer;

h. policy guidelines to avoid material conflicts of interest involving board or staff;

In all instances where an organization's business or policy decisions can result in direct or indirect financial or personal benefit to a member of the board or staff, the decisions in question must be explicitly reviewed by the board with the members concerned absent.

i. no material conflicts of interest involving board or staff;

j. a policy promoting pluralism and diversity within the organization's board, staff, and constituencies.

Organizations vary widely in their ability to demonstrate pluralism and diversity. Every organization should establish a policy, consistent with its mission statement, that fosters such inclusiveness. An affirmative action program is an example of fulfilling this requirement. The formal or abridged statement of purpose should appear with some frequency in organization publications and presentations.

2. Purpose: The organization's purpose, approved by the board, should be formally and specifically stated.

3. Programs: The organization's activities should be consistent with its statement of purpose.

4. Information: Promotion, fund raising, and public information should describe accurately the organization's identity, purpose, programs, and financial needs.

Not every communication from an organization need contain all this descriptive information, but each one should include all accurate information relevant to its primary message.

There should be no material omissions, exaggerations of fact, misleading photographs, or any other practice with would tend to create a false impression or misunderstanding.

5. Financial Support and Related Activities: The board is accountable for all authorized activities generating financial support on the organization's behalf:

   a. fund-raising practices should encourage voluntary giving and should not apply unwarranted pressure;

   b. descriptive and financial information for all substantial income and for all revenue-generating activities conducted by the organization should be disclosed on request;

   Such activities include, but are not limited to, fees for service, related and unrelated business ventures, and for-profit subsidiaries.

   c. basic descriptive and financial information for income derived from authorized commercial activities, involving the organization's name, which are conducted by for-profit organizations, should be available. All public promotion of such commercial activity

   Basic descriptive and financial information may vary depending on the promotional activity involved. Common elements would include, for example, the campaign time frame, the total amount or the percentage to be received by the organization, whether the organization's contributor list is made available to the for-profit company, and the campaign expenses directly incurred by the organization.

should either include
this information or in-
dicate that it is avail-
able from the
organization.

6. Use of Funds: The organization's use of funds should
reflect consideration of current and future needs and
resources in planning for
program continuity. The
organization should:

a. spend at least 60% of
annual expenses for
program activities;

b. insure that fund-
raising expenses, in re-
lation to fund-raising
results, are reasonable
over time;

c. have net assets available for the following
fiscal year not usually
more than twice the
current year's expenses
or the next year's
budget, whichever is
higher;

Fund-raising methods available
to organizations vary widely
and often have very different
costs. Overall, an organization's
fund-raising expense should be
reasonable in relation to the
contributions received, which
could include indirect contributions (such as federated campaign support), bequests
(generally averaged over five
years), and government grants.

Reserve Funds:
Unless specifically told otherwise, most contributors believe
that their contributions are being applied to the current program needs identified by the
organization.

Organizations may accumulate
reserve funds in the interest of
prudent management. Reserve

funds in excess of the standard may be justified in special circumstances.

In all cases the needs of the constituency served should be the most important factor in determining and evaluating the appropriate level of available net assets.

d. not have a persistent and/or increasing deficit in the unrestricted fund balance.

Deficits:
An organization which incurs a deficit in its unrestricted fund balance should make every attempt to restore the fund balance as soon as possible. Any organization sustaining a substantial and persistent, or an increasing, deficit is at least in demonstrable financial danger, and may even be fiscally irresponsible. In its evaluations, NCIB will take into account evidence of remedial efforts.

Reporting and Fiscal Fundamentals

7. Annual Reporting: An annual report should be available on request, and should include

a. an explicit narrative description of the organization's major activities, presented in the same major categories and covering the same fiscal period as

Where an equivalent package of documentation, identified as such, is available and routinely supplied upon request, it may substitute for an annual report.

the audited financial
statements;

b. a list of board
members;

The listing of board members
should include some identifying information on each
member.

c. audited financial statements or, at a min-
imum, a comprehen-
sive financial sum-
mary that 1) identifies
all revenues in signifi-
cant categories, 2) re-
ports expenses in the
same program, man-
agement/general, and
fund-raising categories
as in the audited fi-
nancial statements,
and 3) reports all end-
ing balances. (When
the annual report does
not include the full
audited financial state-
ments, it should indi-
cate that they are
available on request.)

In particular, financial sum-
maries or extracts presented separately from the audited
financial statements should be
clearly related to the information in these statements and
consistent with them.

8. Accountability: An organization should supply on request complete financial
statements which

a. are prepared in confor-
mity with generally
accepted accounting
principles (GAAP), ac-
companied by a report
of an independent cer-

To be able to make its financial
analysis, NCIB may require
more detailed information regarding the interpretation, applications and validation of
GAAP guidelines used in the

tified public accoun-
tant, and reviewed by
the board;

audit. Accountants can vary
widely in their interpretations
of GAAP guidelines, especially
regarding such relatively new
practices as multi-purpose allocations. NCIB may question
some interpretations and
applications.

and

b.   fully disclose eco-
nomic resources and
obligations, including
transactions with re-
lated parties and affil-
iated organizations,
significant events af-
fecting finances, and
significant categories
of income and
expense;

and should also supply

c.   a statement of functional allocation of ex-
penses, in addition to
such statements re-
quired by generally ac-
cepted accounting
principles to be in-
cluded among the fi-
nancial statements;

d.   combined financial
statements for a na-
tional organization
operating with affil-
iates prepared in the
foregoing manner.

9. Budget: The organization should prepare a detailed annual budget consistent with the major classifications in the audited financial statements, and approved by the board.

    Program categories can change from year to year; the budget should still allow meaningful comparison with the previous year's financial statements, recast if necessary.

NCIB believes the spirit of these standards to be universally useful for all nonprofit organizations. However, for organizations less than three years old or with annual budgets of less than $100,000, greater flexibility in applying some of the standards may be appropriate.

INDEX

395

Burpee, culture of, 110
Burroughs Corporation, restructured, 166
Bush, G., 38, 51, 56, 59, 68, 324
Business deduction, charitable gift distinct from, 29
Business Roundtable, 167–168
Business sector: boundaries of, 12–13; and government, related to nonprofit sector, 41–45; nonprofit sector linked with, 35–49. *See also* Corporations
Butler, O. B., 72

C

California: child care concerns in, 99; community relations programs in, 289; employee volunteers in, 323, 325, 326–327; voluntary organization in, 41
California Regional and Occupational Centers and Programs, 73
Campeau, restructured, 166
Cargill Industries, as radio sponsor, 148
Carnegie, D., 349
Carpenter, S. L., 91
Carter, J. E., 54
Catholic Charities, 38
Cause-related marketing: analysis of, 139–152; background on, 139–140; benefits of, 144–146; and charity exploitation, 141–142; and charity selection, 140–141; and charity visibility, 144; and competitive advantage, 10; concept of, 140; consumer attitudes toward, 146–148; and credibility, 142; criteria for, 142; and critical needs, 145–146; developing program for, 150–152; direct impact of, 146; ethics of, 296; exchange values of, 86; and marketing talents, 144; place of, 353–354; and product promotions, 149–150; risks with, 140–144; sales and image benefits from, 145, 148–149; and short term programs, 142–143; and traditional

giving, 143–144; types of, 148–150.
Celestial Seasonings, and cause-related marketing, 149
Charitable activities, legal standards on, 201–203
Charity: business deduction distinct from, 29; and cause-related marketing, 139–152; corporate contributions distinct from, 250
Chesebrough-Pond's, restructured, 166
Chicago: corporate culture in, 113; neighborhood organizations in, 54; restructuring in, 170–171, 178; voluntary organizations in, 40, 215
Chief executive officer (CEO): and corporate-community involvement, 290–291; and employee volunteers, 324–325; and grant-making, 345–348; and involvement, 123; leadership challenges for, 63–74; notes to new, 121–125; standards for, 378–380; support by, 4, 69–70, 179, 344–345
Chrysler Corporation, culture of, 110–111
Chrysler Corporation Fund, and corporate culture, 111
Citizens League, 94
Civic duty, idea of, 9
Civic index, 15–16
Clean Up the Ghetto, 40
Cleveland, neighborhood organizations in, 54
Cleveland Tomorrow, 73
Cloud, S., Jr., 50
Collins, G. M., 185
Colorado, employee volunteers in, 325
Columbia University, 4, 288
Coman, R., 178
Combined Health Appeal Drives, 157, 160
Committee for Economic Development (CED), 65, 66, 72, 73, 74
Common Cause, 40, 215
Communication: with corporate directors and employees, 197–198;

community institution, 94; and employee volunteers, 312, 314, 315–316, 317; and Gifts in Kind, 163, 297; history of, 28; issues in supporting, 158–159, 233–234; and options, 160–163; resources from, 263; and rise of alternatives, 156–158; roles of, 38, 52, 69, 127; Volunteer Action Center of, 312, 317

Urban Development Action Grants, 54

Urban Institute, 65

Ury, W., 90, 91

U S WEST Communications: community involvement by, 123, 124, 125; culture of, 116

V

Values: in corporate culture, 108–109; and ethical issues, 340–342

Veblen, T., 21, 34

Visa, 149

Vocal Jazz, 40

Volunteer Action Center, 312, 317, 326

Volunteer Centers of California, 326

Volunteers: employees as, 310–331; involvement of, 47; numbers of, 38

W

Walley, W., 140, 148, 152

Wampanoag Indians, trade with, 357

Wargo, M., 163, 164

Washington: corporate culture in, 110; employee volunteers in, 325

Washington, D.C., resource organization in, 229

Webster, P. J., 145, 152

Weisbrod, B. A., 214, 226

Weitzman, M., 38, 48, 214, 226

Westinghouse Electric Corporation, consulting services from, 125

Weyerhaeuser, J. P., Jr., 105

Weyerhaeuser Company, culture of, 105, 108–109, 110, 114

Weyerhaeuser Foundation, and corporate culture, 105, 109, 110

Wilderness Society, 110

Wilson, E. R., 310

Wittbrook, M., 214, 226

Wolch, J. R., 50–51, 60

Women, Infants, and Children supplements, 67

Women's Funds, 157

Workers benefits, evolution of, 25–26

World Bank, 36

World Wildlife Federation, 110

Y

Yankelovich, Skelly, and White, 344–345, 358

Yankelovich Group, 4, 69–70, 74, 179, 181, 344, 358

Young Men's Christian Association (YMCA): corporate rehabilitation of, 111; as hostels for workers, 25

Youth Trust, 94–95